COP LAND
&
HEAVY

# COP LAND
# &
# HEAVY

## James Mangold

*faber and faber*

First published in 1997
by Faber and Faber Limited
3 Queen Square London WC1N 3AU

Photoset by Parker Typesetting Service, Leicester
Printed in England by Clays Ltd, St Ives plc

A CIP record for this book
is available from the British Library
ISBN 0-571-19425-7

The publisher wishes to thank Susan Dalsimer and Kristin Powers
for their assistance in making this book possible.

2 4 6 8 10 9 7 5 3 1

# CONTENTS

# FOREWORD

Part architectural plan, part hard-sell, part recipe, part literature; the screenplay is a proudly *intermediate* art form. It is the only document of original intent. It describes an uncooked film dream.

As a writer/director I have a straight line journey from blank page to finished film. There is no moment when one task ends and the other begins. But there is a moment when the film dream begins to push up against the confines of the real world. The two screenplays published here were not cleaned up or slavishly edited to reflect the finished films. I wanted to share the texts we worked *from*. Because they were my dreams.

While I may write alone, I am bad at being alone. I thrash about – I call people, performing scenes over the phone, inevitably luring them to my home or office to read new pages while I obsessively watch over their shoulders. I am grateful to lifelong friends and collaborators such as Scott Ferguson, F. Ron Miller, Peter Ortel, Douglas Rushkoff and Alex Rubin. Heartfelt thanks to Richard Miller, who toiled for two years with me, producing *Heavy*. Thanks also to Amanda Lasher, my brilliant assistant, and to my representatives, Joanne Wiles, Jason Sloane and Daniel Rappaport, all of whom saw value in my work long before it was apparent to anyone else.

It has become trendy for film-makers to scoff at their film school experiences. But my time at CalArts, Columbia University and Sundance was hardly disillusioning. I have been blessed with great teachers, such as Alexander Mackendrick, Miloš Forman, Stefan Sharff and Gill Dennis. I am grateful for the time and wisdom they invested in me.

Producer Cathy Konrad developed *Cop Land* with an intense and imaginative eye. She believed in the material, fiercely. On the set, she was a true partner, concerned with every detail, yet somehow maintaining a tactician's view of the big picture. For me, *Cop Land* was a gigantic leap in scale and I don't know if I would have survived without a producer who was so steady from beginning to end. If I am lucky, I will never be without her.

Finally, I want to thank my parents, Robert Mangold and Sylvia Plimack Mangold, and my brother Andrew. The level of support and inspiration my family has given to me and my 'projects' – from when I was twelve and my 'hobby' was charming, to when I was twenty-five, unemployed and depressed – is a gift of such magnitude, it is beyond thanks. I can only hope to offer the same kind of love and encouragement to my children's dreams.

James Mangold, 1997

# FOLLOWING YOUR GUT:
## Writing and directing *Heavy* and *Cop Land*

### James Mangold talks to Tod Lippy

Raised in upstate New York, James Mangold earned an under-graduate degree in film from the California Institute of the Arts in Valencia.

TOD LIPPY: *You studied filmmaking at CalArts?*

JAMES MANGOLD: Yeah, I made a bunch of films there – one short every year. One of the years I was there I spent in the acting pro-gram, which was really one of the great parts of my time at CalArts. Sandy MacKendrick was my main teacher; he was one of the few teachers in the film department who was also an experi-enced, classically narrative filmmaker. I was Sandy's TA for two years and kind of his protégé. He died last year. He was a great man and a remarkable and rare kind of teacher. It isn't often – as a student – that you are exposed to an amazingly talented director who can afford, emotionally or financially, to give more than just his time to you. Sandy's career had been cut short by ill health and by the fact that he was so demanding. But instead of feeling sorry for himself, he just devoted himself to being a truly great teacher. He had this tremendous reserve of energy.

The greatest lesson I learned from him was how hard you had to work to make a good film. I would bring in some lame five-page film script, and he would generate seven pages of handwritten text about what I had written. He was also an illustrator; he'd even do sketches of scenes in your film. It was this level of indulgence that made you realize that you were a complete fraud unless you could somehow match his level of application and passion toward your projects with some of your own.

*One of the films you made at CalArts got you a lot of attention in Hollywood.*

It was the last one I made – I'd have to admit to being completely conscious of trying to make a film that would get me hired in the industry. My last year there I was reading about *Amazing Stories*, the TV series that Spielberg was putting together. So I just devised this short film that I was sure was going to get me hired by

Spielberg. It was completely calculated to be kind of *Twilight Zone-y*, with lots of fog, starring a little child; it was a clever film.

And, as wishes often do come true, it got a lot of attention and ended up getting me in a bidding war between Barry Diller and Michael Eisner, between Fox and Disney, and I was represented by Jeff Berg, chairman of ICM. I mean, I was twenty-one at the time, and I ended up with a writing/directing deal at Disney! But I got caught up in an incredibly complex political environment. My only real advocate at the studio was Eisner, who was so high up that you never saw him – he was opening theme parks around the world. The first thing I did was look through this book of their TV movies that were in development for the next year. The one I was drawn to was called 'Deer Story.' It said, 'A fawn lost in Manhattan teams up with some kids.' I was like, 'Oh, this is what I'm gonna do.' And then I set about basically trying to write *The Red Balloon* in Manhattan, with a deer instead of a balloon. The structure was built on the standard template of the Disney animal movie: kid finds raccoon: builds raccoon a pen; gives raccoon a name; loves raccoon but then realizes raccoon needs to go back to nature, so it's goodbye, raccoon. Raccoon saves him once from a cougar and then goes away. In this case, it was all those things except I added an urban twist to it in that it took place in the city with these kids from the projects who had no idea how to return this fragile creature – fawn, who, for them, might as well be from Mars – back to the woods. I thought it was actually a pretty beautiful script, but the problem was that it just wasn't Disney. Actually, it was *very* Disney. But it was not Michael Eisner/Jeff Katzenberg Disney. It was not very talky, it wasn't particularly funny – it was extremely earnest and kind of lyrical and silent. I was trying very hard to do something un-TV.

Unfortunately, the studio detested what I was doing. They thought it was dark and maudlin, and too ethnic and too urban. I got fired after two days of being director. They then asked me to rewrite it and make it more suburban – all this with the promise that I'd get another thing to direct. I was twenty-one and completely confused, so that's what I did. But I never got another chance. Once you become 'damaged,' in the Hollywood context, you are truly damaged. 'What ever happened to that kid with the big deal at Disney?' I was young enough to heed some very bad advice given to me by my agency: keep my firing from the TV movie a secret. So as other studios were talking to me after this incident, I didn't tell them what had happened. Whenever you try to keep a secret like that, you're screwed: there's an incredible hole in your story that's causing everyone to wonder whether you have a drug problem or what exactly happened to you over at Disney. The better thing to do is to say, 'Ah, they fucked me over – goddamn assholes, they got no imagination.'

Ultimately, I think that everyone did me a big favor. 'Coming up through the system' is a completely false model. The dream I think everyone is being sold is this kind of Spielbergian ascent from a small cubbyhole office into big directing jobs. Essentially, he is really the only great director who had that kind of experience. If you think about it, most of the directors you admire made movies on their own first. You simply can't walk into this incredibly intense environment with so little political capital or momentum and make something great. If you are so beholden to the people who are giving you your start, then you really have to just do what they say and follow their orders and hope to God you make a terrific film. When you're twenty-one, lifted out of film school and given an office and an assistant, you assume that what they want is your freshness and your idealism. Yeah, well, sure they do. As long as it doesn't get in their way.

On the other hand, I'm not someone who came up fantasizing about working completely outside the system. I have a fascination with trying to get something great done within the system, but I think you need to have a tremendous amount of knowledge about how that organism works. I got some of that in my first pass through Hollywood – by making a lot of mistakes.

*So that was all you worked on during your tenure at Disney?*
No, I wrote *Oliver and Company*, an animated feature musical they threw me on to work off my deal. This was pre-*Roger Rabbit*, pre-any big successful animated movies. Regardless of the revisionist histories that have since been written about Jeffrey and Michael's reign at Disney, at that point, animation was not considered the centerpiece of the new Disney's strategy, which is why a nobody like me was given the task of writing their regime's first animated feature. In any other situation, they would have hired some

renowned screenwriter. *Oliver and Company* came out three years later. It wasn't embarrassing – and it actually made a decent amount of money. But that was long after I had left the studio. After my deal was finished, I found myself back on the streets, really doubting why I was doing this. I toyed with the idea of becoming a novelist, going back to school, studying writing and just kind of dropping the whole film thing.

Then I had a conversation with the guy who ran the writing school at UC Irvine, who assured me that the writing world sucked, too. He said it was incredibly political and rife with corruption and agents and 'buzz' and 'heat' and hypocrisy – I wasn't going to find any solace there. So I ended up going back to film school. I moved to New York and enrolled at Columbia, which was kind of a goofy thing to do, in the sense that I'd already written a successfully produced studio feature and a TV movie. I don't think anyone at Columbia really believed that all of this stuff had happened to me: 'He was under contract at Disney and then ended up back at *film school*?' I was the physical incarnation of every film student's ultimate nightmare.

At Columbia, I decided to make a film that was the opposite of that last film I'd made at CalArts – the one calculated to get me a job. Now, I was going to make a movie that was as inaccessible to studio executives as it possibly could be. Actually, I wasn't even thinking about them; I wanted to make a movie like the Super-8 ones I made when I was thirteen or fourteen when I would just think of these perverse challenges for myself and then try to meet them. In this case, it was to tell a story that was completely wordless. Not a spoof, or an homage or a nostalgic comedic silent film, but a contemporary and adult story – silent.

*And this was your film* Victor?
Yeah. I figured a lot out for myself with that film. I figured out what my problem had been at Disney; I figured out what was driving me artistically. Writing and directing *Victor* made me incredibly aware of why I was dissatisfied with certain kinds of movies, particularly American films. Most movies we recognize as being extremely 'visual' are actually standard dialogue films with a couple of homages to great cinema in a couple of key sequences – these unique cinematic moments which are dolloped on like sour

cream. But if you want your whole movie to be some kind of unique cinematic moment, then you've got to somehow embed that within writing. It is not the job of the director to make a film visual, it is the job of the writer, because it is the writer who will decide whether the thing is decorated with images or *built* with images.

As I was making *Victor*, this thirty-minute silent film, people kept saying, 'Why don't you just roll some sound while you're shooting, just in case you change your mind.' I was surprised that, even within a film-school setting, you hear those kinds of 'studio executive' voices. When someone asked me, 'What are you going to hear when this movie plays?' I'd say, 'People coughing.' I actually ended up marrying music and ambient effects to the film, but it's almost like I had to stake that severe position – total silence – just to end up where I did.

*Did you write a screenplay for that or just use storyboards?*
I wrote a screenplay for it, and then I storyboarded it. The screenplay was eleven pages long; the movie was twenty-eight minutes long. The page-a-minute thing just doesn't work dependably with image-built films. At least it doesn't for me. That rule of thumb is based on the thirties to forties post-arrival-of-sound screenplay model – that a page, most of it being dialogue, will generally run about a minute.

*You've written an article on what you feel about that and other discrepancies between screenplay and film. It seems that your basic thesis is that the classic screenplay format gets in the way of the content of a film; that the rules that must be followed while writing a screenplay will actually modify the content of the film.*
If you work with graphics and page-layout software, there are these 'intelligent' tools called 'snap-to grids.' As you're laying down objects in a layout, the software forces the objects to sit on the 'one inch line,' or the 'two inch line,' etc. It forces things to stay lined up. It's sort of the same, in a subtle way, with screenplay format. The format has an 'intelligence' of its own, it has grids it wants you to cooperate with. For instance, it just *reads* better ending a scene with someone saying 'fuck you' or 'I love you' than it does with a line of action description like 'Jack looks about the room, tears in his eyes.' For some reason, snappy dialogue as

xiii

scene punctuation is often a stronger 'feeling' choice when you're writing, but not necessarily when you're filming.

I don't mean to suggest that the screenplay format should be abandoned, it's just that you should be aware of how all the 'snap-to grids' within the format are pulling on your words. These paranoias of mine come, I think, from my being first and foremost – since I was a kid – a film-maker. I never considered myself a writer, so I always looked at that process with great suspicion. As a director, as a film-maker, you're continually made aware of how drastically the choices you are making – your crew, actors, rehearsal, location, lens – will affect the final film. In the writing process, you can fool yourself and think you're alone, but you're not. The 'grids' you're working with and against – readability, page count, the layout's natural prediliction for dialogue, etc. – are so universal; they are the voices of unseen collaborators, and if you listen to them all the time, the writing process itself becomes formulaic. For Christ's sake, every one doesn't have to write a movie the same way! I mean, it would be like everyone rehearsing their movies the same way, with all actors – like robots – using the exact same method.

So many writers throw up their hands and deliver the same basic script over and over again. Of course, someone like Paul Schrader is working one way, Robert Towne is working another way, Gus Van Sant another way – many screenwriters do rebel against these standards. A lot of the people making interesting movies are – not coincidentally – pushing and pulling at the format of the screenplay as much as they can.

*You seem to have your own ways of rebelling against it in the screenplay for* Heavy. *First of all, in your directions you introduce a character by name only after that character has been identified in the film. For instance, in the film, we don't know who the two women conversing are until we see Dolly's name tag, and get a full close-up of Callie's face. Instead of introducing her name on the first page, you simply call her a YOUNG WOMAN until that point in the script. It approximates the phenomenological experience of the film.*

Toward the end of my time at Columbia, I was teaching undergraduate writing and directing, and I was always telling my students to write as if they were describing a movie to a blind person.

Yet you've got to be brief, keep things moving along. You can't take twenty pages to describe every nuance of Liv Tyler's [Callie's] face, you need to move on. Essentially, if you don't know a character's name, don't offer it to the reader until they learn it in the course of watching the film. This method of writing is a kind of protection, because you don't fool yourself. If you introduce a character with a lot of detail – 'Into the room walks Hank, a thirty-ish stockbroker, with a hero's smile and a predilection for loose women and fast cars' – you're fooling yourself and all the people you're working with, suggesting you're going to get all of that information into that moment.

*What about using sound effects so prominently?*
That I got from a wonderful writing teacher at CalArts named Gil Dennis. He had us watch five minutes of an existing film and then write the screenplay for the scene we'd just watched; you know, going backwards. What I remember is this powerful scene from Joseph Losey and Harold Pinter's *The Servant*, with Wendy Craig and James Fox. Wendy Craig is seducing James Fox on a butcher-block kitchen table at night, with water dripping from the faucet. The water dripping plays such an incredibly significant rhythmic role in accentuating the tension, counting off the seconds. Transcribing that scene, I realized how much certain sound effects – even things like clocks ticking – have to do with punctuating a movie, and they should, if possible, be noted in the script.

*Victor seemed basically like a sketch, or study, for* Heavy. *The lead character is an overweight, shy photo clerk who falls in love with a young college student, is rebuffed, and then, at the end of the film, seems about to enter into a relationship with a store clerk. When you made* Victor, *did you know you would eventually be doing a feature film with essentially the same lead character in a very similar situation?*
In fact, it was a very interesting genesis, because I had accumulated so much ambition about this character Victor. I had him working days in a photo shop and nights in his mother's restaurant – I had all this stuff going on. I almost couldn't solve the screenplay because I had too many ideas. There was an 'A' story – at the tavern – and a 'B' story – at a photo shop. When I made *Victor*, I just lifted the 'B' plot from *Heavy*. Then when I turned back to *Heavy*, I thought, 'Well, now I'll skip the "B" plot since I did it

already,' and suddenly the 'A' plot made more sense. Your head can be filled with so many ideas that you can drown your film. Sometimes you can break it in two – like an earthworm – and let the two halves live separately.

*Victor* wasn't a 'study' for *Heavy* because I never really had that much confidence that I was going to get a million dollars to make *Heavy*. Making *Victor*, I was just trying to experiment – to reawaken myself to what I liked about making movies. And I was truly astounded at the quality of the experiment, because I really thought it was going to be much more of an indulgent learning experience than a film.

*When did you start writing* Heavy?
The central ideas came out of my post-Disney depression. I had gained fifteen or sixteen pounds, I was living at home, making elaborate breakfasts every morning and avoiding writing, and I was thinking about the place I grew up, which had this tavern where a very heavy guy worked – it was his mother's place. I started assembling all these ideas and added the idea of invisibility because, personally, I'd been so high-profile, and then I just disappeared. The contradiction between being bigger than other people and at the same time being unseen were just spinning off of this – tons of ideas – but I had no idea how to shape them. Then I came to Columbia and I made *Victor*. In my second year there, Miloš Forman selected me for this group of five people he was going to work with. We all arrived the first day without any movies to shoot – it was a directing class, but I arrived without a script! So I started writing ten or twenty pages every week. By the end of the semester, I had a feature screenplay. Miloš's brilliant gift to me, because in his early work he had been doing these incredibly intimate observational movies, was that he *understood* what I wanted to do – in a way that no other teacher or advisor ever had. One day, he said to me, 'This movie is about what occurs on page X.' And I quickly fumbled to page X, and it was the scene in which Victor says, 'She's fine,' after someone asks how his mother – who has just died – is doing. Miloš said, 'There's your event. Stop worrying you've got a plotless movie and just expand on that.' As I was first writing on the movie, I had Victor lying about her death for, like, two days. But when he pointed to that lie as the big event, I realized

I should explore why someone wouldn't tell anyone that his mother had died, and how long he might sustain it. Because the longer it goes, the more dramatic it is.

Anyway, I'd never had a teacher who would isolate these kind of life moments as key plot points; others were more worried about the fact that the 'plot', in a conventional 'bomb under the table' sense, wasn't going anywhere.

I'm much more about trying to collect these organic life moments and trying to figure everything out, which is, admittedly, a much sloppier way of going about writing a movie. Given that I come from a family of painters, it's the only way I can work, as opposed to creating this incredibly severe architecture and then trying to breathe life into it. I'd much rather take life and try to shift it around and figure out an order.

*That was your first draft?*
Yeah, I worked on it a lot after that. I continued working with Miloš after that semester, sending him stuff. The basic idea – this kind of beauty-and-beast relationship with this incredible connection between the two of them, yet with an overriding sense of impossibility about any kind of real love happening – was there. The other central idea that also got crystallized at that point was that this was going to be a movie about a person who moves an inch. This is a fascination of mine, the idea of making a movie in which a small distance is traveled but it feels big. Most movies are about someone moving from a position of possibility to a position of triumph or tragedy. In this case, I was making a movie about someone moving from no possibility to possibility. That was the triumph. A character with absolutely no choices moves to a place where he has a few.

So those central ideas were there. I'd say that three-quarters of the movie as it exists now was written in that context with Miloš. It was very freeing for me: I'd write long sequences of talk-radio dialogue or the 'Turtle crossing the road' scene and he'd say, 'Well, I don't know if this will work or not. Shoot it and cut it if it doesn't.' He knew that I was going to direct it, so there was this inherent sense of playfulness in it all.

*Was the script finished by the time you finished school?*
*Heavy* – the film itself – was actually my thesis. I could have made

*Victor* my thesis, or the screenplay to *Heavy*, but I didn't because I really wanted to stay a part of the film community at Columbia. So even though I'd completed my credits, I went off and shot *Heavy* without having formally graduated.

*Heavy* solidified in the year or so after that class with Miloš. That's when I teamed up with Richard Miller, who produced it. It never changed too much, although I was always messing with it. It's a lesson in how the first burst of energy needs to be respected. I tend to think that you can really mitigate something into the ground, worrying too much. You can gain tremendous amounts from reworking a script over and over, but essentially you are blunting what you originally did. Over and over I find that you end up going right back to where you started, taking some of the fruits of your reworking and plugging them back into the original draft. No matter how much logistical thinking you do later about ways a script could be better, there's primal energy in a first draft. You really need to respect it.

*Once you had the script together, when did you go about getting the film financed and made?*
The fall/winter of '93. I wanted to shoot in 35mm. And I wanted a seven-week schedule, which is rather long for an independent film. But I knew that this kind of silent wordless thing is extremely time-consuming – it requires more set-ups. You can't knock out a page in a two-shot. Also, I'm not a big fan of rehearsing outside the spaces in which the movie will actually take place. Given that we weren't able to trundle all of the actors to upstate New York and put them in the tavern to rehearse, I wanted time to do it in the moment, because when you're making a movie that's all about gestures and props imbued with so much meaning, it becomes a false rehearsal to bring actors into an empty room with masking tape on the floor and ask them to play the scene. It also puts me at a disadvantage, because so much of the architecture of the space – the food slot, the bar, the kitchen implements, for instance – is going to affect the staging. To pretend those things don't matter is to acknowledge the way a lot of modern movies are made: you just pop a 50mm lens on and pan and tilt and dolly wherever the actors move as they chatter away.

*Was this the actual tavern from your hometown you were referring to earlier?*
No, that one wouldn't have worked. It had changed since the old days. Pete and Dolly's Tavern was tough to find – the script made so many specific demands on it. It had to physically conform to the script, because we didn't have the money to be knocking down walls. When we finally found that tavern, the one in the film, I could just see these scenes getting played out in it – with only a few small modifications. The house where Victor and his mom lived didn't so much have to look a certain way – I didn't care whether it was an old house or a fifties house – but I was concerned with where the doors were, where the hallway was, where the kitchen would be, the way these spaces played. I finally decided on this house that had a cupboard that opened on both sides – it was like the food slot in the tavern. To me, the movie was endlessly about looking through something at something.

*That's very clear in your camera directions.*
I have a personal little mantra I'm always repeating to myself: variety is not the spice of life. There is a beauty to ritual. When you're making a movie about someone who moves a small distance, who doesn't talk much about how he's feeling, one of the ways to extrapolate what's going on with him is to watch him doing the same thing many times over. Of course, each time he's doing it, he's doing if differently, because he's changing.

Anyway, it's the same with limiting the number of locations. Often, plays are written and imbued with a real claustrophobia – it is all jammed into this one room – and that's great for a movie, too. If you make an *Uncle Vanya* where suddenly everyone's wandering all over the fucking place, you've destroyed part of its power. In *Heavy*, Dolly sits in this armchair in the kitchen and then – later – she's dead. Then, Callie is sitting in the same chair, weeping, and then – later yet – Leo comes in and sits there and eats cheese. Because that chair is so leaned upon throughout the movie, it gains a certain power that wouldn't exist if you were always trying to keep things moving to different places for variety's sake. These little micro-discoveries and micro-struggles with spaces, doorways or chairs are really very fruitful. I learned this from the films of Ozu, who really wasn't afraid to keep playing with permutations of the same space. He'd take you through elaborate transitions from one space to another, but wouldn't necessarily try to break the movie out into new spaces all the time.

*The traces the characters leave on spaces, as well as objects, play a significant role. For instance, the toothmarks on Dolly's toast, or the shots of a door swinging in a frame after someone has walked through it. Then there are the scenes of them driving to the overlook near the airport, where, instead of viewing a car driving into the frame and parking, you simply see car lights briefly hitting a 'No trespassing' sign.* Sometimes those short cuts seem simply like short cuts – laziness – if you don't reinvest in them, ritualize them. But there is a level where, if you confidently repeat the same gestures, the same cinematic contractions, people begin to understand that there's some system of logic at work in the film. Besides, you can't, in movies, always have people arriving and leaving; you need to find ways in and out faster.

*Can you talk about the fantasy sequences – Victor's rescue of Callie and the subsequent appearances of 'Wet Callie'? You never really indicate that what we're watching is any different from the rest of the film's action.*
I'd argue with that; the music indicates it. But, you're right, it's not telegraphed. It's not clear that this isn't really happening. Which essentially was my little game with the *Psycho* iconography: Who killed her? Jeff? Victor? I really enjoy that cheat. I think there's an interesting emotional flow in the movie. In that scene, where he sees her lying in the water, it's the first time the movie is clearly Victor's. It's an ensemble movie up until that point. Then, finally, you're in Victor's head. I really didn't want to just say on a literary level: 'This is what Victor's thinking right now.' I wanted to invest in the beauty of the fantasy, which is all the better if *you* believe it. If you're like, 'Wow, this is kind of sexy, the way he's pulling her back to life.' And then suddenly having to deal with the fact that it didn't happen.

*Regarding music; you obviously take a great interest in underscoring the moods of your films with their soundtracks. In* Victor, *you used some pieces by Erik Satie to create an elegiac tone, and Thurston Moore's soundtrack for* Heavy *has a similar effect.*

One of the things I was most concerned about was that *Heavy* would end up being perceived as a sort of a Rust Belt ensemble film – a *Last Picture Show* remake. Yet it had all these dreamy lyrical elements to it: fantasies, the guy in the hospital, the invisibility issues. I didn't want a country-western, upstate-New York soundtrack. Thurston's score did everything that I was hoping it would. It staked a much more modernist ground for the movie and, at the same time, kind of sutured a lot of thematic ideas together.

*How did you come up with the premise for* Cop Land?
I had been thinking about making a movie like this for some time. I grew up in a town in the Hudson Valley of New York where a lot of cops and firemen from New York City had bought one-acre plots. It was during the seventies, when there was this 'white flight' from the city. Many of the friends I went to school with were children of civil servants in New York City, so I was exposed to a lot of this anger about the Brooklyn and Queens neighborhoods that had changed – gone ethnic – and the city that had betrayed them – gone liberal – and how these changes had caused them to set out and make a new home for themselves and their families. I remember going on a field trip to see *The Nutcracker* in New York City, and was amazed to find that many of the kids I went to school with had never been to Manhattan. They lived an hour and a half away from the biggest city in the world, their parents worked there, and yet these kids had no exposure to the city other than to know to fear it. Everyone shopped in Paramus.

As I would tell people about this odd population of my home town, it always occurred to me that there were certain parallels with the issues of the frontier and the Old West. A new land, a fresh start for some gun-toting men and their families, a sense of community – being with others of like minds and similar anger – and a uniting fear of what they had escaped catching up with them. I asked myself who would be the most interesting character to follow in a town full of cops, and the answer I came up with – already feeling the Western vibe of the setting – was the local sheriff.

Also, around the time I started writing this, the news was filled with stories about the Rodney King incident in LA and the Mollen Commission Hearings on police corruption in New York City. And there was a consistent theme that ran through many of these stories: often these cops-gone-bad were commuters – 'Hessians,' as they're called by other cops in New York City – who found themselves risking their lives protecting a place they had no personal stake in.

*In some ways, this was quite a departure for you from* Heavy.
After writing *Heavy*, I wanted to write a movie that wasn't so ephemeral, if that's the right word, something that drove me and the story a little harder. Yet what I was uninspired by were the formulas of current action films. I found myself continually attracted in the thought process to Westerns, because to me they somehow have this very formal quality, and a lot of character – certainly a lot more than modern action films. When people think back about certain Westerns, they often remember them being more high-octane than they actually were. They were generally these amazing character pieces about a man caught in a real moral crisis – where, in a sense, law, righteousness, right or wrong, were all up to him to define. And of course there were other really beautiful big themes, like redemption, or revenge, or religious freedom. The films that rang over and over in my head when I was writing this were *Shane* and *3:10 to Yuma*.

High Noon *has been mentioned in several reviews of the film.*
Everyone talks about that film. *High Noon* was much less important to me in making the movie than the two I mentioned.

*What about* Bad Day at Black Rock? *That film also features an emasculated sheriff who's been bullied into submission by the bad eggs who run the town.*
After I'd written *Cop Land*, people suggested I look at it. I hadn't before I wrote it, though. To me, *High Noon* and *Bad Day at Black Rock* are great films, but they didn't pack the emotional wallop I wanted. Ultimately, though, I think that *Cop Land* has turned out to be more like those films than *Shane* or *3:10 to Yuma*. Part of what I came to understand while making the movie was that when you have a piece with so many characters, you can't be centered in enough on one person to effect the kind of single character emotionality you find in those films. In *Heavy*, there are lots of supporting characters, but they're all pretty marginalized. It's a fine difference in *Cop Land*, but with the addition

of all of these plot elements, there are things you have to explain – the interstices of the modern world, how law enforcement works, people plotting against one another – which take your attention away from Sylvester Stallone's character.

Actually, what's interesting to me is that almost every major event on a plot level in the movie is discreet from the separate character story of this guy living on the outskirts. I mean, if you didn't have Freddy in the film, you'd pretty much have a cop movie. Freddy is the Western. I don't know, maybe I can't put my finger on it that cleanly; I'm still processing it, just like I processed *Heavy* after it came out.

*We'll talk more about this later, but since you brought up* Heavy, *do you find that you went through a similar process, from first draft to finished film, with* Cop Land?
The kinds of changes that occurred between the screenplay and the finished film were pretty much the same with both *Heavy* and *Cop Land*. As a writer/director, I don't really feel the evolution of the film is a succeeding or failing of the screenplay. The screenplay is a draft of the movie, the shoot is a rewrite, and the cutting is the final draft. Not to be New Agey about it, but it's interesting to take this journey of discovery and see what lives and what doesn't through this process.

In both movies I excised a further internal investigation into the private life of the protagonist. At some point the story engine took over and was not going to let me indulge in, for instance, Freddy's world of music or Victor's drink-mixing or cookery. These private activities on some level took away from the obvious story goals. In *Heavy*, the guy's lonely, and he desperately wants to make a connection with someone other than his mother. But by suddenly focusing on his cooking too much in the middle of the movie – as I did in the script – his relation to Liv Tyler's character was being minimized emotionally. In *Cop Land*, if Freddy's attachment to classical music had more to do with the central plot lines of the movie, which are so strong, then it somehow would've lived. But it really became a frustrating denial on Freddy's part regarding everything that was going on around him. Actually, that Glenn Gould stuff was added on much later. I don't know if this is true for other writers, but when you sit with the screenplay for a while, you can start over-tweaking, throwing extra stuff in. A good friend of mine is a Glenn Gould fanatic, and I got inspired one day to shovel that world into the screenplay. But when you live with the movie, you realize Freddy's preoccupation had to be that he dreams about being a cop, not a classical music aficionado.

*When did you write the first draft?*
I wrote it in 1993, and Miramax bought it that same year.

*It sounds like your focusing on character habits is a tool you use to get to the fundamentals of plot.*
The truth is, I resist plot, and my inspiration for a script tends to be a collection of character beats and interactions between spaces and people – I tend to back into the plot. Once I dramatize these scenes – put them up on their feet – I begin to realize the kind of tangent I've gone off on. I just don't like it when I see the script making too much of a beeline. I get really scared, so I start throwing these kinds of wrenches in the script. Some are true, but some aren't. It's the difference between a novel and a screenplay. Internal moments in film are very tricky. All these dangers are increased when you have characters like the ones I write, who hesitate to take standard screenplay action. It's one thing for them to hesitate; but it's something else to have them further embed themselves in activity that's peripheral.

If you look at *Taxi Driver*, at some point Travis Bickle goes into this intensely private period, where he starts playing with guns, writing diaries, following newspapers – but all of that is in line toward action. Every one of these little private explorations is a preparation for action, not an avoidance of it. Like the gathering of a storm.

*Why did you decide to set* Cop Land *in New Jersey?*
Well, I wanted to put the movie in New Jersey so I could see the city across the river, because I was thinking about the importance of geography in the Western – that kind of big town/little town thing, looking for smoke signals over the mountain, knowing every path between the two settlements. I was talking to Lester Cohen, the Production Designer, and I told him that if this were a book, the endpages would feature a map of the world it depicts: The Town on one side, The City on the other and The Bridge span-

ning the two. That's almost all you need. The men in this town commute across that bridge every day into this city they hate, wondering if they'll make it home alive to this new frontier, this suburbia, they've established. To see that compression of geography – have it just be 'there' all the time – was really important. But I've always been a fan of compressed geography, and not only in Westerns. I mean, think of *Rear Window*, or almost any of Hitchcock's other films, except for *North by Northwest*.

*I noticed a disclaimer at the end of the film stating that it's actually illegal for New York City policemen to live outside of New York State.*
Well, I never felt like I was making a Sidney Lumet movie. For one thing, I didn't want to jump into that sandbox and have to compete. And besides, I didn't want the movie to be an absolutely realistic depiction of modern law enforcement: I barreled through the constraints of what actually could and could not happen pretty quickly as I wrote this.

*You obviously did some pretty extensive research, though.*
I did a lot of research, but I think you can know too much. For me, it's such a troubling thing when, for instance, you know something is best for the story if it goes a certain way, but then you find out it's not possible because they just passed a law last year making it illegal. That disclaimer was put at the end of the movie in anticipation of the media's usual reaction to a film that happens to be about real-life issues. It's going to be perceived, no matter what I say, as an 'issue film,' and suddenly any breaches with reality are going to be attacked.

I think I was making this movie for people who don't live in New York, because I knew there was a level to it which people who actually live here would have all kinds of problems with. It's different with the Western. None of us ever lived there, so the film-maker has this tremendous freedom, even more so than doing a science-fiction movie, because in sci-fi you have to justify every bit of technology. But you seldom question the way things are depicted in the Western, even though there are often gigantic holes: 'Oh my God, there wasn't a gold-rush that year after all,' or 'Wait – the Indians weren't hostile at all in that area.' I mean, nobody sat George Stevens down and told him he'd gotten it wrong.

So one of the sad facts of modern film is that, unless you put something in outer space, you're setting yourself up for all kinds of problems. This slavishness to current fact causes anyone with an imagination to run into a land of complete make-believe – and it inhibits storytelling.

Have you ever noticed how people always exaggerate when they're recounting something that happened to them? Like the classic case of the guy describing the size of the fish he caught? Well, there's a reason people make the fish bigger – why they heighten the drama when they're telling a story about something they experienced. It's because they want to impart upon the listener the feeling they had, the sense of wonder or excitement they felt when they lived through it. And when a storyteller makes everything accurate, it's boring. I remember when *Jaws* came out, there was all this discussion about the fact that great white sharks had never been found near Martha's Vineyard, or that they couldn't grow to be as big as the one in the movie. Give me a break! It's so stupid. I think it comes from the fact that drama – what makes it work, the ways in which we're drawn to it – is so undiscussed, that generally, people's approach to criticizing drama is as if they're criticizing an article in *Newsweek*.

*How did you come up with the whole 'diagonal rule' metaphor Figs expounds upon throughout the film? Was that police department lingo you came across while doing research?*
No, I didn't do my research until after I'd written two passes on the screenplay. That to me was a lesson in how you can get to truth through total bullshit. It came from the way I always walked around Manhattan. When I was standing on a corner, with one sign saying 'Walk' and the other saying 'Don't Walk,' I would always go wherever it said 'Walk,' just to keep moving. You enter into a rhythm, where you don't want to stop in one of those sweaty packs of people on the curb. So I thought of this as my own little 'diagonal rule' of walking around Manhattan, and I wrote it into the first draft as dialogue for Figs. But later on, after Mike McAlary and some other cops read the script, they all commented on the diagonal rule idea as being so true to how cops talk and think.

*How did you come up with the character of Figs?*
Well, for all my love of wordless – or at least less articulate –

characters, I myself have a very big mouth and can go on big rants when I feel like it, so I wanted to find that part of myself in somebody in this movie. Also, in some ways he's the other half of Freddy: they're the same guy, enmeshed in ambiguity. Figs is just more active about it, scheming, going behind people's backs, that kind of thing. And he's always constructing theories in an attempt to rationalize his way out of everything.

*Can you talk about the similarities between Victor, the protagonist in* Heavy, *and Freddy Heflin? Both seem trapped in a certain stasis when we first meet them, and both, as you put it in the* Heavy *interview, end up 'moving an inch,' although the repercussions of Freddy's transformation are much greater.*

No matter what anyone says about similarities between the two characters, Freddy is much further along than Victor was. When I look at *Cop Land*, I don't imagine the lead character is a virgin, or someone who's never dated a girl.

*Well, he's also had this moment of glory in his youth, when he rescued Liz from the submerged car.*

But also, he has responsibility and functions, and he doesn't have Shelley Winters yelling at him all the time. But there is the same kind of melancholy to his character. One thing that makes me mad is when people talk about my characters as 'retarded' or 'slow.' It's the same thing when people ask me, 'What's the deal with fat in your movies?' Well, all I'm trying to do is actually put people in movies who seem like the people I see in the real world. But there's this grid system in movies: everyone's so beautiful. I mean, when Liv Tyler's playing the dowdy sister in *Inventing the Abbotts*, you know there's something crazy and skewed going on in terms of aesthetics of beauty and the way movies are cast. Liv was great in that movie, but that just proves my point. If one of the most beautiful women in the world can inhabit that kind of role, it shows the strange relationship between the audience and beauty on film. When you're working with movie stars, it's more important to close the gap between their glamour and the characters they play. Sly is not fat in *Cop Land*; he just went from having a Mr Universe body to the body of a regular guy.

Also, we're so used to characters who have a weapon for everything in their bat belt, or who have a retort for every smart remark.

Those are all such well-worn rituals in movies now that suddenly when you don't do that – when your character receives an insult and doesn't come back with anything – some people might think of him as dumb. The fact is, when people hit me verbally, I usually just don't know what to say, and I'm a pretty smart guy. Besides, whose actions in the movie are more stupid? Ray Donlan's, Figs's or Freddy's? The person conducting himself with the most intelligence given the quandary he's in is Freddy Heflin. What's he going to do, ruin his life and arrest all of his friends because one guy he barely knows tells them they have Mob connections? And while almost everyone else in the film has such a clean agenda, like Tilden, for instance, Freddy has no big prize waiting for him if he does the right thing. I tried to explore that notion of how we all do things for such fucked-up reasons in the late part of the film. Freddy thinks, 'Well, if I do this, maybe Liz will really like me.' And she makes it clear she doesn't want to get involved with it. Even his deputies don't support him.

*I've noticed that there is a certain amount of expanded dialogue, as well as several entirely new scenes, for some of the characters in the script published here, compared with an earlier, slightly leaner draft from 1995 you sent me a while ago. Did that have something to do with securing the participation of people like De Niro and Keitel?*
I'm trying to remember. Which scenes in particular?

*For instance, there's an entire scene added into this script (and the film) in which De Niro's character, Moe Tilden, has a brief, tense confrontation with Harvey Keitel's character, Ray Donlan, in the Garrison town deli.*
Actually, I wrote a draft long before Bob was involved which opens with Moe Tilden in the bar with Freddy, where he lays out this central challenge to Freddy in the first ten pages. But that really destroyed the chance to set up the town first. But I think even that far back I saw the importance of having the Tilden character actually come to Garrison. I will say that, in part, understanding the power of the actor playing the part does suddenly free you to imagine that it doesn't have to be a big dialogue-heavy scene, it can just be a scene where he grins and hands out his business card and leaves.

xxviii

*In that earlier draft, you also have Figs, in the scene where his house has caught fire, arriving home in time to burst into the house and carry Monica back out, as Freddy stands by watching, pretty much paralysed, on the sidelines.*

To tell you the truth, I had to cut back on that scene to get the budget down. What I loved about the original scene was Figs running into the fire while Freddy is facing the limits of his own bravery. I liked the idea of Freddy witnessing the 'can-do-ness' of these New York City cops, and Figs, in particular, on his own turf.

*There seems to be more exposition in this script, particularly regarding the interconnections between Ray Donlan, the town of Garrison and the Mob, than there was in earlier drafts.*

Well, the draft that's published here is the 'everything in the kitchen sink' draft. This draft has scenes I wrote that I never folded into the shooting script. I wanted people to see where my mind was rambling. I don't understand the usefulness of published screenplays when they're tailored to reflect what appeared on-screen, so I thought with both *Heavy* and *Cop Land* I'd go in the opposite direction and show the reader everything I was thinking.

*Can you talk about the evolution of the long interrogation scene in this draft, in which De Niro's character is first introduced?*

Until three weeks before we started shooting, I had always started that interrogation scene just as they were finishing up. Basically, Tilden shut down the discussion and said, 'Let's take a break,' and then he left and had another short conversation with Carson in a different office. What happened was, the week before production began, Bob and I got to hang out at Internal Affairs, and they staged a mock interrogation with a cop for us. It was fantastic, and it inspired the shit out of us.

So Bob and I went back and called in all the other actors who were in the interrogation scene. Based upon what I'd taped during the mock interrogation, I wrote, like, five pages of bantering, interrogating – this, to answer your earlier question, was definitely a function of falling in love with Bob De Niro and wanting to see more of him. Then we got together in a rehearsal and worked on the five pages, which I boiled down to the three in this script. It was really intense – Bob, Malik Yoba, Victor Williams, the guy who played the cop and Bruce Altman, the lawyer, were all great. The problem was, you just can't stay anywhere for that long in a movie like this. If you saw that scene you'd say, 'Wow! That's great!' But when you drop it into the movie, it's like, 'Where the fuck is this movie going?! What is the point?'

*Speaking of exposition, in this draft there's also a moment in which Freddy, looking in the direction of the water tower, suddenly realizes that Superboy has been hiding there all along. In the film, he needs a little help from Rose Donlan, who tells him where her nephew is hiding when he goes to visit her. I liked the subtlety of the first solution.*

I loved it, too. There is a war that goes on between the beautiful language of cinema and the realities of exposition. The way it was originally written would have made a really nice film moment, of him looking toward the water tower and then cutting to him climbing it. But you had to concretely understand how Freddy knew Babitch was in the tower. As Sandy MacKendrick often told me, 'Sometimes you have to kill your babies.'

*How many rewrites did you do on this script?*

In terms of really major revisions of the movie, maybe three. And I'd do reworkings of specific scenes, or I'd take stabs at things – like sticking De Niro's character in the bar – and then I'd bail.

*How did Stallone become involved?*

Essentially, Miramax was very torn between holding out and trying to find a really big star for the movie, which would justify making the movie at a higher budget level, or doing it with a real, real low budget – maybe $6 million – with a cast of actors you'd probably heard of, but who wouldn't guarantee box office. I was busy rewriting at that point, but the early drafts were generating a lot of 'buzz' in Hollywood, even though there were still obvious problems with the script: it had a great opening, and a great ending, but not much of a middle. The other thing with Miramax is, they're not going to pay a major actor his normal rate, so when Harvey Weinstein believes that the cast could be really stellar, you've got to find people who love it enough to want to do it for less.

One day I got a call from Arnold Rifkin, who was Sly's agent at the time. He said Sly had read *Cop Land* and really liked it, and had also responded strongly to *Heavy*. And I said, 'You've gotta be kidding me. The guy doesn't make movies like this. I mean, he's a great actor – he was amazing in *Rocky* – but he's only making these humungous action movies now. Not only that, if he *were* going to do it, he would have to lose the buff body and gain a lot of weight. And I've heard frightening stories about stars who are this big who take over movies – this would have to be *my* movie, and follow my direction, and the screenplay couldn't change . . .' I hit Rifkin with this flurry of paranoia, and I was shocked when he said to me, 'Tell him. I'll put the two of you together.'

So Stallone flew to New York to see me. We met for dinner at the Four Seasons. I remember rounding the corner in the restaurant and seeing him sitting alone at a table, looking very sweet. I knew immediately he was going to be in the film. I sat down and told him all my reservations, and he countered each one of them, telling me how tired he was of making the same kind of movies. 'I want to wake up and not be sure I can handle the work of the day.' He wanted to feel alive again. I got really attached to him that night, and it seemed clear to me from our conversation that he would really be on my side, and would actually function as a sort of 800lb gorilla who would protect me.

I mean, beyond all that, it was an incredible opportunity for me to roll the dice and see if I could try to collaborate with this megastar and come out with something different.

*What did you need Stallone to protect you from?*
This was my first big movie, and someone as powerful as Sly aligning himself with my vision of the film merely meant that that vision would be further secured. It was less about him defending me against adversaries than it was about me sensing that this relationship was an alliance, and would be a source of power in getting the movie made the right way.

*Did his commitment lead immediately to this cavalcade of big guns attaching themselves to the movie?*
Well, one thing to keep in mind was the fact that if you have Sylvester Stallone playing a fallible, 'weak' man in a film, you don't want little-known character actors playing the people who are pressing against him and intimidating him. You want the playing field releveled, with actors with enough weight to make his vulnerability in the film seem justifiable.

Right after we did a press conference announcing Sly's involvement, we all went upstairs and sat in this conference room, going through who might be good for the other roles in the movie. I remember in my own glib way saying, 'Harvey, why don't we send this to Bob De Niro; he'd make a great Tilden.' He said to me, 'How long would it take him to play this role?' I was like, 'Five days.' Of course, it ended up being two-and-a-half weeks. So Harvey started chasing him around with the script. I met him in LA, and we got along. And then it started falling into place. Cathy Konrad [the producer] had the idea of casting Janeane Garofalo as Cindy, and I'd just seen her in *The Truth about Cats and Dogs*, which I thought was great. So we put in a call to her, and it turns out she was a big *Heavy* fan. Ray Liotta had been tracking the script, and loved it, and I thought he'd make the perfect Figs. At that point, the casting of the movie had become this sort of 'happening.'

Although Harvey Keitel was on the top of our list to play Donlan, he had been committed to another movie, but then it fell apart. The first time I met him was on Bob's rooftop in TriBeCa. Bob and I were talking about who might be right for this part, and he just got on the phone and said, 'Harv, come up here, I've got somebody for you to meet.' So Harvey came up to the rooftop, without his shirt on, and he looked fabulous: 'Hey, how you doin'?' It was the most amazing experience. There are moments when you pinch yourself: 'I'm sitting on a rooftop with Bob De Niro and Harvey Keitel.'

*You didn't have any actors in mind when you were writing?*
Van Heflin. That's it. The hubris involved in imagining four years ago that actors of this caliber would be in my movie – I mean, I may have lots of confidence at times, but I don't have that much confidence.

*Wasn't there a concern on your part about feeling a bit overawed by these actors?*
It's like painting with really good brushes or cooking with the best ingredients. Everyone came in feeling they had something to learn or gain. And Sly really wanted this collaborative process, which isn't to say he was just putty in my hands – he's a very smart guy, and had lots of great suggestions, as all of the actors did. Every one of them was so willing to give their best to this.

I'll give you an example. You might have noticed that in this script, in the scene in which Freddy comes to visit Moe Tilden at the Internal Affairs office, Tilden isn't eating a sandwich, as he is quite entertaining in the film. What happened was, we had been rehearsing the scene, and it was really flat. We all felt pretty awful. There are times during production when the results are just not great, regardless of who you're working with. Those moments are utterly humanizing – you're just stuck with each other and you've got to figure a way out together. Anyway, I asked the actors to stay through lunch so we could keep working on it, and the caterers brought up sandwiches. Since Stallone was the only one on his feet in the scene, he couldn't eat his while he was rehearsing. So Bob was opening his sandwich, and I said, 'Let's run through it one more time. I just want to hear it again so I can figure out where we're going wrong here.' In the middle of the scene, after Sly had finished this impassioned plea, Bob suddenly looked up, with mayonnaise all over him and says, 'I need a napkin.' And I was like, 'That's it!' What a great signal that he's completely shut this guy off. By the way, I'm sure Bob knew exactly what he was doing at that moment. Maybe not consciously, but in some powerful, intuitive part of his brain he was trying to find an effective way to physicalize the scene. I immediately ran and ordered twenty-five sandwiches for the afternoon.

That scene gets a lot of laughs, and I think part of the reason it's such a big relief for the audience is that a character of tremendous authority finally calls Freddy on what we as an audience have become increasingly impatient about. When he says, 'You blew it,' it's almost like he's saying, 'You blew the movie. It's an hour into it, and you're supposed to be doing shit already.' Any time the audience is feeling something that is not at all acknowledged on the screen, a distance is set up between the audience and the film. And if at no point the film turns around and says, 'Oh, that distance? I know about that distance, I know what you're thinking. I've got this story under control,' you're going to lose the audience. Anyway, to me, that's a great example of how you can get in trouble and find your way out by keeping your eyes open. So you see, in working with actors of this caliber, the working day is just like it is with anybody else. There are moments where you get frightened, and others where you get elated. It was only later, in dailies, where I really had the opportunity to register the fact that I'd been working with these icons.

*I noticed that, among all the actors, Keitel was the only one who was absolutely faithful to your dialogue, even down to the 'ums.'*
Harvey is very fastidious.

*Having read through or heard about all the ideas you had while you were writing and shooting the film, I'm curious to know how you managed to boil it down to a 95-minute film in the editing room.*
Cutting is an extremely painful process for me, because what moves me to get involved in movies is so much more about character and images than it is about plot. I still don't think of myself as a screenwriter. I could not, I think, write for hire; I have a very messy process. Every frame in a movie informs the audience so much more than you realize. For instance, in our first preview, it was amazing to me how quickly audiences 'got' Freddy as a character – without further scenes spelling it out for them. And then there was the pulling over of the black kids in the Suzuki.

*That's a four- or five-page scene in this script.*
That's a big one. I loved that scene, because beyond all the drama, it was a scene that united the geography of the town. As the Suzuki drives through the streets, it goes past the cops playing softball, and Cindy and Bill in the Sheriff's office, and Freddy and Figs pumping gas, and one by one they jump into their cars and start following it. I remember Cathy Konrad saying to me during the writing, 'You know, I'm not sure that scene has a function any more.' And I would be like, 'But it's so cool! I bet it'll be in the trailer!' I had the most childish reaction; I thought it was so important, but for all the most feeble reasons. At that point, you already know these guys are evil, and you've gotten the sense of racial division – it's all much more subtle without it. Also, that scene sort of stopped the plot engine for a little while. Where was Babitch? What was going to happen to him? The editor, Craig McKay, kept saying in the cutting room, 'Babitch *is* the storyline, and every time we leave him for more than one scene you are going to feel like the movie has stopped.'
The funny thing is, Miramax *did* put that scene in the trailer. It

was perfect, because anybody who saw the TV ads or the trailers were walking into the film with this sense of exposition about what this town was without me having to fuck up the narrative by actually showing the scene.

*Besides adding De Niro's voice-overs at the beginning and end of the film, you also managed to take care of some exposition by relegating it to TV or radio broadcasts, which, as in* Heavy, *are spread throughout the film.*
Some of those were actually in the script. Yeah, any way I could get it in. That information was there, basically, just to satisfy the questioning part of our nature. It's like parsley on a steak. Some of it was critical to relate, and some of it was just to tell the audience that the film-maker is aware that there are holes, or that there is stuff happening out there that isn't worth the investment of an entire scene. Also, in order to present a silent beat of storytelling to today's audience, I've found that you need to tickle their ears with music or information, or they might disengage. The second there's silence, you can get in trouble with an audience reared on television.

*There's a moment like that in the film that seems to have been the result of a decision on the set, because it's not alluded to here in the script: during Superboy's funeral, there's this incredibly elaborate network of glances – between Rose and Joey Randone (the adulterers) and Donlan and Liz (the cuckolds) – that reminded me of the scene in* Nashville *where Keith Carradine sings 'I'm Easy' and Altman captures all the women his character has slept with eyeing him and each other. It was immensely satisfying, and very funny.*
Yeah. That beat expanded on the set. It's one of those moments inspired by my love of silent moments in film. If you noticed, the music track is very heavy there – you've got to use sound really aggressively when there's no dialogue. I mean, if I hadn't had the talk radio playing during certain scenes in *Heavy*, I think people would have started making calls on their cell phones. In this day and age, the level of stimulus people require is so incredible – you feel like you've got to literally massage their thighs while they're watching the film.

*Near the end of the script, after Freddy has collected Superboy from the water tower, he has a long confrontational scene with Ray Donlan at the Four Aces Tavern, where he enters and tells Ray, 'I've found Superboy,' and then proceeds to inform him that he's bringing him in to Internal Affairs the next morning. In the film, that scene is brought forward almost twenty pages – right after Superboy has appeared at his front door – and his line of dialogue is changed to 'Superboy came to see me last night.'*

I shifted that scene in the cutting room. Part of this has to do with who's playing Freddy. Because Sly has played so many heroes who are great at anticipating the moves of their adversaries, the perception of Freddy being 'dim' was accelerated at certain points, and this was one of them. When we screened the first cut of this, there was a *giant* reaction to that scene near the end. 'Why the hell is he volunteering the fact that he's got Babitch to a proven killer?' The audience was frustrated he would do that, and sabotage himself. There was another problem, though: I was sensing that, structurally, I had kept Freddy in his cocoon for too long. And it turned out that both things could be solved by moving the scene forward.

However, I lost some of my Western motif by changing it around. When we shot that scene, I had him walking down the center of the street – with a big crane shot – and entering the tavern. The idea there, which I cherish, was to feature a character who will walk into his own death, and say what he feels, maybe even hoping it puts a stop to everything. But however I intellectualize it, it just didn't work that way.

Quite honestly, it's so easy to jump over these things as I'm answering you and make myself sound like a smarter writer, but let me tell you what I overlooked. I'll use *3:10 to Yuma* as an example: Van Heflin has to get Glenn Ford to a train which leaves at 3:10. But it's only two o'clock, so he has to sit for over an hour with Glenn Ford while all of the bad guys figure out how to try and stop him. The problem in my film is, all those limitations of the Western genre don't exist in the modern world. There are telephones, there are cars, there are bridges, there are tunnels. If you don't call Moe Tilden, why not call the FBI, or the State Police? It was so frustrating to me. I was this dog with my teeth clamped shut on this bone of an idea that I was making a Western. At every juncture, I was fighting the logic of the modern world, and it was a real battle. If it had been physically impossible for Freddy to get

Babitch across the river before 6.00 a.m., the scene would have worked. I racked my brain trying to come up with something.

*The ending of the film is quite different from the one in this script. Several things have been added on. For example, the very last scene of Freddy, by the river in Garrison, looking over at Manhattan. Personally, I really liked the ending to the 1995 draft I read, which closes with a crane shot of the car with Freddy, Figs and Babitch moving across the George Washington Bridge.*

Actually, in the first draft from 1993 there is a car chase into Manhattan, all the way to Internal Affairs, and then there's a series of wrap-up scenes in the town with Liz, with Cindy and with Freddy sporting a new hearing-aid. Anyway, the coda scene in the film I just improvised. I felt like the movie lays itself out as the story of this one character kind of growing up and, frankly, the ending of Freddy going into the Internal Affairs building would be the equivalent of ending *Heavy* with Victor crying and Liv Tyler driving away. I tried to construct the most economical, unspoonfed kind of thing, which to me was very much a Western thing.

*I think the coda worked. My bigger problem was with the voice-over montage of news reports immediately preceding it, during which many loose ends are tied up. We hear that the Mob has been indicted, and Freddy has gotten his hearing back, etc. It was a little too much closure for my taste, and it really pulled the film away from Freddy.*

Well, when I realized I wanted to use that coda to see Sly's character develop this much more mature relationship with the city across the river – as a sort of bookend to the earlier scene – I knew I had a problem: how do you get to the coda right out of him walking into the Internal Affairs office? You couldn't – there's no way to go from one to another. Sometimes you have to do something that is bumpy in order to get to the gravy on the other side. I mean, if you watch the films you think are great, you'll find those bumpy moments in most of them, which I find to be a great lesson in giving yourself a break.

My hope with my movies is that, in ten or fifteen years, when people look back at them, and they represent a time and place that no longer exists, and the movie stars in them have moved on or are doing other things, there's a resonance to it all that's impossible to perceive now. When I took *Cop Land* on, I had no idea what the whole package was going to end up being. Once I understood the scale of this movie, I was just throwing everything in and seeing what came out the other side. It's the most perverse feeling in the world. You're following your gut, and you've got all these people looking at you, wanting your gut to be a dramatic fact.

*While you were editing* Cop Land *did you ever feel like you were steering the film toward the expectations of a general audience, as opposed to how you would have liked to see to play?*
It's never more complicated than this: if you pick out a pair of pants, and you think they're really cool, and really *you*, and then you go out into the world and everyone laughs at you, you don't wear them again. It's not like you gave up your identity, unless your identity is that you want people to snicker at you. Part of the search for your identity, or your sense of language as a film-maker, is your search for a way to express yourself that doesn't ostracize you, so you can reach somebody.

*But there's always going to be* someone *who likes your pants.*
But then, when you find yourself only in their company, are you happy? I mean, here is a movie that questions some of the fantasies of white flight and suburban bliss and it's playing right in the heart of suburbia. That's more exciting than preaching to the converted. Besides, art-house audiences can be lemmings, too. I learned that with *Heavy*. When we showed it at Sundance, the response was good, but a bit perplexed. It was a whole lot more passionate when Janet Maslin (*New York Times* lead film critic) gave it a great review and explained to everyone that the film was *supposed* to be wordless and subtle. She gave them a handle on it. My goal is really simple: to make decent films. That doesn't mean art-house. That doesn't mean mainstream. It just means 'my films.'

(The *Heavy* section of this interview was excerpted from vol. 1 no. 3 of *Scenario* magazine, 1995.)

# Cop Land

# CREDITS

INT. FOUR ACES TAVERN – GARRISON, NJ – NIGHT

The walls of this suburban bar are lined with NEW YORK CITY POLICE PARAPHERNALIA and FRAMED NEWSPAPER STORIES – tales of police heroism clipped from the major New York dailies.

A SCOTCH AND BEER MUG upon a *Lethal Weapon* PINBALL MACHINE. Danny Glover and Mel Gibson leap about a blinking triptych of high octane police action. The score tallies into the millions. Strips of tape line the side of the machine, noting high scores, almost all of which are attributed to – *Freddy*.

FREDDY HEFLIN (42), EYELIDS HEAVY, LEANS LOW OVER THE MACHINE. Fingers on the buttons, he paddles the silver ball skillfully. A belly hanging over his belt, he is a slump-shouldered man, puffy, wilted. Dull with booze, HIS EYES ARE FOCUSED ON –

A NEARBY TABLE WHERE – A HARD-JAWED WOMAN (BERTA, 38) AND A BALDING BRIGHT-EYED MAN (GARY 'FIGS' FIGGIS, 44) sip drinks. Both have the peculiar posture, gestures and vocabulary of the NYPD, though they are in civilian clothes.

> BERTA
> – but this Armenian guy, he's from the other side over there. 'Told her she's dead – that she'll be dead by morning –

> FIGS
> uh huh.

> BERTA
> – so, he drops off this box at her apartment –

> FIGS
> – and they call bomb squad –

BERTA
(nods)
– and we X-ray it – on-scene. But I can't see
anything. So I cut a little hole. And there's
something in there.

Freddy nimbly holds the ball on the flipper, straining to listen in.
SENSING FREDDY'S STARE, BERTA GROWS UNCOMFORTABLE.

Some white fuzz – and something pink. But I can't
figure what it is. And *suddenly* I realize I'm looking
at a *tongue*. A fat pink tongue – sticking out at me.

FIGS
Shit.

BERTA
The guy put a goat's head in there.

Freddy sends the ball back into play.
Figs sighs and takes an NYPD ATHLETIC BAG from beside Berta's
chair. Though unimpressed by her story, Figs is always happy to
pontificate – and he does so – as he rummages through the bag:

FIGS
*This* at the end of the twentieth century. H. G. Wells
– he'd roll over in his grave to think at the start of a
new millennium – that some Iranian –

BERTA
– Armenian.

Figs snaps the bag closed, putting it down beside *his* chair.

FIGS
– some Armenian be delivering a *goat's head* to the
door of the woman that he loves.

BERTA
'From a backward culture.

FIGS
We're all backward. Our machines are all modern
and shit – but *our minds, Berta* – our minds are
*primitive* –

4

AN ATTRACTIVE CUBAN WOMAN (32) emerges from the rest room, sniffling. From a distance, she is sexy. But as she sashays behind FIGS, kissing his ear, we see her vacant eyes.

> Come on, Monica. Sit down.

> MONICA
> I want to go home. We gotta go to your place – and I still gotta drive back to –

> FIGS
> Hey. I'm waiting on the *call*, baby.

*Beep!* FIGS REACHES FOR HIS BEEPER, looking at the display. Berta's eyes meet Freddy's eyes, *watching*.

> BERTA
> Excuse me – Do you mind? *Do you mind?*

FREDDY'S PINBALL DROPS INTO THE GUTTER. LED's blink 'DEPOSIT QUARTER TO CONTINUE' Freddy searches his pockets for quarters.

> FREDDY
> Hey. I'm sorry.

Figs rises, finger in the air, waving off the tension.

> FIGS
> It's cool, Berta. Freddy's good people. 'only got one good ear anyway.

Freddy steps back from the pinball machine. Woozy.

> CUT TO:

FREDDY AT THE BAR – HE PULLS A BILL FROM HIS WALLET.

Through the FOOD SLOT, the COOK washes dishes. There is no one behind the bar.

FREDDY LOOKS AT – BERTA, who lights her cig, watching Freddy. MONICA hovers over the jukebox. Flipping the electronic menu. FIGS stands at the pay phone by the door, *on hold*.

Freddy approaches Figs, unsteadily, dollar in hand.

                    FIGS
Quiet tonight, huh?

                    FREDDY
'at that bachelor party. Across the river.

                    FIGS
Yeah. Whoop-de-doo.
                    (into phone)
No, no. I'll hold.
                    (back to Freddy)
What is this, Freddy?
'You celebrating long distance?

Freddy thinks a moment, numb with liquor. DELORES THE
BARMAID enters from outside. She takes an empty mug from
Freddy and notices the dollar in his hand.

                    DELORES
Don't look at me. The register's closed and I put
two more in the goddamn meter.
                    (sashaying off)
It's his birthday. He needs quarters. He's going for
high score over there.

                    FIGS
Oh yeah? Happy Birthday, Freddy. Let me see what
I got.

Freddy nods.

Figs digs through the change in his pockets.

So – Where's your new girl? Your little 'deputy' –
*Wendy*.

                    FREDDY
At her mom's. *Cindy*. I wasn't into making a big
deal, you know? After the party – the ten-year thing.

Figs nods, disinterested, cradling the phone, pushing through
some change. *A voice squawks on the phone.*

                      7

FIGS

Hey, Frankie. How's it hanging? Yeah.
(empty palm to Freddy)
. . . *sorry, Freddy.*

Freddy nods, stoic. Blinks.

CUT TO:

EXT. FOUR ACES TAVERN – GARRISON, NJ – NIGHT

FREDDY HEFLIN fumbles with a LARGE RING OF KEYS.
HE UNLOCKS A PARKING METER. QUARTERS SPILL OUT INTO HIS HAND. SOME ONTO THE SIDEWALK.
Freddy kneels, picking them up.

FIGS
(off-screen)

'Two kinds of people in the world – pinball people. And video game people.

FIGS stands in the tavern doorway. He smokes a cigarette. Freddy looks up, bleary-eyed, drunk.

You – Freddy – are pinball people.

Freddy blinks, smiles sadly. Figs crosses to –

A SQUAD CAR at the curb. On the side, it says –
SHERIFF – TOWN OF GARRISON.
Figs opens the driver's door, beckoning Freddy.

Come on. It's bedtime, Sheriff.

CUT AWAY TO:

INT./EXT. SCORE'S NIGHT CLUB – MANHATTAN – NIGHT

The thumping of dance music.

COLORED LIGHT. A STRIPPER AT A POLE, ANOTHER GYRATING ON A MAN'S LAP. A CROWD OF MEN, IN OFF-DUTY NYPD GARB, HOLDING BEERS, BOTTLES OF SCOTCH. A BLACK MAN IN AN NYPD JACKET (RUSSELL) SLAPS GOODNIGHT TO –

Take care, Superboy.

BABITCH

Alright, Russ.

MURRAY 'SUPERBOY' BABITCH (32) MOVING TOWARD THE DOOR
– SHIT-FACED – confetti around his neck. He nods goodnight to
others and moves out through the door.

Babitch shuffles through the LOT PACKED WITH CIVILIAN AND
PATROL CARS – *the civilian cars all sporting Patrolman's Benevolent
Association bumper stickers.*

A HONDA sits in front of a hydrant. AN NYPD PARKING PLACARD
poised on the dash. Babitch unlocks the door.

*A dull sound; muffled gagging.*
Babitch looks into the darkness, groggy, squinting. *Music throbs.*
But there is something else, *something near,* in the ungroomed
bushes that run the perimeter of the lot.

Babitch pulls a FLASHLIGHT and PISTOL from his glove box.
He holds the flashlight, arm cocked over his ear.

THE BEAM FINDS – A RED-HAIRED COP (JACK RUCKER) IN AN
UNBUTTONED UNIFORM kneeling in the bushes. He looks up into
the light, his chin wet. ANOTHER COP (LAGONDA) STANDS BESIDE
HIM, SMOKING.

BABITCH

Hey guys.

LAGONDA

Hey Superboy.

BABITCH

Is Jackie okay?

RUCKER

Fine. I'm fine.

Babitch sighs and moves off. He turns off the flashlight and throws
it – along with the revolver – onto the seat of his Honda. He backs
the car onto the street.

9

Suddenly: SMASH! HIS FRONT TIRE CRUSHES A BEER BOTTLE.
Babitch leans out his door, looking at the shattered glass.

                         BABITCH
     Fuck me.

                                                  CUT TO:

INT./EXT. BABITCH'S HONDA – GW* BRIDGE ON-RAMP – NIGHT

THE BRIDGE APPROACH GLOWS blue-green under the mercury
lights. MURRAY BABITCH drives, his head against the glass. *The
radio dribbles sports scores.* He slows, moving through a red light.

IN A LOT, THREE FIGURES MOVE EFFICIENTLY AROUND A CAR;
ONE STANDS WATCH BY THE BROKEN GLASS AS ANOTHER RIPS AT
CABLES FROM INSIDE, AND A THIRD PRIES THE TRUNK WITH A
CROWBAR.

Disgusted, Babitch pulls onto the ramp.
SUDDENLY – *krunch!* – HIS HONDA IS SIDE-SWIPED BY A RED CAR.

Jolted, Babitch swerves into opposing traffic. He reels, glaring out
his window at the damage.

                         BABITCH
     Mother fucker!

*Honnk!* – A TAXI'S LIGHTS FLARE, HEADING STRAIGHT FOR
BABITCH. Babitch twists the wheel, lurching his Honda over the
shallow concrete meridian, *bottoming out,* and back into his lane.

Up ahead, THE SPEEDING RED CAR, A MAZDA RX7, SNAKES
CRAZILY, MOVING OUT ACROSS THE BRIDGE.

BABITCH STEPS ON THE PEDAL.

HE PULLS UP ALONGSIDE THE MAZDA – *thumping house music.*
TWO BLACK TEENS, WILD-EYED, ON A JOY RIDE.

BABITCH GLARES, ROLLING DOWN HIS WINDOW.
HIS EYES MEET WITH ONE OF THE TEENS. BABITCH UNFURLS HIS
BADGE.

        NYPD! Pull it *OVER!*

* George Washington.

THE KIDS LAUGH AND THE MAZDA RIPS FORWARD. One of them leans, waving A DARK OBJECT, aiming the barrel at Babitch. A GUN.

BAM! – BABITCH'S FRONT TIRE BLOWS OUT.

*WIDE-EYED,* BABITCH DUCKS – (assuming it was a gun shot) –

> *shit* fuck *piss!*

HE SWERVES, SCRAPING A CONCRETE DIVIDER.
> (voice cracking)
> Mother *fucker!* MOTHER FUCKER!

BABITCH STICKS HIS PISTOL OUT THE WINDOW – *FIRING* – BAM – BAM – BAM – BAM – BAM!

THE MAZDA'S REAR GLASS SHATTERS. AND THE RED CAR SKIDS WILDLY ACROSS THE BRIDGE. IT CAREENS INTO A BRIDGE SUPPORT. *THUNK.*

*SMASH.*
BABITCH'S HONDA SLAMS AGAINST A JUTTING CONCRETE DIVIDER. HE HITS THE WINDSHIELD AND ROCKS BACK, HIS FACE BLOODY. Steam rises. The bridge is quiet.

> CUT AWAY TO:

INT./EXT. A GARRISON SQUAD CAR – ALONG THE RIVER – NIGHT

HEADLIGHTS CASCADE OVER A 'DEER CROSSING' SIGN.

A MOVING SQUAD CAR – ON THE SIDE, AN INSIGNIA – S H E R I F F – T O W N  O F  G A R R I S O N.

*The car stereo plays a Sibelius piano sonata . . .*
*Bleary,* FREDDY HEFLIN drives, straddling the double yellow. HIS EYES ARE NOT ON THE ROAD – he stares longingly out toward –

THE LIGHTS OF NORTHERN MANHATTAN AND THE GEORGE WASHINGTON BRIDGE REFLECT IN THE CHURNING WATER.

Freddy turns back to the road.

A YOUNG DOE STANDS ON THE DOUBLE YELLOW – EYES GLOWING – FREDDY'S CAR CAREENING TOWARD IT.

FREDDY SLAMS ON THE BRAKES – BUT – *SCREEEEECH!*
HE WILL NOT STOP IN TIME, THE DEER FROZEN IN HIS
HEADLIGHTS.

> FREDDY
> *Shit!*

FREDDY JERKS THE WHEEL. HIS SQUAD CAR SKIDS OFF THE ROAD,
HEADING FOR A RAVINE. HE PULLS THE WHEEL THE OTHER WAY,
HEADING FOR AN EMBANKMENT. FREDDY DUCKS DOWN.

THE SQUAD CAR SMASHES THROUGH THE BRUSH AND SLAMS INTO
THE EMBANKMENT. *Crunch.*

> CUT AWAY TO:

EXT. NYC – GEORGE WASHINGTON BRIDGE – NIGHT

*A chorus of honking, sirens.* Dead traffic. Vapor lights spray through
suspension cables. EMERGENCY VEHICLES, cherry-topped.

THE MAZDA RX7 sits, steam rising from the hood, impaled by a
bridge support. A PAIR OF MEDICS GRAB BAGS FROM THEIR
AMBULANCE.

THE RED-HAIRED COP (JACK RUCKER) pokes over the medics'
shoulders as they tend to THE PASSENGERS – THE TWO BLACK
TEENS: THE DRIVER gurgles, his ear a sopping trench. THE OTHER
KID sits, his forehead sprinkled across the dash.

RUCKER drops A CRACK PIPE AND VIAL INTO A PLASTIC BAG. A
HISPANIC MEDIC nudges him out of the car.

> HISPANIC MEDIC
> Traffic incident. *Bullshit, man.*

The medic glances at the rear window of the Mazda. It is shattered
by bullet holes.

> OTHER MEDIC
> Nobody said they were popped.

RUCKER PUSHES OUT THE SHATTERED GLASS, smug, wordless.

ANOTHER NYPD, RUSSELL (THE BLACK COP), sets flares, his eyes moving heavily from the accident to – THE GRIDLOCKED TRAFFIC.

A BARREL-CHESTED OLDER COP steps from the gridlock on the Jersey side, a cell phone to his ear. As he gets closer, we see his eyes. Deep blue. Saucy. His badge reads: LIEUTENANT RAY DONLAN. Cops nod as he moves, unfettered, toward –

MURRAY BABITCH (SUPERBOY), who stands slumped behind his SMASHED HONDA, gesticulating wildly to A FAT COP (LAGONDA).

Short, pot-bellied DETECTIVE LEO CRASKY (50) crosses, a squawking radio in his hand. He meets eyes with Russell.

> CRASKY
> What you're thinking, Russell – swallow it.

> RUSSELL
> Hey. 'he saved five babies at Red Hook.

> CRASKY
> That's right. Black babies. Mashed potatoes don't
> mean gravy.

CUT TO:

ACROSS THE BRIDGE – BABITCH, LAGONDA AND DONLAN –
(CONTINUOUS)

CLOSE ON – BABITCH, his BADGE clipped to his jacket, a bandage on his nose, eyes wet. He gulps for air, sucking a cigarette.

> BABITCH
> – a million of 'em holding candles. I'm gonna be the
> fuckin' poster boy for the CCRB. I'm dead. My life
> is fucking over. They're gonna string me up by my
> balls, Ray – just like Tunney.

LAGONDA meets eyes with RAY DONLAN, THE SAUCY-EYED LIEUTENANT. Donlan takes Babitch's head, his thick fingers in his hair.

> DONLAN
> We ain't gonna let it go down like that. I'm here this
> time.

13

**BABITCH**

Tunney didn't even get to the Grand Jury.

**LAGONDA**

Fuck the GJ. You're Superboy. You saved what *six black babies*? That shit plays.

DETECTIVE LEO CRASKY arrives, listening to his squawking radio.

**CRASKY**

The car was hot.

Donlan nods, pleased. Babitch stares, dull-eyed, at the sunrise.

**BABITCH**

Three babies.

CRASKY holds his walkie in the air. A woman's voice squawks.

**CRASKY**

– Miss DKNY says there's a jurisdictional question. If it *began* on the bridge, it's PA – if it began on the ramp, it's ours.

**LAGONDA**

– on the ramp.

**CRASKY**

(into his radio)

One at a time please!

(looking up)

I got PA on another channel, the Mayor's Office, Assistant DA, Press up the ying-yang; the only reason they're not here now is we got gridlock – from Cross Bronx to the Palisades.

**DONLAN**

We're lucky. We have time.

RUCKER (THE RED-HAIRED COP) returns from the crumpled Mazda. He whispers something to DONLAN. Babitch watches them.

Donlan looks to Crasky. Crasky hands Rucker a set of keys.

CRASKY

In my trunk. In a Grand Union bag.

BABITCH

Ray. You don't have to. *I saw it.* He pointed the fucking piece at me. I *heard* the shot.

Rucker departs.

CRASKY

The kid had a *steering wheel lock* in his hand.

BABITCH

*I heard the shot –*

CRASKY

– your tire blew. No. *Listen to me. Your tire blew.* You fucked up and you wasted a pair of shitbags who aren't worth the hair in the crack of your ass. So cool it with the patty-cake morality because – without me – those two stiffs'll put you in a room where you will fuck your uncle and everything he's built.

15

                         DONLAN
    Hey. Hey. Leo, easy.

Crasky and Donlan exchange glances.

                         BABITCH
    I don't drop dimes.

                         CRASKY
    Oh yeah? How much blow you do tonight? I heard
    they had a fuckin' brick.

                         BABITCH
    Fuck you.

                         CRASKY
    Fuck *you*, little boy. The black van's gonna be here
    in a minute and I haven't done shit. What I'm doing
    is highly –

                         DONLAN
    Sympathetic. It is.

                         CRASKY
    Damned right. I've been standing on this bridge
    popping pimples. But *fuck it*, you're Ray's nephew –
    'Superboy' – saved ten black babies – and I caught
    the case. I caught the case and now I want it simple
    'cause this racial shit *eats you alive* –

                         DONLAN
    – if it plays the wrong way.
                         (to Babitch)
    It could eat all of us, Murray.

Crasky's eyes meet Jack Rucker's as he passes with a CRUMPLED
BROWN GRAND UNION BAG. Murray Babitch's expression falls.

                                        CUT AWAY TO:


EXT. A GARRISON SQUAD CAR – ALONG THE RIVER – NIGHT

FREDDY'S SQUAD CAR SITS, pitched against the embankment,
steaming, its front end crumpled, the driver door open. *The*

                            16

*concert piano continues to play . . .*

ANOTHER SHERIFF'S SQUAD CAR – WITH THE SAME MARKINGS AS
FREDDY'S – PULLS UP ALONGSIDE. A TOUSLE-HAIRED DEPUTY
(BILL GEISLER) SHINES A HOODMOUNTED LIGHT INTO FREDDY'S
CAB.

                         BILL
    Freddy?

But the car is empty and Bill moves on, slowly, scanning the brush
with his light.

THE GREAT GRAY BRIDGE RUMBLES OVERHEAD. A path leads
down from the accident site – toward –

                                        CUT TO:


EXT. GARRISON, NJ – UNDER THE BRIDGE – NIGHT

FREDDY sits at the river's edge. He faces the water and the lights
of the great city beyond. The water moves slowly, hypnotically.
Tears run down his cheeks.

THE CITY ACROSS THE RIVER. A SIREN SOUNDS and one can see
the lights of emergency vehicles on the George Washington
Bridge.

Suddenly: SPIRALING RED LIGHTS MOVE ACROSS THE BACK OF
FREDDY'S HEAD, THE SIDE OF HIS FACE. THE SIREN IS HERE.
Freddy turns, wiping his cheeks.

DEPUTY BILL'S SQUAD CAR PULLS TO A STOP. A door slams.

DEPUTY BILL emerges. He shines a flashlight over the landscape.

                       DEPUTY
    Freddy? It's Bill.

                       FREDDY
    Over here.

Freddy, who wipes away his tears – and blood – on his sleeve.

                                    CUT AWAY TO:


17

EXT. GW BRIDGE – INSIDE THE CRUMPLED MAZDA – NIGHT

The GRAND UNION BAG under his arm, JACK RUCKER pushes his way around the TWO MEDICS. He kneels at the feet of the dead kid, gracelessly pantomiming – *the finding of a semi.*

> RUCKER
> Ooo baby. Look at that.

> HISPANIC MEDIC
> What are you *doing?*

> RUCKER
> I found their piece.

Rucker is red-faced. *A very bad liar.*

> HISPANIC MEDIC
> Bullshit, man. You can't do that.

> RUCKER
> Do *what?* It was sitting there.

> HISPANIC MEDIC
> No, it wasn't.

> RUCKER
> Yes, it was.

Rucker moves to take the semi out of the car. BUT THE MEDIC GRABS THE GUN BY THE BARREL.

> RUCKER
> MOTHER FUCKER. *Hey!*

> HISPANIC MEDIC
> YOU CAN'T DO THAT!

There is a moment of struggle, both men gripping the weapon.

AT THE OTHER SIDE OF THE BRIDGE – CASKY TURNS. LAGONDA, DONLAN AND BABITCH stand behind him, watching the face-off. LaGonda's sleepy eyes widen.

> LAGONDA
> Oh, *shit* . . .

Crasky clips his radio to his side, moving off.

> CRASKY

Jesus Christ!

He waddles toward THE MAZDA, his hands waving.

Panicking, tearful, BABITCH steps backward, to the railing.

> BABITCH

I told you guys. Fuck. Fuck. I told you guys to let it
*be*.

ACROSS THE BRIDGE – AT THE MAZDA – THE MEDIC JERKS THE
GUN AWAY FROM RUCKER. He steps out of the car, carrying the
weapon toward the railing.

> RUCKER

Put it down!

THE OTHER MEDIC WAVES TO HIS PARTNER –

> OTHER MEDIC

Hector! What the fuck are you doing?!

CRASKY MOVES IN, HIS HAND IN THE AIR.

> CRASKY

*Hey, hey, hey*! Cool it, boys. Everyone should just be
doing their jobs here.

RUCKER PULLS HIS WEAPON ON THE MEDIC.

> RUCKER

Put it down, Chico! *Now*!

THE HISPANIC MEDIC (HECTOR) CONSIDERS THIS, GLARING AT
RUCKER –

> HECTOR

Why? You gonna shoot me?

RUCKER SAYS NOTHING, HIS PISTOL TRAINED ON THE MEDIC.
*Sirens rise.*
ACROSS THE BRIDGE – RAY DONLAN turns to the sound.

*From Manhattan* – lurching through opposing traffic, A BLACK POLICE CHIEF'S VAN AND A DARK SEDAN APPROACH, lights swirling.

AT THE RAILING – BABITCH faces the water, eyes wet. He looks like he might throw up – or *jump* . . .

>                    BABITCH
> I'm going down, Uncle Ray. *Just like Tunney* . . . *I'm going down.*

Ray Donlan turns, watching the vehicles approach, his mind racing behind his blue eyes. He tosses keys to Frank LaGonda.

>                    DONLAN
> Frankie – get me started up.

BACK AT THE MAZDA –

>                    RUCKER
> PUT IT *DOWN!*

HECTOR SMILES SPITEFULLY AND TOSSES THE GUN – *out and over the edge of the bridge.*

STUNNED, CRASKY RUNS TO THE SIDE OF THE BRIDGE. *Plop.* The guns hit the water below.

>                    CRASKY
> SHIT!

RUCKER LEAPS, PUMMELING THE MEDIC WITH HIS PISTOL. The other medic struggles to break it up, Russell restraining him.

NYPD BRASS AND MEN IN SUITS EMERGE FROM THE DARK SEDAN.

> Motherfuck.

>                    DONLAN
>                   (off-screen)
> Oh my God! OH MY GOD! LEO! JESUS!

LEO CRASKY TURNS – ACROSS THE BRIDGE – RAY DONLAN LEANS, ASHEN LOOKING OVER THE RAILING – DOWN TO – THE HUDSON RIVER.

DONLAN

    – he just – *jumped* –

CRASKY JOINS HIM AT THE RAILING. Others look up.

    – he hit the water – and he went *down.*

TWO HUNDRED FEET BELOW – THE RIVER CHURNS – GREASY, SILENT.

CUT AWAY TO:

INT. FREDDY HEFLIN'S SUBURBAN HOUSE – DAWN

THROUGH WINDOW – Birds flutter as the sun rises over the bridge. But it is oddly silent. Dead silent.

On the porch of a nearby house, A YOUNG MAN WITH AN NYPD BAG (TONY) kisses his WIFE goodbye as – A CAR POOL OF COPS IDLES.

PULLING INSIDE – A BEDSIDE ALARM CLOCK. The hammer strikes the bell, furiously – *but silently.* Beside it – A BOX OF BAND AIDS. AND SEVERAL DOG-EARED WAMBAUGH-ESQUE PAPERBACKS.

ON THE DISHEVELED BED – FISTFULS OF QUARTERS among the sheets – FREDDY HEFLIN lies, eyes open – a bandage on the bridge of his nose, a brown stain at its center. As he pulls his head from his pillow – exposing his good ear – THE NUMB SILENCE IS FILLED BY THE RINGING BELL, THE BIRDS, THE WORLD.

CUT TO:

INT. FREDDY HEFLIN'S HOUSE – MORNING

AN ELABORATE OLD TURNTABLE AND TUBE AMPLIFIER. A record spins. *Piano tinkling. Hauntingly.*

Scattered around the room – YELLOWED CLASSICAL RECORD ALBUMS. On many of the jackets, A BENT-EARED PIANIST – *Glenn Gould.*

THROUGH THE KITCHEN WINDOW – AN UNBLEMISHED SQUAD CAR pulls in the drive – on the side it says:
S H E R I F F – T O W N   O F   G A R R I S O N.

BILL GEISLER (THE TOUSLE-HAIRED DEPUTY) CLIMBS OUT.
He wears his gray uniform.

In his robe, smoking, FREDDY sits at the kitchen table.

Bill enters the house without knocking. He holds a newspaper. He
drops a grocery bag on the table. He takes bowls and spoons from
the cupboard. He pulls covered coffees, a box of Fruit Loops, and
a quart of milk from the bag.

Freddy sits there as Bill pours himself some cereal.

> FREDDY
> How long's the car gonna take?

> BILL
> Lenny won't know – till the parts guys gets in. Take
> the number two. Y'told Cindy you'd show her the
> new radar today.

> FREDDY
> (nods)
> What did you tell Lenny? – about the accident.

> BILL
> (eating)
> 'chasing a speeder.

Freddy looks up, touching his ear.

> FREDDY
> Excuse me?

> BILL
> *'Sheriff was chasing a speeder.*

Freddy nods.

> How's the nose?

> FREDDY
> Fine.

Bill is itching to say more. But Freddy avoids Bill's eyes. He looks
to the DAILY NEWS on the table.

# HERO COP TAKES PLUNGE
*Shoots teens, jumps off bridge.*

Picture of Murray Babitch inset against a still of the GW Bridge.

Freddy sucks on his cigarette, reading intensely.

CUT AWAY TO:

INT. PDA* ANTEROOM – NYC – DAY

A WINDOW – LOOKS FROM NYC – ACROSS THE RIVER – TO JERSEY.

A HANDSOME MAN IN A DARK SUIT checks his tie-knot in the window's reflection. He is PDA PRESIDENT LASSARO. AN AIDE stands beside a door to a CROWDED PRESS ROOM.

> AIDE
> No wife. 'was from Jersey City.

Lassaro, turns, smiles, and moves toward the PRESS ROOM DOOR.

> LASSARO
> And he's Ray's nephew, right? – So put the service in Garrison. He owns the locals – then we got the seating plan.

> AIDE
> (smiles)
> You know, Vince, it's a good thing this hero jumped. Two black kids, unarmed – it coulda' played a whole 'nother way.

> LASSARO
> Let's go.

CUT TO:

INT. ENTRANCE/LOBBY – PDA PRESS ROOM – DAY

A POKER-FACED COP STANDS BEFORE TWO GLASS DOORS. HE CHECKS REPORTERS FOR PASSES. *Each time the doors open we hear a fragment of the press conference inside:*

* Patrolmen's Defense Association.

THROUGH THE GLASS – BEFORE THE PDA EMBLEM – PDA
PRESIDENT LASSARO reads a statement to THE THRONG OF
REPORTERS.

> LASSARO
> – was a hero cop. He deserved a fair hearing. But *he
> knew* this would not happen – not in this city, under
> *this Mayor* –

*Door closes.* SUDDENLY, A REPORTER DIALING A CELLULAR
PHONE EXITS the conference, *pulling the door open again.*

> – we all learned from the Tunney tragedy that for
> cops in this city –

*Door closes.* The reporter speaks into his cell phone, pacing.

> REPORTER
> – No – the jumper – *Babitch*. 'Pulled some babies
> from a fire last year – in Red Hook.

> POKER-FACED COP
> Three *black* babies.

The Reporter nods to the Poker-Faced Cop.

> REPORTER
> – they say he jumped cause of the Tunney thing. So
> tell Myra, she was on Tunney right? I need a recap –
> Glen Tunney – two years ago – shot a kid holding a
> water gun, lynched in his cell waiting GJ – *No*, to
> date – otherwise I could do it myself – Well, get her
> off it. Fuck the asbestos.

*Doors opens.* A MAN WITH GREEN EYES exits the conference.
He looks back once, weary, meeting eyes with the Reporter.
The green-eyed man's look has *weight.* He moves off.

> LASSARO
> – the suicide rate is a direct result of a hostile
> bureaucracy, a hostile public, a hostile press. Cops
> have rights too.

*Door closes.*

POKER-FACED COP
Damn straight.

INT. ONE POLICE PLAZA – NYC – A CORRIDOR – DAY

THE HISPANIC MEDIC (HECTOR) sits, uneasy, on a bench. His face is *bruised*. He smokes a cigarette.

Some key-carved letters peek out from beneath a telephone on a nearby coffee table. Hector pushes the phone aside.

*Yellow betray blue* – reads the carved graffiti.

Across from Hector, THE OTHER MEDIC sits, stiff. He sighs, feeling the stares of passing Detectives. Among them, LEO CRASKY. Crasky holds a long look at Hector, moving off.

A SIGN ON AN ADJACENT DOOR READS:

OFFICE OF SPECIAL SERVICES – INTERNAL AFFAIRS

HISPANIC MEDIC
No way that guy jumped. No way.

Hector sighs, pushing out his cigarette. He looks toward an interrogation room, the blinds drawn –

CUT TO:

INT. ONE POLICE PLAZA – NYC – INTERROGATION ROOM – DAY (CONTINUOUS)

RUSSELL (THE BLACK COP) sits in a wooden chair that won't sit level. It rocks, knocking on the floor. Exhausted, he looks –

THROUGH THE DRAWN BLINDS – HECTOR sits out in the hall.

A few feet behind Russell, his PDA ATTORNEY. A BLACK DETECTIVE (CARSON, 35) sits on the edge of a table, looking at some notes on a steno pad. A Marantz-tape recorder sits on the table.

Russell's eyes drift to – THE GREEN-EYED MAN AT THE WINDOW –
LIEUTENANT MOE TILDEN. He wears a white shirt, sleeves rolled,
and a bureaucratic tie. He listens as he looks out.

> CARSON
> – so – – on the way home from the strip bar – at 0200
> – you get this call on your cell saying something
> happened to Superboy on the bridge. And you
> should get over there – to assist.

> RUSSELL
> Yes.

> CARSON
> And you went.

> RUSSELL
> Yes.

> ATTORNEY
> Along with many others.

> CARSON
> But you don't know who called you?

The PDA ATTORNEY puts out his hand, stopping Russell.

> ATTORNEY
> Wait a minute. I'm gonna object. We went through
> this. He has been up all night. How many times – I
> mean – let's remember there was a tragedy on that
> bridge last night.

At the window, TILDEN SCOFFS. He mouthes the word 'tragedy'.

> He already – my client already stated that he has no
> recollection of the –

> CARSON
> Objection noted. Counsellor. I know you want a
> recess – I know you're tired – but I need a better
> answer to this –

ATTORNEY

– he's conceded – at his administrative peril – that
he was drinking excessively –

MOE TILDEN TURNS FROM THE WINDOW. HIS EYES BRIGHT.

TILDEN

*We understand he was drunk, Counsellor.* The officer
was drunk.
(to Russell)
You were drunk. So why then – Officer – drunk as
you were – did you respond to a *call to duty – over
your car phone* – from a stranger at two a.m.?

RUSSELL

I don't know. I heard Officer Babitch had an
accident – and the impulse made me go.

TILDEN

Didn't you take occasion to wonder *why* the
response *was not* being coordinated over *department
radio* by *sober, on-duty officers?*

RUSSELL

No. No. I did not.

TILDEN

You did not.

RUSSELL

No.

TILDEN

You're gonna have to give me a better answer than
that. Your job is in jeopardy. You're gonna have to
give me a better answer than that.

RUSSELL

I didn't take the time to notice how it was being
coordinated . . . No . . .

This is a dull silence. Carson looks to Tilden. Tilden backs off.
Carson crosses to Russell.

27

CARSON

Have you ever been to Garrison, New Jersey?

ATTORNEY

That is another question entirely –

CARSON

Excuse me. Have you ever been to Garrison, New Jersey?

ATTORNEY

I don't understand why –

CARSON

*Counsellor.*
(back to Russell)
Would you consider the PD on the bridge your friends? Are these white boys from Jersey your friends? *Bro?* 'You looking for a 'summer home' in Jersey?

ATTORNEY

Oh come on, Detective. I object. I object.

CARSON

Or do they *scare you*? Is that it? Does Ray Donlan scare you?

RUSSELL

*Bro?* You in the 'Mod Squad'?

A shouting match erupts. Tilden steps toward the tape machine.

TILDEN

All right. I'm gonna call a recess.
(pressing stop on the tape machine)
Listen, Counsellor. I'm gonna tell you right now. If he doesn't answer the questions he's gonna be out of his fuckin' job, okay? Pure and simple. He's gonna be out of a fucking job. What does he think he's talking to – a bunch of fucking morons? Huh? Does he think he's talking to a bunch of fucking morons?

(to Russell)
What's the matter with you?

ATTORNEY
– all I'm saying to you is that I believe –

TILDEN
Shut the fuck up. You listen to me, Counsellor. The PDA may pay your fuckin' bills – and they don't want this thing spreading – fine – but this guy – *your client* – is about to lose his job. If he wants to fuckin' save his ass – he better tell us what we want to know. *Because we know it anyway.* You hear me? Now you can think about it. We'll give you a little time to think about it – like about five minutes.

ATTORNEY
I think we need a recess, Lieutenant.

TILDEN
I'll decide when we have a recess or not. Not you! Not you!

TILDEN exits – crossing into the next room as –

CUT TO:


INT. ONE POLICE PLAZA – NYC – WAR ROOM – DAY (CONTINUOUS)

Tilden enters (from the interrogation room). He moves past HECTOR THE MEDIC – who looks up at him –

HECTOR
Hey. Are we gonna talk or what – ? I want to talk to you.

TILDEN
(still moving)
When your lawyer gets here.

Tilden moves through the maze of desks.
OTHER INTERNAL AFFAIRS DETECTIVES look up at Tilden, getting out of his way, deferential. He looks at a Detective at a desk.

29

Can you call EMS* about his rep?

IA DETECTIVE #2 (RUBIN)
Moe. Harbor – they found one of Soup-y-boy's
shoes.

TILDEN snorts. He takes a cigarette from a pack on a desk.
He enters HIS OFFICE AND OPENS A PACK OF FILES.

CARSON pokes his head into Tilden's office.

CARSON
Rucker's coming at nine tomorrow.

TILDEN
What about Donlan?

CARSON
Coming in next week. His lawyer – from PDA – he
says –

TILDEN
Who's that? Who's his lawyer?

CARSON
This guy Sloane –

Moe Tilden smiles. He crosses to A MAP.

TILDEN
Sloane. Big gun. Big gun.

CARSON
– he says Donlan's grieving for his nephew.

Carson crosses to Tilden – at the map.

I don't know. If the Superboy's alive – he's the
fuckin plague, y'know? – why bring him home with
you? I mean – *You don't shit where you eat,* right?

Tilden turns – his green eyes bright. He speaks quietly, his jaw
barely moving, smoke trickling from his lips.

---

* Emergency Medical Service.

TILDEN
But I do, Carsie. *I live in a house – and in it – I shit
and I eat.*

Tilden twirls his thumb and finger on – A CHINESE COCKTAIL
UMBRELLA PINNED IN – THE TOWN OF GARRISON, NEW JERSEY.

CUT AWAY TO:

INT./EXT. GARRISON PATROL CAR/SHOULDER OF ROAD – DAY

The abandoned water tower rises high above the trees.
G A R R I S O N,  N J – it says in fading letters. A TOYOTA CRUISES
QUICKLY PAST A SUBURBAN SCHOOL BUILDING oblivious to THE
GARRISON SQUAD CAR at the shoulder.

SHERIFF FREDDY HEFLIN opens his puffy eyes. He wears a gray
uniform. He sits in the patrol car. He looks down as –

A FEMALE HAND withdraws from his thigh.
DEPUTY CINDY BETTS cups her *newly freed hand* over a RADAR
display. She clocks the Toyota at 45 mph.

*The school zone sign says '30'.*

Cindy has a round face, rosy cheeks. Bright eyes. She looks at
Freddy expectantly.

FREDDY shakes his head, watching the car recede.

FREDDY
It's Gratto.

CINDY
Freddy. This whole town is cops. We gotta pull
someone over.

Freddy winces, pressing on the gauze taped to his nose.

FREDDY
Why?

Cindy sighs. Thick-armed, she is uncomfortable in her uniform
and pulls at the polyester bunched under her armpits.

31

*Another car rips past –* A BLUE OLDS DELTA 88. The radar shows – SEVENTY TWO MILES AN HOUR.

Cindy glares at Freddy.

CUT TO:

INT./EXT. OLDS DELTA 88/ROUTE 36 – GARRISON – DAY

Riding shotgun, JACK RUCKER sprays Dristan up his nose. RAY DONLAN, driving, stares in his rear view at –

A MAN LYING DOWN ACROSS THE BACK SEAT, his legs sliding out, his face obscured. He is missing one shoe . . .

Rucker joggles with the air conditioner, turning it on. He finds Donlan glaring at him.

> RUCKER
> Ray. I'm burning up here.

Suddenly, in the rear view, SPINNING RED LIGHTS.

> DONLAN

Oh, *fuck this.*

> MAN IN BACK
> What? – *What?*

RUCKER smiles at the obscured Man in Back.

> RUCKER
> Don't freak. It's our munchkins.

DONLAN PULLS THE OLDS OVER TO THE SHOULDER.

Awkward, DEPUTY CINDY BETTS steps out of the patrol car. She shuffles toward the Oldsmobile.

THE DRIVER'S WINDOW OF THE OLDS HUMS DOWN TO REVEAL – RAY DONLAN, GLARING, SWEATY AND RED-EYED.

> CINDY
> Turn off the car please?

> DONLAN

I got the air on.

Donlan smirks. He does not shut off the car. He holds out his
wallet, unflapping it to reveal – AN NYPD LIEUTENANT'S BADGE.
A pause as Cindy stares at the badge.

> CINDY

You were on the job?

Rucker leans over from the passenger side.

> RUCKER

No – we're coming from Forest Hills, honey. I'm
John McEnroe. That's Jimmy Connors.

Cindy takes the wallet from Donlan.

> CINDY

Is your license in here? Can you pull it out for me?

> RUCKER

Oh Christ!

Cindy hands the wallet back to Donlan.

> CINDY

You know. This is a School zone.

> DONLAN
> (reading Cindy's tag)

Listen Miss . . . Betts – You're new, right?

> CINDY

New here. But not on the job. I was a municipal
Deputy in Elmira.

> DONLAN

*Freddy!* FREDDY!

Freddy climbs out of his squad car, approaching the Oldsmobile.

See, honey, *in Garrison* – when the car you're gonna
tag has got a PDA sticker – I'd advise you to think to
yourself – *'hey, that's one of the good guys, I think I'll
go catch me a bad guy.'*

THE MAN IN BACK pulls on Donlan's collar. Nervous.

> MAN IN BACK
> Christ, Ray. *Don't make a scene.*

> CINDY
> If we let every PD go by, there might not be a single
> violation in this town.

> DONLAN
> (smiling)
> 'Fine by me.

> RUCKER
> The problem in this town ain't the people who live
> here, honey . . . it's the element that visits.

Freddy leans in the window of the Olds, from the other side. He
looks in the car at Rucker and Donlan. He notices – The Man in
Back – obscured – lying still.

> FREDDY
> New car, Ray. It's nice. I didn't recognize it.

> RUCKER
> Come on, Freddy. I want to go home. Tell your
> cupcake to heel.

> CINDY
> Listen buddy. I'm not –

Freddy shakes his head at Cindy, cooling her jets. He backs her off
with his hand. She turns and storms back to the squad car.

> FREDDY
> Take care, guys. I'll see you later.

Donlan salutes Freddy. He notices Freddy's bandage.

> DONLAN
> Hey. What happened to you, Freddy?

Freddy smiles, bashful.

> FREDDY
> Oh. 'Little fender bender.

The Oldsmobile lurches away and, as it does – Freddy notices – THE MAN IN BACK RISING FROM HIS 'SLUMBER' – STARING OUT THE REAR WINDOW OF THE OLDS. The man wears a bandage on his nose – a mirror of Freddy's wound. Except for the gauze, it is the same face from the morning's paper – BABITCH (SUPERBOY).

Freddy touches his own bandage, thoughtfully. The Oldsmobile disappears round the bend, leaving Freddy standing on the shoulder.

CUT TO:

INT. DAY – SHERIFF'S OFFICE – CLOSE ON A CLUTTERED DESKTOP

IN SOMEONE'S HANDS – THE DAILY NEWS opened to the article on Babitch's 'suicide' – THE PICTURE OF MURRAY BABITCH . . .

A mass of OFFICIAL PAPERWORK.

A collection of THUMB-WORN WAMBAUGH-ESQUE PAPERBACKS.

AN OPEN TAPE CASE filled with classical cassettes.

A smoldering cigarette.

A ONE-HOUR PHOTO ENVELOPE – SCATTERED SNAPSHOTS –

*A party. A banner –* SHERIFF FREDDY – TEN YEARS STRONG! – *Freddy with NYPD and families.* A PHOTO OF RAY DONLAN HIS ARM AROUND FREDDY. *They hold water guns to their heads – wearing goofy grins.*

> CINDY
> (off-screen)
> How do I know that guy?

At his desk, a fresh bandage on his nose, FREDDY HEFLIN READS THE PAPER, INTENSELY. He turns with a start, closing the paper, putting his hand – protectively – over the picture of Babitch.

But Cindy is looking over Freddy's shoulder at the snapshots on his desk. She refers – sarcastically – to a photo of Freddy.

> Not bad for forty-something. 'Looks like he might
> be a jerk sometimes. But there's hope – in his eyes.

Cindy smirks and sashays over to an outer room, sitting before the dispatch radio, paperwork piled high around her.

We are in the Sheriff's Office at Garrison. Once a garage, it has been re-fitted, complete with jail cell in what was once tire storage. Citations and framed clippings line the walls.

Freddy looks up to see –

MOE TILDEN (THE GREEN-EYED IA DETECTIVE) peers in the window of the Sheriff's office. He moves on, flicking a butt, crossing the street – toward the DELI.

The second hand on the big wall clock sticks. Then snaps free. *It is three thirty.*

*Rinnng.* The dispatch phone.
Cindy knocks a basket of papers, reaching for the receiver.

> Shit.

Struggling to keep the papers from spilling, she knocks the radio into alarm mode. *Dweeep, dweeep, dweeep . . .*

Freddy sighs, looking out through the window –

THROUGH THE GLASS – ACROSS THE STREET – A SCHOOL BUILDING:

A BEAUTIFUL BROWN-HAIRED WOMAN (35) EMERGES FROM THE
SCHOOLYARD, her hair blowing, a CHILD in her arms. The child
holds a PLUSH TURTLE. The woman struggles to fasten her child in
a safety seat. She takes the turtle and puts it on the roof of her van.

*Dweeep, dweeep, dweeep* . . .
>                    (shutting off the alarm)
>            Dispatch. Can you hold a second?

THROUGH THE GLASS – DONLAN'S OLDS PULLS UP ALONG SIDE
THE WOMAN. She smiles and nods at DONLAN, RUCKER AND
LAGONDA as they cross into – THE TOWN DELI.

THE BEAUTIFUL WOMAN CLIMBS IN HER VAN, STARTING IT,
UNAWARE OF THE TURTLE, STILL SITTING ON THE ROOF.

Freddy watches it all, riveted.

>                                            CUT TO:

INT. TOWN DELI – GARRISON – AFTERNOON

DONLAN, RUCKER and LAGONDA buy coffees, haggard, up all
night. DONLAN turns – tense, as he sees –

MOE TILDEN mixing milk and sugar at the counter. Tilden smiles.
Donlan smiles. But his comrades glare, uneasy.

>            TILDEN
>    Hey, Ray.

>            DONLAN
>    Hey, Moe.

>            TILDEN
>    I'm sorry about your nephew.

>            DONLAN
>    Yeah. He was a good kid. We were up all night with
>    it.
>            (crossing to mix his coffee, beside Tilden)
>    Uh. I know you need to talk to me. I'll come in next
>    week some time, how's that? Jackie here's comin' in
>    early for you – tomorrow.

TILDEN
(offering his hand to Rucker)
Hey. How ya doing? Moe Tilden.

RUCKER
(wary)
Yeah. Hey.

DONLAN
Moe, here, was my classmate – at the Academy –
back in the day – before he fell in love with this
redhead at IA and transferred.

TILDEN
Is that how it went, Ray?

DONLAN
So. What brings you to our fair city? Checkin' up on
us?

TILDEN
'heard it was a way of life over here. 'Wanted to see
it first hand.

DONLAN
What are we – like the Amish, now?

TILDEN
(smiles, putting the cover on his coffee)
When does that Arby's open up?

DONLAN
'couple months.

TILDEN
(moving to the door)
'gonna take a chunk outta this place.

DONLAN
I'll still be here.

Tilden nods. Exits.

CUT TO:

EXT. MAIN STREET – GARRISON – AFTERNOON

THE SIGN SAYS – 'NO PARKING'.

> TILDEN
>
> Shit.

TILDEN pulls a PIECE OF PAPER from his windshield. It looks like a parking ticket. He holds it close, reading it.

> *JULY 4th CELEBRATION! BRING THE FAMILY! AT*
> *BORDEN'S FIELD.*
> *Sponsored by the Garrison Volunteer Fire Department.*

Tilden smiles. He looks up, meeting eyes with –

SHERIFF FREDDY HEFLIN, walking up the street – THE TATTERED PLUSH TURTLE IN HIS HANDS. He moves it to his side.

> TILDEN
>
> 'thought you gave me a ticket.

> FREDDY
> (moving past)
>
> *Hm?*

> TILDEN
>
> 'You the Sheriff?

> FREDDY
>
> Yeah.
> (noticing something)
> *One second.* Gordon!

A GRUNGY KID sits with his friends in an alley, smoking, sipping sodas from bags. They look up.

– get outta there. Go on.

The kids comply.

Freddy turns back to Tilden, touching his bandaged nose. He sticks the turtle under his arm, awkward. Tilden smiles.

> TILDEN
>
> 'How long you been Sheriff?

                    FREDDY
Hm? Oh. Ten years.

                    TILDEN
That's great. (beat) 'Lotta cops here, huh?

                    FREDDY
Yeah.

                    TILDEN
It's a great gig.
                    (pulling out his card)
Well. I'm sure you're busy. But let me give you my
card. I'm with a special unit – in the city. In case –
you know – you want to talk about something.

Freddy examines the card: MOE TILDEN – NYPD INTERNAL
AFFAIRS

He looks up as Tilden drives off.

                                        CUT TO:

INT./EXT. GARRISON HOUSING TRACTS – LATE AFTERNOON

FREDDY DRIVES HIS SQUAD CAR. He listens to news radio as he redoes the bandage on his nose.

> RADIO
> (voice-over)
> – and our top story – a hero cop jumps off the GWB after two African American minors, reportedly unarmed, are shot in a pre-dawn gunfight on the bridge.

On the seat beside him, THE STUFFED TURTLE. Filthy and mangled.

Split-level houses sit in rows upon manicured plots, a basketball net above each garage door.

We pass a MAILBOX that reads: *Tunney.*

Freddy drives on, he pulls into a driveway –

The mailbox reads: *Randone.* A DOBERMAN ON A CHAIN BARKS. FOUR GARBAGE BAGS sit slumped in a RUSTED METAL TRASH BIN.

CUT TO:

EXT. RANDONE HOUSE – FRONT DOOR – LATE AFTERNOON

Freddy knocks. *No answer.* Knocks again. He stands there, slumped, holding the turtle. There are voices inside. The Doberman continues snarling.

> FREDDY
> Hello!

*No answer.* Freddy turns, walking back down the drive.

> LIZ
> (off-screen)
> Jesus. I'm sorry.

THE DOOR SWINGS OPEN. In sweats and v-neck tee, THE BEAUTIFUL BROWN-HAIRED WOMAN – LIZ RANDONE. She holds her hair against the breeze. She smiles, warm – a tooth poking out

tenderly – against her lip. *A child sings in the background.*

Freddy re-approaches, his eyes bright, smiling bashfully.

> FREDDY
> That's okay. I heard voices. I was gonna have base call you back.

> LIZ
> (noticing the turtle)
> Oh, Freddy. Look what you found.

Liz takes the stuffed animal. She smiles.

> She's gonna be so happy. Her daddy won her this at the fair last year. I left it on –

> FREDDY
> Yeah. I saw. From my window.

Liz smiles wider, infected by Freddy's dopey grin. Suddenly her smile disappears.

> LIZ
> That's awful about Ray's nephew, huh.

*Suddenly, the child in the other room is yelling. Loud.*

> Hey! Caroline! Come on, now. *Daddy's trying to sleep*!

Liz is exasperated, not by Freddy, but by life in general. Despite her distracted manner, her dry smile charms; A SMALL STUDDED CROSS HANGS AROUND HER NECK. Moving with her.

Freddy breaks his stare.

> I heard they're gonna do the service here.

Freddy nods. Liz notices his bandage, touches her nose.

> – Ouch. What happened to you?

> ### FREDDY
> Little accident. 'Chasing a speeder.

*The child's yelling grows louder. 'Mommy – come see – come see!'*

> ### LIZ
> – *one second.*

Liz crosses into an adjoining room with the turtle. '*Baby, look what the Sheriff found.*' The child calms.
> (off-screen)
> Freddy. You want some coffee?!

> ### FREDDY
> No. I'm fine.

Freddy takes a timid step into the foyer.

PICTURES ON THE WALL – A CHILD'S DRAWING – 'MY FAMILY' AN ACADEMY PHOTO OF LIZ'S HANDSOME HUSBAND, JOEY, IN UNIFORM. AND A PORTRAIT OF LIZ (16) – BEAUTY QUEEN'S CROWN ON HER HEAD.

> ### LIZ
> (off-screen)
> So. I hope you caught him.

Liz re-enters the room.

#### FREDDY

Hm? – Who?

#### LIZ

The speeder.

#### FREDDY

Oh. Yeah.

#### LIZ

. . . you know . . . I was thinking of calling you. I
mean – not you – but one of your –

#### FREDDY

Why? What's up?

#### LIZ

Oh. Someone's been dumping garbage. Garbage
bags.

She gestures toward THE FOUR GARBAGE BAGS BY THE ROAD.
Freddy eagerly pulls out his pad.

#### FREDDY

Uh huh. Is that them?

#### LIZ

There's just one. The rest are mine.

#### FREDDY

Okay – they threw *one* bag in with yours.

#### LIZ

This isn't the first time. They've been pulling this
shit for weeks, slipping it in. Why? That's enough,
isn't it?

Freddy erases something in his book.

#### FREDDY

Enough? Yeah. A beer bottle's enough as far as I'm
concerned.

#### LIZ

Damn right – I use white bags. Theirs are black.
Some cheap shit.

Freddy nods, scribbling in his pad.

> I don't tell Joey – cause he thinks he's gotta take care
> of it. Not that he doesn't think much of the local –
> you guys – but . . .

FREDDY

I'll take care of it. He's got the city to worry about,
right?

Liz nods, smiling. Freddy smiles back, his eyes sparkling.

CUT TO:

EXT. END OF RANDONE DRIVEWAY – LATE AFTERNOON

FREDDY pushes through THE BLACK GARBAGE BAG with a pencil.

LIZ watches from a window. She stands there, then moves away.

Freddy flips through the pieces of trash. *Paper plates. Bottles of beer.*
He comes upon a stained envelope; A PHONE BILL. Leafing it
open:

*A name: RAYMOND DONLAN*
*An address: 31 DALLAS DRIVE*

CUT TO:

EXT. DONLAN HOUSE – 31 DALLAS DRIVE – LATE AFTERNOON

The mailbox says: *Donlan.*

FREDDY STANDS AT THE DOOR OF THE SPLIT LEVEL HOUSE, the
soiled phone bill in hand. Before him, A BUSTY MIDDLE-AGED
WOMAN, ROSE DONLAN (46). Hand on hip, she sucks a cigarette.

ROSE

What if I said I don't know where it came from?

FREDDY

I'd take your word for it, Rose. Um. *Is Ray home?*

ROSE

'Taking care of our little visitor.

45

Freddy plays with the envelope in his fingers, letting this cryptic remark hang in the air. Rose stares at the envelope.

I get my garbage picked up every Tuesday.

FREDDY
Alright. Thanks for your time.

He walks back toward his car.

ROSE
You tell Joey to come here and talk to me about it if he thinks I've got no right.

Freddy turns around.

FREDDY
Rose. I want to believe you when you tell me something.

ROSE
Oh you do, do you?

FREDDY
Did you dump these bags or not?

ROSE
This is not a law problem – if you catch my drift. You tell Joey Randone that if he doesn't like my garbage he should stop soiling my sheets.

Rose is miraculously nonchalant – her eyes riveted boldly on Freddy; relishing his discomfort.

FREDDY
Rose, you can't just dump garbage on other people's property.

ROSE
But glamour boy – he can throw away a woman like she was garbage and that's okay – is that what you're saying, Freddy?

A pause. *The phone rings.* They stand there.

Are you gonna tell Ray about this?

46

Freddy shakes his head. Rose takes a drag of her cigarette. *The phone still ringing.* She spins around, slamming the door.

INT./EXT. DONLAN HOUSE – LATE AFTERNOON

As Freddy backs his SQUAD CAR out of the Donlan driveway, – THE BLUE OLDS DELTA 88 PULLS IN.

RAY DONLAN, THE SAUCY-EYED LIEUTENANT – the only occupant – steps out of the driver's side.

> DONLAN
> What's up, Freddy?
> 'Decided to give me that ticket.

Freddy shifts to park, the engine running.

> FREDDY
> No . . . Uh. Someone's dumping garbage.

> DONLAN
> Oh, a felony.

Freddy smiles, tense.

Donlan salutes. Freddy nods, backing out onto the street.

> CUT TO:

INT./EXT. FREDDY'S SQUAD CAR – MEADOWLANDS – ROADSIDE – SUNSET

Driving along the marshlands. Manhattan in the distance. The Garrison water tower against the orange sky. Up ahead – FLASHING LIGHTS – ROADSIDE.

FREDDY slows.

DEPUTY BILL GEISLER has pulled over a RUSTED IMPALA. He stands at the driver's window.

Freddy's headlights illuminate the cab of the Impala. A BLACK MAN AND WOMAN LOOK INTO THE FLARING LIGHT, ANGRY.

> BILL
> (over the radio)
> 'a few over. I'm checking docs.

Freddy nods, waving to Bill.
He lights a cig and pushes in a cassette. *A piano concerto.*

Freddy turns and looks out his window toward –

A GARBAGE STREWN WATERWAY sits, oil-slicked, under A
GRAFFITI-COVERED OVERPASS.

MOVING CLOSER ON – FREDDY – he stares at the marsh.
*The sound of heavy equipment rises. The piano continues.*

CUT TO:

A MEMORY: MARSH – GARRISON MEADOWLANDS – DAY (1975)

THE SAME WATERWAY BENEATH I–80, ONLY PRISTINE.
ON THE BILLBOARD – A 70S family before a ranch house.
'A NEW LIFE IN NEW JERSEY!'

THE WATER narrows under the OVERPASS UNDER
CONSTRUCTION.

YOUNG FREDDY (19) SITS BENEATH THE OVERPASS, eating a bag
lunch.

OUT THE MOUTH – IN THE DISTANCE – A CONSTRUCTION SITE –
YOUNG MEN MAKING THEIR WAY TO THE BIG MACHINES.
Suddenly: *screeeeeech! thunk! splash!*

YOUNG FREDDY TURNS AS – OUT THE OTHER END OF THE
OVERPASS – A GREEN FORD ROCKS IN THE WATER, NOSE DOWN.

FREDDY STANDS, AWESTRUCK.

With a flurry of bubbles, THE FORD SINKS INTO THE WATER.

CUT TO:

PRESENT DAY – CLOSE ON – FREDDY IN HIS CAR – EYES RIVETED
ON THE MARSH – THE MUSIC CONTINUES . . . BUT THERE ARE
VOICES . . .

THE RUSTED IMPALA ROLLS SLOW AS IT PASSES FREDDY'S SQUAD
CAR. TWO ANGRY BLACK FACES SPIT WORDS:

| BLACK WOMAN | BLACK MAN |
|---|---|
| We come here to watch the | – speeding – my ass – |
| sunset and you pull this – | fuckin' *racist pigs*! |

Freddy receives this, unblinking. THE IMPALA LURCHES AWAY.
Freddy touches his bandage.

Bill walks to his patrol car. He nods to Freddy – 'all done'.

                                                      CUT TO:


EXT. MAIN STREET – GARRISON – TWILIGHT

The bank clock blinks. 7:32, 7:32, 7:33 · · ·

The Arby's under construction. Light traffic.

In civilian clothes, CINDY BETTS crosses to the GARRISON
SHERIFF'S OFFICE, KEYS IN HAND.

                                                      CUT TO:


INT. SHERIFF'S OFFICE – NIGHT

FREDDY sits hunched, on the phone. His collar loose.

                         FREDDY
          Liz – All I'm saying is that I think it's gonna stop.

                          LIZ
                       (on phone)
          It was his little bitch, wasn't it? Sending messages.

*ka-chunk* – the door opens. CINDY BETTS peers inside.

                         FREDDY
          Uh. One second. Can you hold a second?

Freddy looks up, hitting the 'hold' button on the phone.
Cindy crosses to Freddy, sitting beside him.

          I'm on the phone.

                         CINDY
          I can see that.

FREDDY

How 'bout I meet you across the street in fifteen
minutes?

Cindy makes a face.

Look, *I'm sorry*. How 'bout tomorrow. I take you
someplace nice. Okay?

Cindy lets this hang in the air. Then she crosses to the door.
*klunk – the door shuts as –* Freddy pushes on the 'hold' button.

Liz – *Liz?*

LIZ
(on phone)
What?

FREDDY
– Do you want me to talk to Joey?

There is a long sigh on the phone. Freddy glances at –

A FRAMED LOCAL NEWS CLIPPING ON THE WALL, yellowing with
age:

LOCAL BOY SAVES DROWNING TEEN
*Hero in hospital with infection from icy waters*

A PHOTO shows a YOUNG FREDDY standing by the waterside, a
bandage over his ear. AN INSET – a high school portrait of A
YOUNG WOMAN, a beauty queen's crown on her head.

LIZ
(on phone)
Talk to him? Why, Freddy? – you didn't marry him.

FREDDY
No – but – I'm your friend.

LIZ
(on phone)
Freddy. I gotta go. (*click*)

*dial tone*. Hanging up slowly, Freddy stares at –

THE FRAMED NEWSPAPER CLIPPING – CLOSE ON – THE PICTURE OF YOUNG FREDDY, standing by the water, bandage around his head, smiling wide . . . a hero . . . full of dreams . . . *a proud hopeful young man.*

CUT TO:

INT. THE FOUR ACES TAVERN – GARRISON, NJ – NIGHT

A cigarette dangling from his fingers, FREDDY HEFLIN sips a drink at the bar, doing crosswords. *A long way from that hopeful boy.*

We are in the same NYPD-paraphenalia-decorated tavern from last night, only *tonight*, IT IS CROWDED. TWENTY OFF-DUTY COPS move about – crossing from the rest room, the tap, the TV, the entrance, the rear tables – engaged in loud conversations – loud enough to clear the jukebox.

Across from the tap, Freddy's equidistant to everything – but strangely marginal . . . and alone.

FRANK LAGONDA ENTERTAINS SOME ROOKIES BY THE VENDING MACHINES –

> LAGONDA
> – no – *this EMS mother fucker* – 'thinks he's *Zorro* – takes the gun in his hand – *state's evidence* – and he 's waving it –

SMOKING NEAR THE MEN'S ROOM DOOR, LEO CRASKY WITH ANOTHER COP –

> CRASKY
> – you're using the *short form*. Nah. For cops, there's tons of deductions –

Crasky loses his train of thought as –

FIGS emerges from the men's room, wiping his nose. He too is alone. Unaccompanied. He makes his way toward the bar.

AT THE DART BOARD – A THIN COP PULLS DARTS WITH JACK RUCKER –

THIN COP
I heard he wanted off the job so bad, he's begging
Tommy O. to shoot him in the *leg*.

Rucker laughs, also watching Figs shuffle toward the bar.

Figs takes a seat beside Freddy. Freddy turns, nodding to Figs,
but is distracted by –

A YOUNG COP AT THE BAR CHATS WITH A FRIEND –

YOUNG COP
– not from that height. Thirty-five flights? The bone
liquefies – looks like strawberry yoghurt.

Figs sips his drink sloppily. He winks at Freddy – aware that
Freddy's listening to all the other conversations – *avidly.*

DELORES – the barmaid – fills a mug for COP #1.

DELORES
How they gonna bury him? With no body.

FIGS
– Ray Donlan'll bury his baseball card collection *if
he has to.* 'Don't want to delay the ceremony – *you
lose the media.*

COP #1
'They know who the kids were?

FIGS
Bebos. From Newark.

DELORES
Who's Bebos?

FIGS
(chuckling)
It's not a guy, Del.

FREDDY
Bebos are a drug gang, Del. Jamaicans. 'Short for
'Who you be, bro?'

Impressed, Figs winks at Freddy. Freddy smiles.

ON THE TV – *the Eleven o'clock News* – Someone turns down the jukebox . . .

> REPORTER
> (on TV)
> – Cyril John met with the parents of the slain teens, calling for a human blockade on the bridge tomorrow –

THE ENTIRE BAR FALLS SILENT, RAPT WITH ATTENTION.

> 'A drunk cop jumps off a bridge, that don't erase the *murder* of two *children.*

There are hisses from the back.

> Attending the Giants–Jets pre-season finale, Mayor Farelli responded to reports of cops planting evidence on the bridge.

> MAYOR
> (on TV)
> – Yes. We're looking into it. There may have been some irregularities and we're looking into it.

There are boos from the back.

> REPORTER
> (on TV)
> In a moment, Chip Mackenzie with the weekend weather . . .

AS A COMMERCIAL COMES UP ON SCREEN, *conversations resume* . . .

Figs turns from the screen, shaking his head.

> FIGS
> The diagonal rule.

> FREDDY
> The what?

Figs turns away to the door as – someone calls out '*Joey!*'

A STRIKINGLY HANDSOME COP ENTERS THE BAR. JOEY RANDONE, 35. (*Liz's husband – we saw him in the pictures in Liz's foyer.*)

                              FIGS
                          (distracted)
The diagonal rule. '*Red light? Don't fight. Make a
right.*' More important the golden rule. 'If
Superboy knew that, he might still be alive.

Figs smiles at Joey Randone – who moves this way.

        Hey, Jo-jo . . .

But Joey Randone ignores Figs, crossing past him – toward a bowl
of pretzels beside Freddy.

                              JOEY
        Freddy. Heard you saved Ollie the Turtle.

Freddy nods, smiles, playing with his stirrer. He looks up at Joey,
serious.

                            FREDDY
        Yeah . . . Uh . . .

                              JOEY
        What happened to your face, Freddy?

Freddy touches the bandage on his nose.

                            FREDDY
        Oh. Nothing. 'little accident. (beat) Listen. Joey.
        There's something – uh – we should prob'ly talk
        about.

Joey loads a napkin with pretzels.

                              JOEY
        What's that, Freddy?

Figs grins at Joey. He speaks in a taunting sing-song.

                              FIGS
        Pretty boy *Jo-jo*. 'against the Bulls? What are you –
        some kind of high roller?

Joey turns to Figs.

                              JOEY
        Fuck you, Figs. I had twelve points.

                               54

Figs speaks louder, his eyes roaming the tavern for an audience. Some cops look up.

> FIGS
> Against the Bulls? Twelve points was twelve reasons for you to become a child. To revert to a pre-pubescent state – 'shoulda prayed before bedtime those pussies.

> JOEY
> – I didn't have to pray for anything. I had *twelve fucking points.*

Freddy turns to the pretzels, taking himself out of it.

> FIGS
> – *Against* the four time NBA champions. You night boys, you watch too much Oprah when you should be catching zees.

There are chuckles from the back. Joey moves off toward the back tables, holding his middle finger in the air.

> JOEY
> I ain't the one pissing my money away.

> FIGS
> That's your 'inner child' making that wager, Joey – little Joey with a sixty-nine Mets poster taped above his bed.

At the back tables, Joey spins around, grabbing his crotch.

> JOEY
> Figsy, why don't you unzip me and bite my 'prepubescent' state. You bite it, baby, hard and thick.

Cops in the back react – *Oooooooo.*

> FIGS
> Fuck you, Joey. Thick is a word reserved for things which are thick.
> (turning to Freddy, low)
> 'God-damned child. With a badge.

Huh?

FIGS
(loud – for Joey)
With a badge. That's how shitheads argue. They
point to their cock.

Jack Rucker walks out the rest room, throwing Freddy a disdainful
look for the company he's keeping – *Figs*.

A dumb fuck like that – PD – how does that make you
feel? With his connections – that's a detective you're
looking at – 'Four-five years – he's a climber –

FREDDY
I don't give a shit.

FIGS
Yeah? 'You like eating donuts?

Freddy shrugs, smirks.

I say it's okay to be jealous. It's a very – you know –
primeval – primitive emotion. I mean – you save a
chick's life. From it, from risking yourself – from
saving her sorry ass, you go deaf – as a result.

FREDDY
In one ear.

FIGS
*In one ear.* Then you have to watch as this chick you
saved – this beauty queen – marries this cocksucker –
(gesturing to Joey)
– this child – this *kumquat* – who reaches for his
pencil dick – the one he pokes her with – whenever
his dim guinea brain seizes up. And you with your
ear – you can't even get a desk on the force. You're
fucked. Be jealous. Let it shine. I would. Purge.
Cleanse yourself. It's fucking cleansing. I guess you
did that last night, huh?

Freddy smiles, sucks his cigarette. He enjoys Figs' intensity.

*Voices rise from the door.* Figs turns away as Freddy speaks.

RAY DONLAN enters the bar.

> FREDDY
>
> I'm not that jealous. I have a very – y'know, this is
> not a joke, here. I mean – sometimes it bugs me, not
> him, but in general –

Men at the rear offer Donlan a seat, deferential.

> FIGS
>
> Oop. Gotta go, Freddy.

Figs moves off, suddenly leaving Freddy alone at the bar.
Freddy sips his drink, looking at his empty pack of cigs.

Delores wipes the bar, glancing toward the rear tables.

> DELORES
>
> *They're* pretty randy –

Freddy nods, pushing out his last cigarette.
> (low)
> – considering one of their friends just killed himself.

> CUT TO:

INT. THE FOUR ACES TAVERN – LATER – NIGHT

Popping quarters into the cigarette machine, FREDDY nods to –
THE MEN AT THE BACK TABLE – DONLAN, RUCKER, LAGONDA,
FIGS, JOEY, CRASKY AND OTHERS. Freddy pulls the lever.

> CUT TO:

BACK AT THE BAR – Freddy lights a cigarette. ON TV – AN *NYPD
BLUE*-STYLE CRIME SHOW – A title montage: Cops in cherry-
topped squad cars race through Manhattan.

Freddy's eyes wander back to the rear of the tavern where *voices
are rising intermittently.* A shouting match breaks out between
RUCKER and FIGS.

> FIGS
>
> Bullshit. What is this, 'omerta'?

DONLAN

Sit down, Gary.

FIGS

If IA's gonna hang me by my balls, it ain't gonna be over missing evidence from –

LAGONDA

Six grams missing – that ain't no white socks violation.

RUCKER

You bought that big ol' house. Maybe you're lookin' to get out from under.

DONLAN

Hey. Jackie.

FIGS

You're damn right I am. What is up your ass, Jack? You getting by without gravy? *Fuck*! I was putting out Ray's fires when you were sucking on your Mama's tittie.
        (raising his arms for a search)
Ray? What is this? You want to toss me?

DONLAN

Sit down.

RUCKER

– or even better – get the fuck out.

FIGS

Fuck *you*, you fuckin' child.

RUCKER

'Least I'm not shackin' with a PR whore.

*Laughter.* FIGS STANDS.

You're supposed to fuck 'em, Gary, not open a methadone clinic.

Rucker snickers, looking about to his peers. They are silent.

58

What?

Suddenly, FIGS LEAPS ACROSS THE TABLE, PUMMELING RUCKER. *Everyone stands. More chairs fall backward.*

FREDDY RISES FROM HIS STOOL.

HIS FACE BLOODIED, RUCKER SUDDENLY DRAWS A REVOLVER, waving it about wildly. LAGONDA STEPS BACK.

STILL SEATED, DONLAN WAVES HIS HAND IN THE AIR.

> DONLAN
> Oh, for Christ's sake!

BUT RUCKER DOES NOT PUT DOWN HIS WEAPON. AND FIGS DOES NOT BACK OFF, ignoring the gun pointed at his chest. HE TAKES RUCKER BY THE SHIRT AND SHOVES HIM FACE FIRST AGAINST THE DART BOARD.

FREDDY SHUFFLES FORWARD.

> FREDDY
> Hey, hey. Guys.

FIGS PULLS A DART FROM THE DART BOARD AND STICKS ITS TIP UP RUCKER'S NOSE, HOLDING HIS HEAD WITH A FISTED GRIP ON HIS HAIR.

> RUCKER
> Owwwwwwww! Jesus *Chriiist!*

> FIGS
> You got a problem – me helping a girl in trouble?
> You got a problem with that?

> RUCKER
> No. NO! You're a fuckin' humanitarian.

RUCKER LOWERS HIS GUN, MOVING WITH FIGS' EVERY GESTURE, YELPING – TRYING TO KEEP THE DART TIP FROM RIPPING HIS NOSE OPEN.

> FIGS
> You think you're so bad, little boy.

Figs presses Rucker's face against a portrait of a young blue-eyed cop. The nameplate reads 'Officer Glenn Tunney'.

FIGS

Y'see that? That was my partner. *That's a cop.*

The only man still seated, RAY DONLAN RISES FROM HIS CHAIR.

DONLAN

*Enough.* Let go of him, Figsy.

Crasky takes the gun from Rucker's hand. Hesitant, Figs removes the dart from Rucker's nose. Rucker falls to the floor.
(glaring at Figs)
*Go home.*

Figs looks up, his lip bleeding, meeting eyes with Donlan.

Freddy, get him out of here.

FREDDY

Come on, Figsy . . .

Figs shakes off Freddy's hand with a spin of the shoulder.

FIGS

Ray. *Don't shut me out.* Okay. Yes – you're still the big man – you found us a sweet town. Got us the low interest. Finessed the residency requirements. *Hey.* I was grateful – I *am* grateful – but don't forget who it was – two years ago –

Donlan's eyes are flaming. LaGonda moves to stand but – with a simple gesture Donlan keeps him in his chair.

Figs points to the portrait of *Officer Glen Tunney.*

It's not *my* fault you can't look at him. You sit in *that chair.* With your *back to him.* You want it to go away. *But I'm still here, Ray.* In for a penny, in for a pound. Just don't *shut me out.*

Figs moves to the coat rack, donning his PD jacket.

Freddy follows Figs to the door. Everyone else watches, frozen, until Figs, taking his sweet time, fixing his sleeves, exits.

But Figs spins around, facing Freddy through the cracked door.
(low, smiling)
Shoulda' hit me, Freddy. Ray woulda' liked that.

CUT TO:

INT. FOUR ACES TAVERN – NIGHT – LATER

DONLAN looks toward – THE DOOR – JOEY RANDONE chats with
COP #1. Pulling on his jacket. Randone breaks eye contact with
DONLAN.

FREDDY carries a bottle of beer from the bar toward – RAY
DONLAN at a small table with JACK RUCKER, who dabs his nose.

###### RUCKER
(picking up the dart)
*Someone's* dropping a dime . . . We just can't keep –
(looking at Freddy)
– *it* here for two weeks – waiting –

FREDDY sits down beside them. DONLAN smiles, terse. He winces
as Rucker continues . . .

I mean. Freddy's new girl pulls us over – Tilden
shows up here with that grin – I mean – we got some
*loose ends.*

###### FREDDY
Cindy's cool. She didn't see nothing.

Donlan is uncomfortable with this topic in Freddy's presence.

I'm sorry.

Freddy stands.

###### DONLAN
Sit down, Freddy.

###### FREDDY
That's okay. I don't want to interrupt –

###### DONLAN
Sit down. Freddy.

Freddy sits down. He sips his beer, taking too much. Rucker chuckles at Freddy. Freddy wipes his mouth. Donlan glares at Rucker.

– Freddy – you know that polyp they took out of my ass?

Freddy nods, uneasy, unsure of where this is going.

Well – sometimes – when I look at Jackie, here –

Rucker grins, proudly.

– who did such a *masterful* job on the bridge last night – sometimes – I think – someone planted that polyp, watered it, gave it a badge – and now that piece of my ass is sitting here grinning at me like a fucking hyena.

The smiles disappears from Rucker's lips. There is a silence. Freddy peels at the label on his beer.

RUCKER
You know I'm the man, Ray.

DONLAN
*Freddy's* my man. Unfortunately, he's on the wrong side of the river.

FREDDY
(low)
'Don't mean you can't trust me, Ray. With *anything*.

DONLAN
(smiles)
I do *trust* you, Freddy. I trust you to keep the kids from killing themselves on prom night. I trust you to suggest a good opera record for my sister at Christmastime.

Freddy looks disappointed by this.

FREDDY
I'm serious, Ray.

DONLAN
(looking up)
Freddy. Everyday – when I'm away – I trust you
with *my town*. Maybe I don't trust you with *anything*.
But I trust you with my home and *my family*. And –
to me – that's *everything*.

Donlan points *the dart* at Freddy. Freddy squirms, glancing back
at – Joey Randone, exiting.

Donlan rises, crossing to the dart board. He pushes THE DART
back into the cork. *The sharp tip squeaks.*

CUT TO:

EXT. FOUR ACES TAVERN – NIGHT – LATER

FREDDY emerges from the tavern. He sighs.

A GARRISON PATROL CAR pulls curbside. DEPUTY BILL leans out.

BILL
Freddy. We got – um – a domestic.

CUT TO:

INT./EXT. SQUAD CAR/RANDONE HOUSE – NIGHT

THE DOBERMAN ON THE CHAIN BARKS AS – JOEY RANDONE – in
boxer shorts – pounds on the front door of his house.

JOEY
Come on, baby . . . *Fuck!*

LIZ
(off-screen)
Fuck you!

LIGHTS RISE. Joey paces, then takes a seat on the porch steps,
running his fingers through his hair. He looks up into –

THE HIGH BEAMS OF A LOCAL SQUAD CAR. Freddy and Bill
emerge. Freddy shines a flashlight. Joey has two cuts on his neck.

JOEY

Go home, Freddy. Everything's hunky dory.

FREDDY

Y'mind it we check up on Liz?

JOEY

Yes, I mind.

Freddy knocks on the door. Bill kneels, examining Joey's neck.

BILL

Oooo. Nasty. I'm gonna get the kit.

Bill heads back to the squad car. Freddy knocks again.

LIZ
(off-screen)

Fuck you!

FREDDY

Liz? *It's Freddy.*

Joey looks up, sullen.

JOEY

Does *Ray* know?

Freddy does not reply.

She hit me with a Listerine bottle.

Bill returns with the kit.

BILL

I thought those things were made of plastic now.

Bill dabs at Joey's wound with a pad. Freddy knocks again.

JOEY

She ain't opening that door.

THE DOOR PULLS OPEN A CRACK, stopping with the chain lock.

LIZ
(off-screen)

God dammit.

                              (her face appears)
        Hey, Freddy.

                              FREDDY
        You okay?

Liz nods sadly. Her eyes are red.
Joey pushes away Bill's bandage. HE CHARGES THE DOOR.

                              BILL
        Hey, hey!

JOEY BREAKS THROUGH THE CHAIN AND STORMS PAST LIZ AND
FREDDY, bolting up the steps:

                              JOEY
        – Freddy's here to rescue you again.

*A door slams*. Liz sighs.

                              FREDDY
        Maybe you and the baby need a place to stay – let
        him cool down. I could take you over to the
        Ramada?

                              LIZ
        Why? He didn't do anything. I threw a bottle at him.

Freddy writes on the back of a card.

                              FREDDY
        Well. Promise you'll call me if there's a problem?
        'Doesn't matter what time.

Liz takes the card. She looks up, her eyes filled with tears.

                              LIZ
        Eight years of marriage. And he's running around
        with that fucking spider woman.

Freddy smiles sadly, meeting her eyes. They hold this tender gaze.
Freddy wipes a tear from her cheek with his thumb.

Bill wanders about the porch, giving them space.

                                                    CUT TO:

                               66

INT. FREDDY'S HOUSE – NIGHT

*A needle drops on a piano concerto.*

FREDDY sits, slumped, on his couch, taking off his uniform.
He lays his holster on the muted playing television beside –

A TROPHY – FROM THE KNIGHTS OF COLUMBUS – INSCRIBED:
TO A YOUNG HERO – FREDDY HEFLIN

Freddy lies back on the couch, sighing. He looks –

OUT HIS WINDOW – THE GEORGE WASHINGTON BRIDGE – and
beyond – the twinkling lights of Manhattan . . .

CLOSE ON – FREDDY CLOSES HIS WEARY EYES . . . *as the lilting
music carries us into –*

TRANSITION TO:

MEMORY: MARSH – GARRISON, NJ – DAY (1975)

WE ARE UNDERWATER. LOOKING UP AT THE SUNLIGHT.
There is a big splash – and YOUNG FREDDY swims toward us.

IT IS QUIET. We hear nothing but young Freddy's heart
pounding.

FREDDY'S CHEEKS PUFFED WITH AIR, HE SEES IN THE MURK –
THE SUNKEN GREEN FORD, NOSE DOWN.

Freddy pulls open the door. A LILY WHITE HAND EXTENDING *to
him from the driver's side.* A BEAUTIFUL BROWN-HAIRED GIRL sits,
bent in the cab, her head cut near the hairline, blood swirling in
the water.

Young Freddy takes the girl, tight, one arm around her shoulder.
BUT SUDDENLY, THE CAR TIPS TO THE SIDE – THE ONLY EXIT
BLOCKED.

FREDDY LOOKS ABOUT THE WATERY SILENCE, WILD-EYED,
bubbles bursting from his mouth. He desperately pulls at the
driver's door, looking for an exit. Jammed. His heart pounds
louder.

FREDDY BEATS THE SIDE OF HIS HEAD AND SHOULDER AGAINST

THE GLASS TILL – *crack* – IT BURSTS UPWARD, GIVING WAY.

HE PULLS HER UPWARD TOWARD THE LIGHT.

TRANSITION TO:

INT. FREDDY'S HOUSE – DAWN

*A distant siren rings through the air.*

FREDDY OPENS HIS EYES, LOOKING ABOUT.
HE LIES ACROSS HIS COUCH.

THE TV PLAYS – A 'HOW TO PLAY BLACKJACK' INFOMERCIAL.
*The siren rises.* RED SWIRLING LIGHT through the drapes.

Freddy sits up.

A SQUAD CAR SCREECHES IN FREDDY'S DRIVE.
Bill Geisler rushes out.

CUT TO:

EXT. A BURNING HOUSE – DAWN

LEAPING FLAMES REFLECTED IN THE GLASS – FREDDY AND BILL
jump out of their patrol car.

AN OLD HOUSE ENGULFED WITH ORANGE FLAME.
THE VOLUNTEER FIRE ENGINE FEEBLY SPRAYS THE ROARING
TIMBERS.

The mailbox reads: FIGGIS.

CINDY AND A FIREMAN stand behind – TWO PARAMEDICS working
on *someone*.

> CINDY
> Freddy. She's in bad shape.
> 'Was in the basement.

> FIREMAN
> (nodding to the water tower)
> If that tower still held water . . .
> – *We got no pressure.*

68

Freddy peers around the medics –

MONICA – FIG'S GIRL – is burnt, bloody. Past pain. Her eyes flutter eerily.

> FREDDY
> Oh Jesus. Where's Figs?

> BILL
> 'On his way back. Cindy beeped him.

A CHEVY CITATION swerves to a stop in the drive. FIGS stands a moment in shock – taking in the spectacle – then noticing the crowd on the lawn, the medics – he sprints wildly toward them –

Freddy steps back as –

Figs – TEARFUL – kneels beside Monica down in the grass – He looks down at her, tortured. He brushes back her blood-clotted hair. She looks up at him, pushing away the oxygen mask.

Figs is choked with emotion.

> FIGS
> Baby. What were you doing in there?!

Monica speaks in a rasp . . . She smiles vaguely through the pain, her fluttering eyes meeting Figs.

> MONICA
> . . . *hey* – I came to *see* you . . . I needed some . . . I wanted to see you . . . you weren't *there* . . .

> FIGS
> (weeping)
> I was *working*, baby.

The medics struggle to keep her on the oxygen, but she weakly pushes it away from her mouth.

> MONICA
> . . . I missed you . . . – went down . . . to listen to the CB . . . See if I could *hear* you . . .
> . . . I fell asleep . . .

They press a mask to her face. But she stops breathing.
They begin to administer CPR. They push Figs away.

FIGS LOOKS UP AT FREDDY – HIS EYES WILD, WET.

                                                        CUT TO:

INT. SHERIFF'S OFFICE – DAY

FREDDY at his desk, filling out an ACCIDENTAL DEATH REPORT.

FIGS sits numb and puffy in a chair beside the dispatch radio.
He chews the rim of his paper cup.

CINDY makes a new pot of coffee.

                          FIGS
          The bastard's getting pay-back.

Freddy looks up.

                          CINDY
          Who's that, Gary?

Figs says nothing. He looks out of the window at –

THE MAIN INTERSECTION. RAY DONLAN PATS JACK RUCKER on
the back. They conclude a serious talk. LAGONDA stands by,
smoking. DONLAN crosses the street, heading this way.

                         FREDDY
          Lenny said it wasn't suspicious.
          'Said it looked electrical.

Figs snorts, his eyes still riveted out the window.

                          FIGS
          Lenny's a mechanic, Freddy.

FREDDY FOLLOWS FIGS' GAZE TO – DONLAN WHO CRACKS OPEN
THE DOOR.

                         DONLAN
          Figsy. I heard what happened.

Figs nods, avoiding eye contact.

Look at me, Figsy.

Figsy looks up, wet-eyed. Donlan's face softens.

> DONLAN
> Did you call in?

> FIGS
> I'm not on till Tuesday.

> DONLAN
> I'll call Lassaro. Buy you a couple weeks.

Figs says nothing.

Donlan smiles sadly at Freddy – and exits.

Freddy looks to Figs: '*See – he's not so bad*'

CUT TO:

INT. IAD CONFERENCE ROOM – DAY

In a smoked glass conference room – RAY DONLAN sits at one end of the table with a LAWYER and LASSARO'S AIDE.

At the other end of the table – MOE TILDEN sits quietly – behind an IA INSPECTOR and ANOTHER BUREAUCRAT (Mayor's office). A COURT STENOGRAPHER types in the corner.

> INSPECTOR
> – so – then you don't *know* he jumped. I mean – Ray
> – how do you *know* he jumped if you didn't see him
> jump?

> DONLAN
> – He was there. And then he wasn't there. I made an
> educated guess, Larry.

The men in the room look at one another. Some smile at Ray's charm. The Bureaucrat looks at Tilden – who is not smiling – then leans forward.

> BUREAUCRAT
> Alright. Let's wrap this up. Lieutenant – You *are*
> aware that your residency across the river –

71

DONLAN
It is *not* illegal.

BUREAUCRAT
– yes – but it violates the *spirit* of a law written to
insure that the men who patrol our streets are also
members of our community.

DONLAN
We've been living there ten years and it is not illegal.

BUREAUCRAT
We are a cop-friendly administration – you know
that – but there's a lot of mob influence across the
river and some people at IAD believe that another
Garrison resident – Glenn Tunney – was murdered
two years ago to prevent him from talking about any
connection between you and –

LASSARO'S AIDE
Where are we going with this? I thought this was a Q
and A about the bridge.

DONLAN
– Glenn Tunney was murdered by an inmate at
Rikers –

BUREAUCRAT
But if Murray Babitch had not taken his own life
and instead chosen to talk to IAD –

DONLAN
I would be very happy. Because my nephew would
still be alive.

The Bureaucrat sighs. He nods to the Inspector.

INSPECTOR
Okay. Well. Thanks for your time, Ray.

Everyone begins to pack their papers. Ray, Lassaro's Aide and the
Lawyer move to the door. MOE TILDEN has not moved from his
seat. He scratches his chin.

TILDEN

Um. I have a question. If that's alright. Is that
alright? I don't want to cause a rumpus.

Everyone stops – looks at Moe.

LASSARO'S AIDE

I think the Inspector said we're done.

INSPECTOR
(turning)
Is this brief, Moe? Ray's been generous with his time
and I –

TILDEN

It's brief.

Tilden unfurls his photo of Ray with Toy Torillo.

Can you tell me what's going on in this photograph?

DONLAN

Sure. That's a meeting I had with Toy Torillo.
About a year ago.

Tilden looks up at the men in the room. They look uneasy.

TILDEN

– And you're aware Torillo is affiliated –

DONLAN

– with a well-known crime family – Yes. I know,
Moe. He's a mobster.

TILDEN

Then – what was the purpose of this meeting?

ATTORNEY

This is way outside the line of inquiry –

Donlan waves away concern.

DONLAN

It's okay, Lloyd. I told Torillo he was moving
merchandise through my town and it had to stop. I
told him to keep his shit out of Garrison.

73

**TILDEN**

And what were you offering in return? – in return for
the sanctity of Garrison – in looking the other way at
the powder he's moving through your precinct?

**ATTORNEY**

This is not right. This should be coming from a
superior officer – not someone –

**DONLAN**

Let's cut the shit.
			(turning to the stenographer)
You stop typing. Stop – typing.

The stenographer stops. Donlan looks to the Inspector.

This is not about my nephew. When his body
washes up, this won't stop. Because this is personal
– between me and Moe. This is about the town my
friends and I built –

**TILDEN**

– with mob money. Through a bullshit loophole.

**DONLAN**

			(shakes his head, looking about)
– and it's about envy. Fifteen years ago all Moe
wanted was to get out of the 3–7 – get a white shield
and a clean desk. But me and Leo were making all
the busts. Moe wasn't making the grade. So one
night – across the pillow – he whispers a little
something to this red-head receptionist working
down here – something about the real estate Leo
and I were going in on – and suddenly – *surprise,
surprise* – there was a *fat file* – on me and the boys
and we're getting our pictures taken everywhere we
go – and *suddenly Moe Tilden is a Detective* – at IAD.
			(eyes flashing)
But guess what – fifteen years later – you still got
nothing.

74

TILDEN
Because the men who'd talk keep dying. (beat) You
got lost, Ray. You told these lies so long, you believe
them.

LASSARO'S AIDE
Excuse me. Are you aware of this man's [indicating
Donlan] record? How many lives he's saved? It's a
fucking phone book.

INSPECTOR
Alright, alright, guys . . . Yes. We're aware, Lloyd.

Donlan has not stopped glaring at Moe.

DONLAN
You're the one who's lost. You hide behind a rule
book written by the over-educated and the
underprivileged, waiting for one of your old friends
to fuck *up* so you can move *up*. You look at me like
I'm a monster. But you're the monster. You are a
*cannibal*, Moe. *You eat your own.*

Tilden's eyes flame with frustration.

ATTORNEY
I think we're done.

CUT TO:

INT. FREDDY'S HOUSE – NIGHT

FREDDY sits on the couch beside CINDY.

There are Chinese food containers on the coffee table.
Cindy has her head on Freddy's shoulder as they watch TV.

CINDY
I don't know – I've been going through the
violations – and three quarters of them are Jacksons,
Johnsons, Browns, Washingtons . . .

On the television – A COP SHOW PLAYS . . .
*A TV cop pushes a black perp against a brick wall.*

Freddy sighs, staring at the TV.

> CINDY

> These aren't moving violations, Freddy. Seat belts –
> insurance – expired license; stuff you can't tell until
> afterward – after you pull 'em over.

> FREDDY

> So?

> CINDY

> So you and Billy just pull over black people?

> FREDDY

> Cindy – we got a couple of nasty neighborhoods
> near us. Sometimes people – certain elements –
> drive through, take short-cuts, through town. I try to
> make it clear – you know – if you cut through
> Garrison –

> CINDY

> – and you're black –

> FREDDY

> – and you fit a certain profile – that you're gonna get
> pulled over.

Cindy shakes her head. She sits up.

> You think these guys – they come home from a hard
> day in the city and want to find out their front lawn
> has been turned into some kind of crack alley?

> CINDY

> Oh, come on.

> FREDDY

> What I'm saying is – this isn't racial.

Cindy nods, picking at her food.

> Can we talk about something else?

Cindy looks up, smiling sadly.

Freddy sips his beer. He turns back to the television.

CUT TO:

INT. SHERIFF'S OFFICE – DAY

FIGS lies face up in the holding cell. He has made it into a
makeshift bedroom. *The phone rings.* Figs lies there – he closes his
eyes but the phone keeps ringing. He trudges across to the
dispatch desk.

>                         FIGS
> *Dispatch.* Uh-huh. Uh-huh. Well, tell them they can't,
> Mam. Just cause they're TV people, that don't mean
> they can park in your lawn. Uh-huh. Alright then.

Figs looks out the window at –

FREDDY – STANDING AMID A MASS OF TRAFFIC IN MAIN STREET.

EXT. GARRISON, NJ – TOWN SQUARE – DAY

Badge on his chest, gun at his hip, scab on his nose, FREDDY
directs A LINE OF CARS – headlights on – many sporting PDA
bumper stickers – up the hill.

At the Arby's under construction –
A BLACK BRICKLAYER and his HISPANIC PARTNER watch warily.

DEPUTY CINDY BETTS flags the traffic onto AN ATHLETIC FIELD.

IT IS AN ELABORATE 'TWENTY GUN' BURIAL IN THE TOWN OF
GARRISON. Everyone in full NYPD uniforms, medals pinned to
chests. A sea of navy blue. Like the Saint Patrick's Day Parade.
Families make their way to the cemetery on the hill.

DEPUTY BILL GEISLER chats with cops. Friendly. Laughing.

A LINE OF LIMOS ARRIVES –
NYC'S MAYOR AND DIGNITARIES EMERGE; PDA PRESIDENT
LASSARO ETC. They exchange words, surveying the scene . . .

CUT TO:

FREDDY WALKS WITH CINDY TOWARD THE CEMETERY.

QUIET CONVERSATIONS BETWEEN DECKED-OUT MEN IN BLUE.

Families mingle about in their Sunday best. Many are strangers to Garrison. But among them: DONLAN, RUCKER, LAGONDA AND OTHERS. Black-slaps. Hugs. Whispers. Notes are passed. This is truly a secret society.

FIGS steps out of the Sheriff's office. The throng seems to sweep around him. He catches sight of someone –

> FIGS
> Hey, Charlie . . .

But CHARLIE smiles tersely and moves on. Figs looks away, hurt.

CUT TO:

Freddy and Cindy stroll up the hill – passing –

FRANK LAGONDA with a BOUNCY WOMAN WITH BIG HAIR.

> LAGONDA
> Yo, Freddy.

BEFORE A BLUE TENT – JOEY RANDONE points people to their seats, a chart in his hand. He points LIZ AND HIS DAUGHTER to their places. Liz moves stiffly, her eyes darting to –

Freddy, who smiles tenderly.
But Liz breaks the gaze, her eyes moving to –

ROSE DONLAN, who smokes with SEVERAL COP'S WIVES beneath a tree. Rose adjusts her sunglasses and scarf, covering a BRUISED EYE, dryly explaining to her peers:

> ROSE
> Ray kept telling me we should prune it. I'm chasing the dog yesterday – and bam.

HALFWAY UP THE HILL – RAY DONLAN grabs FREDDY.

He pulls him away from Cindy over to –

PDA PRESIDENT LASSARO.

THE MAYOR stands only a few feet away talking to a REPORTER.

Vincent Lassaro, meet Sheriff *Freddy Heflin.*

Freddy holds out his hand, beaming.

FREDDY
Glad to meet you, Mr Lassaro.

LASSARO
You people did a nice job here. Real nice.

DONLAN
Freddy's a helluva guy – 'was trying to get on the
force for years. But he had this thing with his ears –

LASSARO
You're not a *lip reader*, are you?

FREDDY
(laughing)
No. It's just one ear. When I was a kid –

AN AIDE PULLS LASSARO AWAY.

LASSARO
– Well. You should call me, Freddy. You know.
When Ray Donlan puts his thumb in the air –
(moves in the crowd) – Hey. It ain't the force – but I
got my own guys, you know? Call me.

Lassaro moves off. Donlan throws his arm around Freddy.
Grinning.

DONLAN
Freddy, my boy, that is how things *happen.*

CUT TO:


EXT. GARRISON – TORO HILL CEMETERY – DAY

A big cemetery atop a rolling Jersey hill. Hundreds of stone
markers with flags and emblems on stakes – *a suburban Arlington* –
inscriptions honoring a different kind of buried veteran:

Sgt. Michael Lindsey NYPD   1948–1976
*Heart of the 38th*
Tony Castanza NYPD   1954–1981
*sixteen years of service*
Officer Gary Matursky NYPD   1951–1979
*in the line of duty*

And finally – AN EXTRAVAGANT MARKER – surrounded by
flowers –

Officer Glenn Tunney NYPD   1960–1994
*Martyr to the system, Hero to his peers*

REPORTER
(off-screen)
– Tunney, murdered in his cell, awaiting a Grand
Jury. Two years later – *déjà vu.*

A TV REPORTER stands beside Tunney's marker. A CAMERAMAN
tilts up to a head and shoulders shot of the Reporter, THE BIG
BLUE TENT in the background. – Babitch's ceremony.

– Another hero cop – dubbed 'Superboy' – unwilling
to trust the system that destroyed his friend – leaps
from the –

CUT TO:

UNDER THE BIG BLUE TENT – THE BURIAL CEREMONY –

A LEGION OF OFFICIALS. AT THE CENTER – BABITCH'S MOTHER
holds a tri-folded flag. She weeps. Flanking her – RAY AND ROSE
DONLAN. Rose adjusts her sunglasses, uncomfortable with the
attention her bruise is receiving from –

JOEY RANDONE – who sits with LIZ a few rows back.

RAY DONLAN MEETS EYES with Joey. Joey looks away.

A WINCH LOWERS THE CASKET INTO THE GROUND.

Freddy, Cindy and Bill watch the ceremony from the shoulder of
the access road. Cindy leans to Freddy, whispering:

CINDY

What's in there?

FREDDY

His uniform.

CUT TO:

ON THE RECEIVING LINE – LIZ RANDONE'S eyes are filled with rage as she stands behind – DONLAN AND HIS WIFE – ROSE.

MA BABITCH solemnly accepts everyone's good wishes. *'He was a great man, Gina.' 'Don't you worry about a thing.'* And the band plays . . .

CUT TO:

INT. SHERIFF'S OFFICE – LATE AFTERNOON

DEPUTY BILL watches uncomfortably from the back as –

MOE TILDEN AND CARSON – THE IA DETECTIVES – wander about Freddy's office. CARSON EXAMINES – FRAMED ON THE WALL – THE YELLOWED NEWSPAPER CLIPS OF FREDDY'S HEROIC ICE RESCUE.

TILDEN sits politely on a stool beside Freddy's desk.

Bill exits. Freddy enters his office. Takes off his hat.

TILDEN

Hey. How' ya doing?

CUT TO:

FREDDY – at his desk – examines A FOLDER OF PHOTOS – 8X10S: A GLOSSY PICTURE OF MURRAY BABITCH (SUPERBOY) – A PICTURE OF RAY DONLAN MEETING WITH A DAPPER ITALIAN MAN.

Sitting on the nearby stool, MOE TILDEN FINGERS – THE TRAVEL CASE OF CASSETTE TAPES on Freddy's desk: Handwritten with care on the spines of the cassettes: *Preludes and Fugues 1957. Sonatas I 1958. Sonatas II 1959.*

TILDEN

I didn't think they allowed classical music in Jersey.

81

Freddy ignores Tilden. He holds the 8x10 glossy of Donlan and the unknown man.

> FREDDY
> Who's this?

CARSON leans against the wall, thumbing through ONE OF FREDDY'S PAPERBACK CRIME NOVELS. He looks up.

> CARSON
> Toy Torillo. You heard of him?

Freddy nods. He puts down the open folder. *The picture of Babitch staring up at him.*

> FREDDY
> Look. This guy didn't live here. Sometimes he'd
> stop by for drinks with the boys. But I didn't know
> anything about him –

> CARSON
> You knew Ray Donlan was his uncle.

> FREDDY
> – other than *that* – and that he was some kind of a
> hero –

> CARSON
> (tapping on Freddy's framed newspaper article)
> *Like you.*

Tilden crosses to the window – lights a cigarette. OUTSIDE – THE DISPERSING CROWD. Men in blue. Their families. Move past. TV CREWS pack up. The PROTESTERS shuffle into a van.

> TILDEN
> I don't know how you do it, Sheriff. Keeping all
> these Hessians in line.

Carson picks up THE PACK OF PHOTOS on Freddy's desk. He flips through them – *grinning cops and their families* . . .

> – All blue. Everyone packing. All together. One door
> down from the next. Wives borrowing sugar. You're
> the Sheriff of 'cop land'.

Excuse me?

You're the Sheriff of 'cop land'.

Tilden smiles. Carson has paused on A PHOTO OF RAY DONLAN AND FREDDY. He holds it up for Tilden to see. Tilden nods.

Freddy shifts.

See, Sheriff. I have a sticky problem. My jurisdiction ends – in a sense – at the George Washington Bridge. But half the men I *watch* live beyond that bridge – Where *no one* is watching.

FREDDY

*I'm* watching.

Tilden looks at Freddy, meeting his eyes. Respectful.

TILDEN

I can see that. You got a crime rate here –

FREDDY

– lowest in Northern Jersey.

CARSON

– yet you got Newark there – and Hoboken over here – and Jersey City –

FREDDY

We do a good job.

TILDEN

With a staff of three? No. What you have – Sheriff – is a town that scares the shit out of certain people.

CARSON

This is like that TV show. Who's that guy – *Barney Fife?*

FREDDY

Hey. I told you – *I'm watching* – I mean – 'You see these guys wearing silk shirts? No. Their pools –

they're *above ground*. (beat) You know – You raise
your family somewhere decent – that's a crime now?

Tilden smiles. He nods to Carson – *leave the two of us alone.*
Carson grabs his coat.

INT. THE OUTER OFFICE – AT THE DISPATCH DESK

Entering with a fresh pack of smokes, FIGS looks up to find
CARSON, pulling on his coat.

CARSON smiles at Figs. Figs glares. Carson exits.

FIGS SITS DOWN ON Cindy's desk. He looks to the cracked door of
Freddy's office. TILDEN PUSHES THE DOOR SHUT ON FIGS.
Through the glass, Tilden speaks to Freddy, but his voice is
muffled.

Figs stares at this mute conversation, then exits.

                                                      CUT TO:


EXT. OUTSIDE THE SHERIFF'S OFFICE – (CONTINUOUS)

CARSON leans on a postal box. He lights a cigarette.

ACROSS THE STREET – THE MEN IN BLUE LOOK UP, UNEASY.
GETTING IN HIS LIMO – PDA PRESIDENT LASSARO confers with
DONLAN.

At the unfinished Arby's, the BLACK BRICKLAYER looks up –
meetings eyes with – Carson. *The only other black man in town.*

Figs emerges on the Sheriff's office stoop – watching.

                                                  CUT BACK TO:


INT. AT FREDDY'S OFFICE WINDOW – FREDDY AND TILDEN

                          TILDEN
        So – we buried a *shoe* today. We buried a shoe. And
        that doesn't bother you.

Freddy does not look at him.

84

He jumped off the GWB.

– but his body *never hit the water.*

Tilden lights another cigarette.

And that doesn't bother you? What *does*? That I
investigate cops? Being a man who always pined to
be a cop.

I am a cop.

– pined to be NYPD: Three force 'apps in ten years.
Appeals of hearing tests. You may be *law
enforcement*. So am I. But you are not a *cop*.

Across the street – OUTSIDE THE FOUR ACES – RAY DONLAN,
RUCKER, RANDONE, LAGONDA AND OTHERS converse in a huddle.

Now, I may watch cops. But – tell me if I'm wrong –
*every day, out these windows – so do you.* You watch
cops, too. And because we are both *law enforcement,*
we share a *duty.* Where there's a stink, we must
investigate. We must gather evidence. Because
evidence makes us see the truth. Is this the stink of a
criminal act? Or is it a turd in a bag? Every day, I see
cops who lost their way. And I can tell you – these
lost cops – they are the *minority* – but they tend to
*gather.* They can be family men. Heroes. They can
have their *reasons.* But they are also the cops who
bring cases down. Addicted cops. Cops who look
the other way. Cops who plant. Cops who beat.
Cops who take. Cops who kill. Their ambivalence is
contagious. They infect those around them. They
are like maggots. Where you find one – you often
find a *nest.* Now, I don't like this. I went to the same
fucking Academy with that guy out there. I stood by
Ray Donlan at graduation. He was a beauty. A real
collar-man. And to the cop he *was* – to his memory

– I am loyal. But through the fog of my loyalty – to
*the men – the evidence* makes me see. And these days
– what I see – like an island – out of my reach – I see
a beautiful island – shining through this fog – every
house financed by one of two mob banks – uh-huh,
that's right, Sheriff – what I see is *your town.*

Freddy shakes his head. Tilden takes a deep drag.

OUTSIDE – DONLAN AND COMPANY disperse, some climbing into
cars and driving off. DONLAN AND RUCKER head into the Four Aces.

Listen to me, Sheriff. Babitch ain't dead. You know
it. And I know it. Ray got him off that bridge – alive.
Before he could talk. Ray wasn't so lucky last time –
when the shit hit with Tunney. That one he had to
take care of later.

Freddy turns, overwhelmed.

But *now what? What does Ray do now?* That is the
sixty-four thousand dollar question.

Tilden wiggles his fingers in the air, the answer out of reach.

That's why I want your help. Because you are *inside.*
Because – besides the church traffic and the cats in
the trees – there isn't much here for you, is there? I
look at you and I see a man waiting for something *to
do.* And here I stand. Here I stand, saying *Sheriff, I
have something for you to do.*

Tilden pushes out his cig, moves off. Freddy turns as – *slam.*

Sitting on the stoop – *Figs looks at Freddy, knowingly.*

FADE OUT:

EXT. GARRISON MEADOWLANDS – NEW DAY

FREDDY sits in his squad car, the door open. He watches as –

FIGS stands, slump-shouldered, at the water's edge. He scatters AN
URN OF ASHES into the water, looking out at –

THE GREAT CITY, GRAY ON THE HORIZON.

INT./EXT. GARRISON SQUAD CAR – DAY – LATER

*Moving past through the glass – Sunday in Garrison:* DONLAN, RUCKER, LAGONDA, CRASKY, RANDONE AND OTHERS PLAY SOFTBALL.

FREDDY drives. FIGS rides beside him, despondent and grubby. He sings a 'Mister Rogers' song as the town passes his window.

> FIGS
> *So let's make the most of this beautiful day.*
> *Since we're together we might as well say.*
> *Would you be mine – Could you be mine –*
> *Won't you be – my neighbour.*

Figs continues to stare – red-eyed – at the scenery. Freddy watches him, driving on.

> FREDDY
> You know. You don't have to sleep at the station, Gary. You can stay in my basement – 'til you find a new place.

Figs turns, facing Freddy.

> FIGS
> Billy heard they're having a party tonight.

CUT TO:

EXT. GARRISON – MAIN ROAD – DAY

A SUZUKI TRACKER OUTFITTED WITH THUMPING BOX WOOFERS DRIVES THROUGH TOWN. WE PAN WITH THE SUZUKI AS IT PASSES –

DONLAN, RUCKER, LAGONDA, CRASKY, RANDONE AND OTHERS PLAY SOFTBALL.

THE MEN PUT DOWN THEIR BEERS, BASEBALL MITTS, ETC., WATCHING THE SUZUKI THUMP AND RUMBLE PAST . . .

CUT TO:

INT. SHERIFF'S OFFICE – DAY

Cindy watches out the window as – THE SUZUKI TRACKER RIPS DOWN MAIN STREET, FOLLOWED BY SEVERAL HONKING CARS.

She stands, concerned – she fastens her holster.

CUT TO:

EXT. GAS STATION – DAY

Figs and Freddy pump gas into the squad car as – A STRANGE CARAVAN PASSES –

THE SUZUKI, MOVING FAST NOW – TAILED BY – GARRISON NYPD IN CIVILIAN CARS – *Honking* . . . AND FINALLY – CINDY'S SQUAD CAR, lights flashing.

> FIGS
> What the – ?

FREDDY moves to his SQUAD CAR. Figs follows.

CUT TO:

EXT. GARRISON – CUL DE SAC – DAY

*Screeeech!* THE SIGN SAYS – DEAD END.

Nearly rolling over, THE SUZUKI lurches to a stop. TWO HOMEBOYS SIT INSIDE, terrified. *Music continues to pound.* COPS EMERGE FROM THEIR HOMES, GUNS PULLED. They are surrounded by MEN WITH GUNS AND BATS – RUCKER, RANDONE, LAGONDA, OTHERS; in softball uniforms, Bermuda shorts, sweats – leaning out the doors and windows of their cars.

The younger of the pair, with a backward Knick's cap, stammers:

> KID #1
> Jesus Christ! We ain't doing shit! We just going to Action Park!

CINDY MOVES THROUGH THE CIRCLE OF MEN, pausing beside RUCKER.

LAGONDA rifles through the glove box of the Suzuki.

> RUCKER
>
> Look in their pockets.

> CINDY
>
> I can't do that. I didn't pull them over.

> RUCKER
>
> What do you want, honey, a letter from the Attorney General?

> KID #2
>
> I told you – we going to Action Park!

> LAGONDA
>
> Action Park is in Vernon.

*Slam.* FREDDY STEPS OUT OF HIS SQUAD CAR. Sunglasses on. Figs stays inside. Tense. Holding his Caldor's bag.

> FIGS
>
> I'll wait.

> KID #2
>
> – we stopped to get gas. It's cheaper on this side. They start following us, honking their horns. They ain't got no lights – how we supposed to know? We try to get away – *that's all.* That's the story.

Freddy steps into the ring. He glances at Cindy. He turns to the men; guns lowered. *The music continues to thump.*

> RUCKER
>
> Look in their pockets, Freddy.

Freddy moves toward the kids.

> FREDDY
>
> First of all – turn off the music.
> (pulling off his shades)
> *Do it.*

One of the kids snaps off the radio.

A SECOND GARRISON PATROL CAR ARRIVES. BILL climbs out.

Get out of the car. Get out.

                    JOEY
I think I smell something.

                    RUCKER
Look in their pockets, Freddy.

The Kid takes his place, next to his friend.

                    THIN COP
Search 'em, Freddy!

                    FREDDY
*Now* – um – I want you to tell these men you're
sorry for messing up their weekend.

Cindy looks at Freddy – incredulous. Bill steps up beside her,
watching.

                    RUCKER
Look in their pockets, Freddy.

                    KID #1
This is *whack*.

                    FREDDY
Do what I said.

The Kids stand, tight-lipped.

Jack Rucker strides forward, shaking his head.

                    RUCKER
This is very cute, Freddy. But you have cause and I
want to get on with my day. Tell them to put their
fucking hands on the fucking car.

Freddy stands, stone-faced.
                    (voice of command, to Kids)
'hands on the car. '*HANDS ON THE CAR!*

The Kids obediently turn and spread for a search. Rucker
rummages through their pockets.

Freddy rocks onto the other foot, brooding as –

RUCKER PROUDLY HOLDS UP – A BLUNTIE AND A BAG OF POT.

CUT TO:

FREDDY shuffles to his car.
In background, Cindy and Bill cross with the TWO HOMEYS – IN CUFFS.

RANDONE AND RUCKER MOVE PAST, muttering, laughing to one another, doing an impression of Freddy:

> JOEY
> 'I want you to tell these men you're sorry for ruining their weekend.'

> RUCKER
> What the fuck 'we pay him for?

Freddy stamps out his cigarette. He looks up, holding eye contact with Rucker and Randone. He climbs into the squad car.

CUT TO:

INT. THE FOUR ACES TAVERN – NIGHT

Freddy sucks a cigarette. He stares at the bar television. *The eleven o'clock news* – FOOTAGE OF BABITCH'S BURIAL. For a moment, *Freddy appears on-screen,* shuffling past camera.

In the back, A FEW COPS watch. There is a festive mood about them. But DONLAN AND COMPANY are decidedly absent.

> MAYOR
> (on TV)
> – reminds us of the blue line that separates us from *anarchy*. That's why I'm forming a bipartisan commission to study working conditions of police in our city.

Scattered applause in the bar.

On TV, another political figure:

> COUNCILMAN JONES
>
> If that officer hadn't jumped, the Mayor'd be talking about *in* creasing supervision.

*Boos from the back.*

DELORES the barmaid smiles at Freddy.

> DELORES
>
> Freddy. Was that you on the TV?

Freddy shrugs. He turns.

Deputy Bill stands in the door of the tavern.

> BILL
>
> 'got a call about this thing up at Ray's. 'maybe you should come.

CUT TO:

INT. RAY DONLAN'S HOUSE – A PARTY – NIGHT

*Lights and loud music snap off as –*

JACK RUCKER carries A CAKE WITH A SINGLE CANDLE through –

A SMALL CROWD OF COPS – LAGONDA, RUCKER, CRASKY AND OTHERS. They sing 'Happy Birthday' – *a perverse 'going away' party for –*

MURRAY BABITCH, who sits at the center, grinning, wearing a party hat. He blows out the single candle and everyone applauds.

> COP #1
>
> Congratulations, Murray!

COP #2 spins around.

> COP #2
>
> He's not Murray any more.
> He's Mortimer Snerd – of Tempe, Arizona!

> BABITCH
>
> Atlanta, Georgia.

COP #1

Whatever.

Everyone laughs.

Someone turns the music back on – *Sinatra plays – loud.*

Babitch leans over to a PRETTY WOMAN beside him.

BABITCH
It's kind of cool, you know? Not many people get to
live *two* lives.

COP #2 pats Ray Donlan.

COP #2
I didn't think you could pull it off, Ray.

Ray Donlan nods. Pained.

CUT TO:

INT. DONLAN'S HOUSE – UPSTAIRS – IN THE BEDROOM
(CONTINUOUS)

*Music plays loud from downstairs.*

RAY DONLAN sits on the edge of his bed – on the phone. His
shoulders slumped. His head in his hand. He speaks quietly.

DONLAN
I don't want to go through this again. *I can't.* I told
the boys – I mean – they're downstairs now, saying
goodbye.

LASSARO
(on phone)
So – fine – let them say goodbye.

A shadow plays across the bed. Ray Donlan looks up. ROSE
DONLAN stands in the doorway. Moves on. Donlan looks to
Rucker who sits on a dresser, looking uneasy.

DONLAN
Vince, I –

93

                    LASSARO
                   (on phone)
Who's Vince? What line are we on?

                    DONLAN
It's fine now. 'wired through Leo's garage.

                    LASSARO
                   (on phone)
Look. You tell me you're nervous. You tell me IAD
should lose the file – you tell me you want this rat-
fuck Tilden off your back – and I'm telling you –
that can happen – you were brilliant the other day –
brilliant – they got nothing on you – other than
*Superboy*. Now, I can back them off, Ray – but you
gotta tell me that boy's body washes up –

                    DONLAN
Vince. It's my sister-in-law's kid.

                    LASSARO
                   (on phone)
                    (beat)
Didn't you say he was adopted?

                                          CUT TO:


INT. DONLAN'S KITCHEN – NIGHT

ROSE DONLAN looks up – tense – as someone exits the
bathroom. She is writing something ON A PARTY NAPKIN WITH
A SHARPIE.

                                          CUT TO:


EXT. DONLAN'S HOUSE – NIGHT

*The music booms loudly from inside Donlan's house.*

FREDDY slams the door of his squad car. There are many cars
parked along the street.

Through the windows – *the place is packed.*

BILL also climbs out of the car – but Freddy gestures for him to stay behind. Bill sits down on the hood.

As Freddy approaches the door –

LAGONDA BURSTS OUT THE DOOR with his BIG-HAIRED GIRLFRIEND.

> FREDDY
>
> Hey, Frank. Is Ray in there?

> LAGONDA
>
> – *need 'm' turn it down?*

> FREDDY
>
> I need to talk to Ray.

Freddy moves to the cracked door. *Music throbbing.*

Frank LaGonda sighs. He releases his girlfriend's hand. He moves past Freddy –

> LAGONDA
>
> – stay here –

LaGonda moves through the cracked door – *glimpses of Rose Donlan, and other familiar faces.*

Freddy shifts onto the other foot. Waiting.

AT THE SQUAD CAR – LAGONDA'S GIRLFRIEND, her finger on her lip, eyes DEPUTY BILL. Bill nods, friendly.

> GIRLFRIEND
> – Your guys' guns – are they the same ones they use in the city?

> BILL
> (nods)
> . . . Uh huh. 'Thirty-eights.

BACK AT THE DOOR – RAY DONLAN emerges from the throng, haggard. He shouts over the music. He does not look Freddy in the eye.

> DONLAN
> What's up, Freddy?
> 'You want me to turn it down?

ROSE DONLAN APPEARS OVER HIS SHOULDER, holding a drink wrapped with a party napkin. She moves toward MURRAY BABITCH.

> FREDDY
> Well. It's after midnight.

> DONLAN
> LOU! TURN IT DOWN! No, *down!*

*The music goes down.* LaGonda heads back out to his girl.

> Frank. Don't go yet.

LaGonda turns around.

> FREDDY
> Ray. This doesn't make –

> LAGONDA
> – I gotta take Donna home.

> DONLAN
> (terse)

Take her to the train.

LaGonda receives the urgency in Donlan's eyes. He moves off shaking his head. Donlan turns back to Freddy, trying to smile.

> FREDDY
> – this don't make things very easy for me. I mean.
> This is a pretty big thing you're having – the day
> *after* – I mean . . .

> DONLAN

Freddy. What are you talking about?

Freddy winces.

> FREDDY
> Ray. This guy – from IAD – Moe Tilden – he came
> to see me yesterday. He's got pictures of –

> DONLAN
> Freddy. That guy's had a hard-on for me for years.
> It's a personal thing. He is a scumbag. You know
> how they recruit at IAD? They catch you on the take
> and they tell you – you can either do time or join
> them.

> FREDDY
> Well. He knows – you know – that Superboy –

Donlan says nothing, unblinking. The tacit question being – *and what did you say, Freddy?*

> I told 'em he's dead. I told him he was wrong about
> you. But – Ray – I'm the sheriff. I'm supposed to
> know what's going on. I mean. *How do you think this
> looks?*

> DONLAN
> Go home, Freddy. And don't think so much. I
> heard what happened today with Jack and the boys.
> I'm sorry about that. Everyone's very high strung.

FREDDY

Ray – I can't –

DONLAN

Go home, Freddy. Go home.

Donlan turns away, closing the door on him.

CUT TO:

INT. DONLAN'S HOUSE – THE PARTY – A HALLWAY – NIGHT

Cops all around – ROSE DONLAN presses A DRINK – WRAPPED IN
A PARTY NAPKIN – into MURRAY BABITCH'S HAND. He resists.

BABITCH

I'm fine, Aunt Rose. *I am.*

Rose wipes the faint bruise on her eye, intense.

ROSE

Murray. *I want you to have this.*

Perplexed – Babitch takes the drink – and the napkin.

CUT TO:

INT. FREDDY HEFLIN'S HOUSE – NIGHT

Leaning on a speaker, A BEATEN-UP RECORD JACKET – Glenn
Gould's *Goldberg Variations. The record spins on the turntable as
fingers gently lower the needle.*

FREDDY unbuttons his shirt, lying back on his couch, smoking.
Headlights spray in the windows. Freddy sits up.

THE DOOR OPENS ONTO – LIZ RANDONE – mascara runny, she
wears a thrown-over coat, and holds a pack of cigarettes, one
lit . . .

LIZ

Hi.

FREDDY

Hi.

98

                              LIZ
  Um.

Liz is nervous and upset. She looks over her shoulder.

                            FREDDY
      You get in another fight?

                              LIZ
      We were gonna have '*a big talk*'.

                            FREDDY
  Uh huh.

                              LIZ
                       (starting to weep)
      I had my mom take Caroline. – But Joey calls and
      says he's stuck. That he made some arrest – and
      that –

Liz descends into bawling.

      I mean – I can't *believe* him any more – when he tells
      me something.

Freddy looks about nervously as – *a car passes.*

Liz pulls herself out of it, suddenly matter-of-fact.

      – So – I decided to get drunk. And I remembered
      this bottle of – that you gave us – when we got
      married –

                            FREDDY
      – Sambuca –

                              LIZ
      – and it tasted like licorice. It made me want to
      smoke. So I went out and got cigarettes. And I was
      driving by –

                            FREDDY
      Liz. You want to come inside?

Liz smiles, sadly . . . *she nods – like a little girl.*

INT. DONLAN'S HOUSE – THE PARTY – NIGHT

The music is low, the last people leaving the party.

Uneasy, ROSE DONLAN heads upstairs to bed, looking back toward –

> COPS
> *Take care. Put this behind you, now.*

> BABITCH
> I will. *Thanks to Ray.*

MURRAY BABITCH is at the door saying tearful 'goodbyes' – the drink in his hand. COPS #1 and #2 offer bear hugs.

> COP #2
> Take care, Mur – I mean, *Pete*. You have a *great life*.

> BABITCH
> You too, Mike.

> COP #1
> Send us some – I don't know – what's in Georgia?

> BABITCH
> Peaches.

> COP #2
> (exiting)
> Well – send us some of those.

Babitch hugs goodbye to – OTHER EXITING COPS.

Rucker puts his arm around Babitch, interrupting. He smiles, but appears tense.

> RUCKER
> Ray wants to see you out back.

> BABITCH
> Tell him fifteen minutes.

Rucker looks firm. Babitch is tipsy. There are a few more cops waiting to wish Babitch well.

What? Tell him fifteen. I'm saying my goodbyes
here.

Rucker moves off, pissed.

> ANOTHER EXITING COP
> They taking you away tonight, Mur?

> BABITCH
> I guess so.

> CUT BACK TO:

INT. FREDDY'S HOUSE – NIGHT

Freddy and Liz sit on the couch. Music playing. Smoking. Sipping
drinks. The TV running silently.

Liz holds the beaten-up record jacket, examining it.

> LIZ
> This is pretty scratchy. You can get CD's – you
> know – in stereo.

> FREDDY
> Wouldn't matter to me.

Liz blinks, then gets it, touching her ear, smiling.

> LIZ
> Oh. Right.

> FREDDY
> Isn't he great? He played like that – so fast – without
> even looking at the keys.

> LIZ
> – like Ray Charles.

> FREDDY
> Yeah. Everyone thought he was a genius. But he
> stopped doing concerts after that. Cause he couldn't
> get it perfect, you know?

The music builds. Freddy conducts with his hands.

LIZ

Oh.

Liz watches Freddy in wonder. Barely listening. Buzzed.
Fascinated by *him*, not the music. She touches Freddy's ear.

Which one is it?

Freddy smiles, trying to focus on the music . . . wishing Liz would
do the same.

FREDDY

The other one.
                        (pointing to the album)
Beethoven was completely deaf at the end of – you
know – his career. Gould had this funky ear, too –
see? 'Kind of a goofy-looking guy – But he was a
genius, you know?

Liz sits up. She leans on Freddy's shoulder. Freddy stiffens. She
turns, her lips close to Freddy's bad ear. She whispers.

LIZ

You smell good.

FREDDY

Hm?

Liz smiles sweetly. A bit amazed with herself.

LIZ

Nothing.

Freddy blushes, unsure what to say – unsure of what *she said*.

You know – it's a funny thing – when you owe
someone your life.

Freddy shrugs. Nods. Liz touches his cheek.

Why is it you never got married?

Freddy turns. He looks deep into her eyes.

FREDDY

All the best girls got taken.

Tears drop from Liz's cheeks. They make a quiet popping sound as they hit the record jacket in her hands. Freddy reaches, wiping her cheeks. His eyes drink her in. *A rumbling silence rises . . .*

WE FLASH TO:

THE MEMORY: AT THE EDGE OF THE WATER.

*. . . the music continues . . .*

YOUNG FREDDY leans down, straightening YOUNG LIZ'S HEAD, *brushing back her hair. Lifeless, she lies in the reeds.*

He presses his mouth down against hers.

BACK TO THE PRESENT:

FREDDY AND LIZ ARE KISSING ON THE COUCH.

*Glen Gould plays . . .*

Freddy and Liz tenderly peck at each other. Sweet kisses – each mirrors the last – his cheek, her cheek – his neck, hers, the hair, the forehead. The kisses quicken. Liz and Freddy build a tender rhythm but are somehow unable, unwilling, to move further, like school kids, up against the limits of their experience.

Suddenly, Liz backs away, self-conscious. She puts the back of her hand to her mouth.

LIZ

Um. This is crazy.

Freddy looks at her, longingly. *The music still playing . . .*

CUT TO:

EXT. FREDDY HEFLIN'S HOUSE – NIGHT

LIZ'S VAN PULLS OUT OF FREDDY'S DRIVE.

FREDDY stands in the doorway, watching the van move off.

A GARRISON SQUAD CAR SITS, PARKED IN THE SHADOWS. Inside, CINDY BETTS looks out sadly – watching . . .

CUT AWAY TO:

INT. DONLAN'S HOUSE – BATHROOM – NIGHT

CLOSE ON – BABITCH'S DRINK sits upon a shelf before a bathroom mirror. MURRAY BABITCH rises into frame, splashing water on his face. He looks at himself in the mirror. Then – notices –

THE MARKED NAPKIN clinging to his drink. He peels it off the glass, reading the scrawl. He looks up in the mirror, suddenly terrified, the color gone from his cheeks.

COATS AND HOLSTERS are hanging on the shower rod. Babitch takes a REVOLVER.

CUT TO:

EXT. DONLAN'S HOUSE – NIGHT

MURRAY BABITCH stands at the back door. Shaken.

IN THE SHADOWS, AT THE FAR SIDE OF AN ABOVE-GROUND POOL, RAY DONLAN smokes, tense. The water tower looms against the sky.

Babitch looks at the water tower – then – nervous – stumbles down the steps, approaching the covered pool. He walks along the perimeter, pausing suddenly, talking to Donlan from the opposite side, looking about pensively, terrified . . .

BABITCH
– You know, Ray. It's a great thing you did. Making a place. Where guys could stick together, you know?

DONLAN nods, grim.

I mean – you didn't have to do this for me –
– I mean, you could'a just –
(shrugs)

JACK RUCKER stands at the back door. FRANK LAGONDA joins him. They look at each other and then – out to –

105

DONLAN and BABITCH stand together –

> I always told Ma – Uncle Ray – he doesn't like me
> very much –

                          DONLAN
> I always liked you, Murray. You just sweat too
> much.

Babitch smiles, painfully.

Donlan nods. He looks to Rucker. ON THE STEPS, Rucker looks to
LaGonda.

                          RUCKER
> Everyone's gone?

LaGonda nods solemnly. Rucker nods 'okay' to Donlan.

                          BABITCH
> So. What's gonna happen? We meeting some
> people? I'm pretty buzzed. I mean. I'm all packed
> and everything but –
> (noticing LaGonda and Rucker approaching him from behind)
> – maybe we should wait and do this tomorrow or
> something.

Rucker and LaGonda smile sadly at Babitch.

> Where's Joey?

                          LAGONDA
> 'Working tonight.

Babitch nods, nervous, standing there.

Donlan sucks on his cigarette.

                          RUCKER
> I'm sorry it came out this way, Murray.

                          BABITCH
>         (shrugs, eyelids, lowering)
> Oh. It's not so bad, Jack.

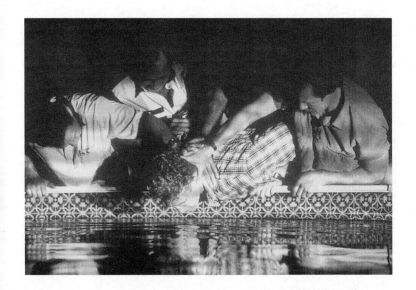

Donlan looks to Rucker. Rucker puts his hand on Babitch's head, his fingers in his hair.

RUCKER

     Yes, it is, Murray.

In a swift motion, RUCKER PLUNGES BABITCH'S HEAD INTO THE SWIMMING POOL, HOLDING HIM UNDER. LAGONDA HOLDS HIS FLAILING ARMS AS – BABITCH THRASHES WILDLY . . . HIS HAND GROPING FOR THE GUN IN HIS PANTS . . .

CUT TO:

EXT. FRONT OF DONLAN'S HOUSE – NIGHT

JOEY RANDONE climbs out of his car – still in uniform – walking toward the door to Donlan's house. It is locked.

*There is a splashing sound* . . . AND SUDDENLY A SHOT . . . *Bang*!

Joey moves quickly around to the back. He comes upon –

RAY DONLAN, RUCKER AND LAGONDA STRUGGLING WITH BABITCH AT THE POOL. BABITCH COMES UP, HIS SMOKING GUN IN THE AIR – CHOKING – SCREAMING – *Bang, Bang*!

107

Rucker and LaGonda recoil from the shots. Babitch springs from the water –

> BABITCH
> JESUS! YOU BASTARDS! *Fuck you!!*

– and runs into the woods.

JOEY RANDONE stands – horrified.

> JOEY
> What the fuck are you *doing*?!

Rucker runs off after Babitch. LaGonda follows. Donlan moves off too but is stopped, by Joey Randon's hand on his sleeve.

> What the fuck, Ray? You said PDA was gonna set
> him up – with a new life.

> DONLAN
> You think I'm all that, Joey? Huh?

Donlan glares, grabbing Joey's face. He moves off. Joey Randone stands there, *devastated*. He looks up to –

The light in Donlan's bedroom switches off. The drapes moving.

CUT TO:

EXT. MOVING WITH RUCKER AND LAGONDA – IN THE WOODS – NIGHT

Out of breath, LaGonda and Rucker look about. Donlan joins them, puffing. They look at one another.

CUT TO:

EXT. MAIN STREET – GARRISON – MORNING

A LINE OF CARS CURBSIDE – PINK TICKETS ON THE WINDSHIELDS.

JACK RUCKER comes out of the deli, a coffee in his hands. He finds a ticket under his wiper blade.

CINDY APPROACHES. She notices the tickets – and Rucker, fuming. RAY DONLAN emerges from the deli, holding a paper cup of coffee.

> RUCKER
>
> What the hell is this?

Cindy shrugs, pointing to the parking sign.

> CINDY
>
> A parking ticket. It's after seven.

> RUCKER
>
> And what? – it's after seven – and what?

> CINDY
> (moving off)
>
> Talk to Freddy. He wrote it.

Rucker yells after Cindy. Donlan's blue eyes are icy, piercing.

> RUCKER
>
> You tell 'Wyatt Earp' – that leg of lamb between his ears – that's for *eating* – not for thinking with.
> (waving the ticket at Cindy)
> He says this is a green car? Does that look green to you. It is *blue*. Carillion Blue. Tell him I don't own no green car – so I ain't paying no fuckin' cupcake ticket.

Donlan takes Rucker by the collar. Other cops look up.

> DONLAN
>
> You pressed yesterday, Jackie – you pressed and he went up into the attic and found his *spine*.
> (Rucker squirms)
> Now – you *chill*. You chill and you find my nephew.
> (moving to his car)
> Think 'Gandhi'.

CUT TO:

INT. SHERIFF'S OFFICE – DAY

THE TWO HOMEYS FROM THE SUZUKI sit – heads in their hands – behind bars in the converted tire storage area.

>                    KID #2
>          This is total racial bullshit, man.

FREDDY ignores him. He reads THE NY POST – PROCLAIMING:

>              BIG BLUE POW POW
>          *Mayor and PDA Prexy to Meet*

>                    FIGS
>          I'm telling you. I'm doing you a favor. Just toss 'em.

FIGS sits on the edge of the dispatch desk, sipping coffee, sorting through the overflowing in-basket with CINDY.

>                   CINDY
>          Gary – you can't do that.

Figs crumples A WAD OF PAPER and tosses it in the trash.

>          Sheriff!

FREDDY looks up from his newspaper.

>                   FREDDY
>          Do what he says, Cin.

Figs grins at Cindy. *She is disgusted.*

>                    KID #2
>                  (off-screen)
>          Yo . . . *Yo.*

Freddy turns as – KID #2 gestures humbly through the bars, bumming for a cigarette.

>                                        CUT TO:


INT. FOUR ACES – MEN'S ROOM – NIGHT

Rucker approaches a urinal beside – Freddy. Freddy nods to him, terse, flushing the toilet. Rucker glares.

'stead of writing bullshit tickets, Freddy, of which I
have no intention to pay – maybe y'should be
looking at that fire. Y'know? With scrutiny. I mean –
my girl at Chase says Figsy was missing payments –
what with the his and her co-co problems and what-
not.

                              FREDDY
Where were you that night, Jack?

Rucker's face goes numb – he zips up his pants.

                              RUCKER
'had nothing to do with it. That'd be retribution –
and that, I leave to God almighty.
                        (smiles)
I'm *Gandhi.*

Rucker throws water on his face.

    *Figs* is the one getting the fat insurance check.

Freddy heads to the door.

                              FREDDY
Say 'hey' to Superboy – if you see him.

Rucker spins around.

Freddy smiles, nervous, in the doorway.

                              RUCKER
Superboy is dead, Freddy. We put him in the
ground.

                                        CUT TO:


INT. FOUR ACES TAVERN – NIGHT

RAY DONLAN sits in back with FRANK LAGONDA, JOEY RANDONE
and a FEW OTHERS. They are quiet. Tense. As FREDDY passes
them –

                              III

DONLAN

Freddy. *Pull up a chair.*

FREDDY shakes his head, stiff, gesturing to CINDY at the bar.
RUCKER returns to his seat, staring at Freddy, uneasy.

Freddy sits down beside CINDY, who picks at a shrimp salad.

CINDY

So – where is he?

FREDDY

Hm?

CINDY

*Where is he?*

Hearing this question, EVERYONE IN THE BACK LOOKS UP.

– *Figs* –

FREDDY

Oh – at my house.

The boys in back return to their business.

Freddy picks at a MEATLOAF SANDWICH before him. He glances to
the men in back.

CINDY

Is he just gonna 'hang around' now?

FREDDY

Hm? I don't know, Cin. Is it a problem?

CINDY

I mean – I know he's got lots of *tips* and all. But
when he's around – I feel like a secretary – with a
gun, y'know?

Freddy sighs. Cindy takes a cigarette from Freddy's pack.

IN THE BACK, JOEY RANDONE SPRINGS TO HIS FEET –

JOEY

– Help find him? – so what? – so you can finish

cleaning your pool with his head? What? – 'you got
something to tell me, Ray. Mr Humanitarian. You
*tell me.*

Donlan glares at Joey, icy. Joey puts up his hands.

I'm going. I'm in at ten.

> RUCKER
> We all are. We got another hour.

Donlan continues staring.

Joey grabs his coat, avoiding Donlan's eyes. He walks out. *slam.*
Rucker looks to Donlan. And Donlan turns to –

Freddy, watching from the bar. Freddy turns back to Cindy – as
she speaks:

> CINDY
> I never should've taken this job. You were sweet
> back then – with your music – and your ear. Doin'
> your job. I told my mom you were like this noble
> turtle. 'thought I found someone who moved at my
> speed.
> (she laughs at herself)
> But now – I mean. What am I – *a door knob?* I mean
> – what are you doing? At least these guys know who
> they are. At least they're not sitting there staring at
> old newspaper clippings. What – you gonna like me
> more if I put on some fuckin' tiara and jump off a
> bridge – let you save me? Is that gonna make you
> feel better?

Cindy crosses to the coat rack.

> CUT TO:

INT. FREDDY'S HOUSE – NIGHT

A bucket of Kentucky Fried Chicken bones and beer cans in the
sink. *'The Passion of Saint Matthew' plays on the turntable.*

Smoking, FREDDY sits at the kitchen table with FIGS. A half empty bottle of scotch between them. And a collection of newspaper clippings, chronicling Babitch's 'suicide'.

> FIGS
> You're lucky your ear kept you off the force, Freddy. It's a deep and dark motherfuck.

> FREDDY
> Whatever. I'd like to have discovered that for myself, you know?

> FIGS
> Well. What you're feeling right now – friendless – angry – nervous – misunderstood – this is it. This is the life.
> (beat)
> City cops ain't nothing but garbage men. 'Pick up the trash, take it away, *dump it*. Next week, 'go down the same block, 'pick up the same trash all over again.

Freddy sucks his cigarette down to the filter. He stares out the window, tears welling in his eyes.

> FREDDY
> If I saw Liz – drowning in the water – if I saw that today? I wouldn't go in. I'd stand there – and I'd *think about it*. And that's the best thing I ever did with my life.
> (pushes out the butt)
> Now – I hear all these voices. Telling me I can't do anything.

> FIGS
> What did you hear when you saved her?

Freddy smirks, shrugs.

> FREDDY
> Music.

Figs smiles. He looks at – A NEWSPAPER PICTURE OF BABITCH.

> FIGS
> So.

FREDDY

So.

FIGS

*So* – you want to sit around listening to Gergen
Gingleshnorts –

FREDDY

– Glenn Gould –

FIGS

– playing the 'Opus to cunt hair number six in G flat
major labia'?

Freddy laughs. Shakes his head.

Or – you want to bring the faggot in? Let him spill.

FREDDY

I wouldn't know where to begin.

FIGS

Y'ever see *Murder on the Orient Express*?

Freddy shakes his head. Figs smiles, eyes bright.

They all did it.

CUT AWAY TO:

MANHATTAN. NIGHT. JERSEY ACROSS THE RIVER. GW BRIDGE

We hear a desperate voice. It feels very close.

WINCING COP
(off-screen)
– ahhh – Christ! – where are you guys?! Shit – I'm
down – and Joey's trying to hold on – but this
bastard – he cut me up –

Like a bank camera, impassive, WE PAN – across the lights, past
the dark buildings between –

– he's a fuckin' monster . . .

– past the loose mortar of this dark rooftop, past a glistening POOL
OF CRIMSON – to find –

WALKIE TALKIE
(off-screen)
(siren in background – static)
On way, Tone. Hold it together.

THE WINCING COP (TONY) LIES ON A TARPAPER ROOF, holding his punctured thigh and neck. HE GRUNTS into a shoulder-clipped walkie.

TONY
– I can't move. I think he cut my tendon . . .

JOEY
(off-screen)
*I need some assist, over here*!

WALKIE TALKIE VOICE
(static)
– Where's Joey? –

TONY
– fifty feet – ah, *shit* – he's in trouble, Jackie.

ACROSS A CHASM – ON THE FLOOR OF THE NEXT BUILDING – JOEY RANDONE IS LIFTED EFFORTLESSLY INTO THE AIR BY A HEAVYSET BLACK MAN IN SWEATS (SHONDEL). They are nose to nose.

JOEY
*You release me* – cocksucker!

Shondel smiles at Joey's feeble temper; a little boy in blue.

SHONDEL
. . . You got a wife?

Joey nods, looking about.

ACROSS THE STREET – PEOPLE ARE WATCHING OUT THEIR OPEN WINDOWS.

Shondel smiles.

'Got a little baby?

Joey nods.

So quit. Tell me you quit. I let go. You go home.
Kiss you wife. Eat you baby's Fruit Loops. And it be
tasting so good. And you thank me, mother fucker.

Joey blinks.

> I can kill you with my hands. I can kill you with your
> gun. I can kill you with my blood. *Tha's right. Or* – I
> can let you go. You 'still be a hero to me. Cause I be
> re-deemed. Re-re-*re*-deemed –
> > (reading his badge)
> – Officer Randon-ee

*A siren rises in the distance. Lights swirl down the block.*
Shonel smiles, angelic, though his grip tightens.
Joey tearful, wipes his mouth on his shoulder.

                                                   CUT BACK TO:

EXT. FREDDY'S PORCH – GARRISON – NIGHT

FREDDY sits on the porch. He watches as – FIGS TIPS A BEER CAN
ON THE RAILING, letting what foam remains dribble out . . .

> ### FIGS
> – a brother's in deep shit – he's down – he's bleeding
> – and you gotta get there – but there's lights – all
> over the city there are *red lights.*

> ### FREDDY
> You go through the red lights.

Figs sucks on his cigarette, disappointed by the response.

> ### FIGS
> Sure, you fire up the roof, you wail, you go through
> the red lights – but it's slow, Freddy, fighting your
> way through traffic. The goal is perpetual motion.
> You want *greens.* But how do you insure the greens?
> *You can't.* As in life, in traffic. So you leave yourself
> an out. At every corner you leave yourself an
> alternative. *You follow?*

Freddy shrugs. Figs sighs, his cigarette hanging on his lip. He

gestures, his hands miming a zig-zag course, approaching the tipped beer on the railing.

> You move *diagonal* – you turn the wheel when you hit a red light. You don't drive *down* Broadway to get to *Broadway*. Life is about navigation, Freddy – motion – *advancement toward your goal.*

Figs rights the tipped beer can. He smiles.

> 'you move diagonal, you get perpetual motion.

FREDDY

> But. How does this apply to –

Figs spins around, impatient.

FIGS

> It applies, Freddy! *Jesus.* It's just as easy to *tail* a man walking *in front of him*. Listen to me. You butt heads with these friends of ours – You come at them head-on? With your pink tickets.

Figs shakes his head, leaning on the railing, looking out at the lights of Garrison.

They got lives, Freddy. Families.
(low)
No. You move diagonal. You jag. It may feel
innately wrong – but like so much in this world,
what feels wrong is innately right.

                                        CUT AWAY TO:

EXT. ON THE STREET – MANHATTAN – NIGHT

DOME-LIGHTS SPINNING – AN NYPD SQUAD CAR LURCHES
CURBSIDE. From out the doors leap SEVERAL NYPD, GUNS
PULLED.

ANOTHER CAR ARRIVES – RAY DONLAN AND JACK RUCKER
EMERGE. Donlan moves slower than the others.

COPS RUN TO THE CORNER, ENCIRCLING – A DULL-EYED WOMAN
AND HER CHILDREN. She points upward, numb, her clothing
ripped . . .

COPS BANG ON STEEL REINFORCED DOORS, pry at them with a
crowbar – trying desperately to get stair access.

ANOTHER COP TRIES TO STAND ON A CEMENT BANISTER,
ATTEMPTING TO PULL DOWN A DECAYING FIRE ESCAPE.

UP ABOVE: THE STRUGGLE CONTINUES . . . Shadows play.
*There is an anguished scream from above. Joey's voice.*

DOWN THE BLOCK – IN AN ALLEY – RAY DONLAN COMES UPON –
AN OPEN DOOR. It leads to A STAIRWELL THAT SPIRALS UPWARD.
DONLAN pulls the door *shut* as – RUCKER AND ANOTHER COP
arrive.

                        RUCKER
Joey's in trouble, Ray.

DONLAN NODS, JIGGLING A PIN IN THE LOCK OF THE (OPEN)
DOOR. *He mimes picking the tumbler.* The other cop is impatient.

                        OTHER COP
Let's break it in!

> DONLAN
> No need. I got it. Just – one – more –

Donlan looks at Rucker, placid, eerie. He holds the door closed one more long beat . . . *then opens it.*

> – second.

UP ABOVE:

RANDONE AND SHONDEL WRESTLE, STRETCHED PRECARIOUSLY ACROSS THE GAP BETWEEN TWO BUILDINGS.
SLASHES ACROSS RANDONE'S HANDS, BLOODY FROM BLOCKING SHONDEL'S SLASHING KNIFE.

From an adjacent roof, RUCKER AND OTHER COPS RUSH TO RANDONE, FIRING IN THE AIR, GRABBING SHONDEL, PULLING HIM OFF JOEY – but – BENEATH JOEY'S FEET – THE BRICK CRUMBLES TO DUST . . .

> JOEY
> Oh, Jesus. Jackie –

JOEY reaches his bloody hand out for JACK RUCKER AS –

HE FALLS BACKWARD . . . PLUMMETING . . .
. . . headlong to the sidewalk
. . . TEN STORIES BELOW. *There is a muffled thunk.*

AT THE ROOFTOP STAIR-BOX – DONLAN STEPS ONTO THE ROOF, winded. He sees the men all staring downward, silent and shocked.

Rucker turns, glaring at Donlan. Donlan winces, looking off.

> CUT TO:

INT. FREDDY'S HOUSE – NIGHT

FREDDY lies in bed – wide awake. The television droning.

The bathroom door is cracked – FIGS running water inside.

*There is a knock at the door.*

Freddy sits up. Checks his hair in his mirror.

HE OPENS THE DOOR ONTO – MURRAY BABITCH – WILD-EYED,
UNSHAVEN.

> BABITCH
>
> You're the Sheriff, right?

Freddy blinks, stunned. He nods, touching his matching nose-
scar.

Babitch speaks in a paranoid whisper, words staggering out his
mouth, his red eyes darting.

> Hey. Um. I'm the guy who jumped. The one they
> buried. I'm dead. Uh. I mean. I need your help.
> *They're trying to kill me.*

> FREDDY
>
> Who?

> BABITCH
> (laughing, *then weeping*)
> *Who?* Are you alive? Who?

Freddy wipes his face with his hand.

> FREDDY
>
> Okay. So. Uh. What do you want to do? You want
> to go to the city?

> BABITCH
>
> Go to the city?! – *Jesus!* – 'You have any idea how
> *connected* he is? *Do you?* Go to the city?! He's
> fucking *everywhere*!

Figs walks out of the bathroom, a towel to his face. Babitch turns,
terrified (*He sees Figs as one of 'them'*).

Freddy meets eyes with Figs. He turns back – but – *Babitch is gone.*

CUT TO:


EXT. ALONG THE ROAD – GARRISON MEADOWLANDS – NIGHT

Rounding a bend, FREDDY (in his robe) and FIGS (further back)
struggle to keep pace with BABITCH, far ahead.

Freddy turns, slowing, looking at an approaching car. Nobody. Just a funkified VW VAN. *It passes.*

Freddy looks about. Babitch has disappeared. Figs joins him. Coughing. Nothing but reeds. And the water tower overhead.

                                                              CUT TO:

INT. FREDDY'S HOUSE – DAWN

THE GW BRIDGE OVER THE RIVER. PULLING FROM A WINDOW – WE COME UPON – A BEDSIDE CLOCK. It blinks: 6:28, 6:28, 6:29. Beside it – A GUN. FREDDY LIES AWAKE IN HIS BED.

Downstairs, in the basement – FIGS sleeps on the couch.

                                                              CUT TO:

INT. FREDDY'S BATHROOM – DAWN

Splashing water on his face, FREDDY stands at the sink. He looks at himself in the mirror. Suddenly, he notices –

A SPRINKLING OF WHITE POWDER on the face of a hand mirror. Freddy runs his finger through the powder, sniffing it.

                          FIGS
                        (off-screen)
          'you waking up? Jesus – I feel like shit.
                        (sniffles)
          Man. Fuckin' allergies . . .

Freddy looks toward the door, dread on his face.

                                                              CUT TO:

EXT. GARRISON CEMETERY – DAY

A CHAPLAIN SPEAKS OVER A FLAG-DRAPED COFFIN.

AS BEFORE – A SEA OF BLUE SURROUNDS THE CEREMONY.

AND AT THE CENTER OF IT ALL – LIZ RANDONE. Lovely and strangely numb, she stands resolute and plain, her hair blowing with the wind, her daughter at her side.

FREDDY watches Liz with obsessive interest as she solemnly accepts everyone's good wishes. '*He was a great guy, Liz*', '*Don't you worry about a thing.*' She finds comfort in Freddy's eyes.

Freddy can't stop staring at Liz.
Over his shoulder, distant, *the old Garrison water tower.*

                                                    CUT TO:


EXT. ONE POLICE PLAZA – NYC – DAY

FREDDY emerges from a PATH TRAIN STATION. He stands under the great arch of Manhattan Borough Hall, Chambers Street behind him, cutting through to the Hudson.

Across the plaza, COPS CRISS-CROSS before A BROWN BUILDING WITH DARK WINDOWS (ONE POLICE PLAZA). The Brooklyn Bridge looms in background. Freddy checks a wad of paper.

FREDDY WALKS PAST – COPS BEFORE A BARRICADE ONE COP WATCHES FREDDY – BERTA – THE BOMB SQUAD COP FROM SCENE 1. Their eyes meet. Freddy nods, friendly, moving on.

                                                    CUT TO:


INT. ONE POLICE PLAZA – NYC – WAR ROOM – DAY

The War room is subdued. TWO IA DETECTIVES whisper, looking back toward –

LIEUTENANT MOE TILDEN – through a doorway – in an ADJOINING OFFICE. He sits, a cigarette burning in his lips, his feet on his desk. He looks glum, playing with a rubber band.

                        IA DETECTIVE #1
                      (unwrapping a lunch)
              What's up? What the fuck happened?

                        IA DETECTIVE #2
          (nods, low, taking potato chips, looking at paperwork)
          PDA went to the Powerhouse – Powerhouse went to
          the Mayor – Mayor's office got to the Inspector.
          'they pulled the plug. 'told Moe if he sets foot in
          Jersey again, he's back in the bag.

CARSON timidly approaches Tilden's door, holding a phone.

                    CARSON
 Uh. Moe.

                    TILDEN
 Yeah.

                    CARSON
 The Sheriff of Garrison, New Jersey, is here to see
 you.

Tilden's face is numb.

   Y'gonna tell him we're frozen?

Tilden thinks. He smiles, wheels turning. He stands. Picks up a
stack of files – and throws it in an empty box.

He tosses another box to Carson, who stands, puzzled.

                    TILDEN
 Put your files in there.

                    CARSON
 What?

                    TILDEN
 Throw 'em in. Do it. We're done.

                    CARSON
 Moe? What the fuck?

Tilden steps into the war room. He turns to Detective #2.

                    TILDEN
 Rubin ? What are you doing?! The case is closed.

RUBIN (DET. #2) looks up, frightened.

                    RUBIN
 Uh. Yeah, but you told me to –

                    TILDEN
 What – I told you what? Fuck you. The case is
 closed. Go to lunch.

Tilden throws Rubin's work in the trash.

*Go – to – lunch.*

#### RUBIN
(looking at his lunch)
But I got –

TILDEN crosses to the map of Garrison on the bulletin board. He rips it down, stuffing it in the trash.

#### TILDEN
GO TO LUNCH!

Stunned, Carson and the others watch as –

Tilden moves along the desks of OTHER DETECTIVES, throwing files to the floor. Everyone looks at him as if he's gone mad.

The case is fucking closed! Get the fuck outta here! All of you!

IA Detectives shuffle out. Carson looks at Tilden, dumbstruck. Tilden grins. Carson blinks.

Carsie – put your work in the box.

Carson reluctantly stuffs 'Garrison' files into his box.

Tilden steps across the mess he's made, moving back toward his office. He slams the door. He puts his feet up, checking once – bright-eyed – over his shoulder as –

CUT TO:

FREDDY HEFLIN enters the war room. He is taken aback by the mess. Files on the floor. The shredded bulletin board.

At his desk, CARSON turns, dumping files.

#### CARSON
Sheriff – what can I do for you?

Freddy looks about, bewildered. He approaches.

#### FREDDY
What's going on? You guys moving?

Carson smiles, cryptic. He continues stuffing his box full of files.

> CARSON
> You could say that.

> FREDDY
> (nodding to Tilden)
> He told me to come down if – you know –

> CARSON
> Uh-huh.

Freddy is confused. He furrows.

> FREDDY
> Look. *You guys were right.* Babitch is alive.

In the back office, TILDEN LISTENS, gleeful, snapping a rubber band. Freddy moves to him but Carson steps in front.

> CARSON
> It's a little late, Sheriff. But – thanks for coming in anyway.

Freddy turns. Confused. He nods toward Tilden.

> FREDDY
> I want to talk to him.

Carson put his hand on Freddy, moving him to the door.

> CARSON
> Sheriff. Look around you. It's out of our hands, now, you *dig*?

> FREDDY
> I gotta talk to him. It's important.

Freddy breaks past Carson – he opens Tilden's door.

> Hey.

Tilden sits there. He refuses to meet Freddy's eyes, lighting a fresh cigarette, turning his back on Freddy, facing the window.

Freddy is perplexed. Carson crosses to Tilden's door, pulling on Freddy's sleeve.

Hey. You were right. They tried to kill him. 'Like you said. But he got away. He's running around in the woods, you know, like Grizzly Adams or something. He's scared to death. We gotta do something.

CARSON

'should be scared. His uncle got this case closed with one phone call.

Freddy shakes off Carson's grip.

FREDDY

Look. I'm sorry – it took so long – to come around, you know? You were right. I couldn't see the truth. 'Like you said. The evidence. My loyalties – they were confused, you know? But I'm ready now.

Tilden is stone-faced.

*What is this?* You come to *me* – to my town – with these speeches.

TILDEN
(still not looking at Freddy)
That was two weeks ago.

FREDDY

What about Babitch?

TILDEN

Fuck him.

FREDDY

What about Donlan?

TILDEN

Fuck him.

FREDDY

What about Joey Randone?

TILDEN

He fell off a building.

Freddy glares.

> Listen to me, Sheriff. I'm very sorry I awoke you
> from your slumber. But it's over. Hands are tied,
> now. *You shut me down.*

**FREDDY**
No, they're not – You can –

Tilden turns, facing Freddy. Red-faced. Intense.

**TILDEN**
*Listen to me.* I offered you a chance. *Listen to me, you
deaf fuck.* When there was still room to move. I
offered you a chance – *to be a cop. And you blew it.*

Freddy speaks slowly, his eyes blazing with emotion.

**FREDDY**
*You people are all the same.*

Tilden is silent. Carson looks to –

Some detectives have assembled outside the door.

Freddy walks off – past them – exiting.

Carson turns to Tilden. Smoke trickles from Tilden's lips.

**TILDEN**
That cupcake makes a mess. We have a case again.

CUT TO:

INT. IA OFFICES – MOVING WITH FREDDY – FROM BEHIND

HE MOVES PAST – STACKS OF FILES STUFFED IN BOXES. ONE BOX
READS: GARRISON/TUNNEY.

FREDDY STOPS – HE LOOKS OVER AT –

A RECEPTIONIST ON THE PHONE, FACING THE OTHER WAY. TWO
DETECTIVES SIP COFFEE BY THE WINDOW.

FREDDY REACHES IN AND GRABS A HANDFUL OF FILES.

CUT TO:

INT. SHERIFF'S OFFICE – NIGHT

CLOSE ON – THE FILES – WE SEE A REPORT STATING THAT THE
CONSTRUCTION IN GARRISON WAS FINANCED BY A MOB-
CONTROLLED BANK. MORTGAGES – ONE AFTER ANOTHER –
DONLAN, CRASKY, RUCKER, RANDONE, ETC.

FREDDY SITS at his desk, hunched over the files. He stares at the
mountain of pictures of Ray and Rucker with Mob figures.

BILL watches through the officer door. CINDY sits on the couch.
She looks through one of the files.

> FREDDY
> Figs was right. The mob owns this town.

> CINDY
> It's *New Jersey*, Freddy. The mob owns everything
> here.

FREDDY EXAMINES – OFFICIAL REPORTS CHRONICLING
TUNNEY'S DEATH. A NEW YORK POST STORY on his arrest, for
using an illegal choke-hold which resulted in a fatality. Another
article stating that Tunney was going to talk to IA.

A PICTURE OF FIGS AND TUNNEY – together – in uniform.

> BILL
> (pointing to the city)
> *They* closed the case, Freddy. If *they* don't have the
> stomach for it . . .

> FREDDY
> They had to. It's all circumstantial.

> CINDY
> You shouldn't be looking at this stuff. It's illegal.
> You stole these.

FREDDY HOLDS THE REPORT on Tunney's murder. *Insufficient
Evidence* is stamped on the report.

> FREDDY
> They need a witness.

FREDDY NOTICES IN A PRESS PHOTO OF TUNNEY'S DEATH – A
CORRECTION GUARD HOLDS UP HIS HAND, blocking the camera.
Freddy opens his party pictures. THAT SAME CORRECTION
OFFICER is arm-in-arm with Rucker. Freddy lowers his head.
Disgusted.

They got rid of Tunney when he was gonna talk.

                        BILL
So why didn't Figs do something about it? Figs was
Ray's right-hand man back then.

                        CINDY
I'll tell you why – he's a coke head.

                        FREDDY
. . . They tried to kill Babitch when –

                        BILL
They were *hiding him*, Freddy.

                        FREDDY
Then they burnt down Figs' house when they
thought he might talk –

                        CINDY
You don't know that. We looked all over that place.

                        BILL
There was no sign of arson.

Cindy moves toward Freddy. She tosses down the file.

                        CINDY
Everything is not some kind of 'hexagonal
conspiracy'. You've been hanging out with Figs too
much. *He's* the one collecting cash on his house.
He's playing you, Freddy. So are those assholes in
the city. There's nothing you can do about this.

                        FREDDY
Yes there is. I can find Superboy and I can bring
him in.

Cindy moves to the door.

I still got my old job back upstate. I don't want any
part of this.
                    (as she exits)
You're not trying to find Superboy. You're trying to
find yourself.

The door slams. Bill looks to Freddy.

                    BILL
Freddy. I don't know about Ray. But everyone in
Garrison is not a murderer.

Freddy looks down to a picture of Ray Donlan and him together,
arm around one another.

                    FREDDY
No. They've just kept their eyes closed. 'kept their
mouths shut. Just like me.

                                        CUT TO:


EXT. GARRISON FIRE HOUSE BARBECUE/FAIR – DAY

CARNIVAL TRUCKS PARKED ON AN ATHLETIC FIELD, SET UP
WITH GAMES OF CHANCE. A SPIDER-LIKE TILT-A-WHIRL SPINS.
Cops' families roam about. There is a GATHERING AROUND A
CHARCOAL PIT.

RAY DONLAN turns the quartered chickens on the grill. He looks
haggard, tense, as he watches FREDDY cross past.

                                        CUT TO:


A BB-GUN SHOOTING GALLERY SET UP IN THE OPEN END OF A
TRUCK. STUFFED ANIMALS hang all around the open end of the
truck. THE UNSHAVEN OPERATOR smokes, watching Freddy warily
as he looks to a BIG GREEN STUFFED TURTLE above.

                    FREDDY
                (putting down cash)
        Two shots in the center?

OPERATOR

'You a cop? 'rules are different for cops. I'm losing
my shirt here.

FREDDY

What do I gotta do?

OPERATOR

*Five out of six.*

Jack Rucker approaches from behind, a full plate in hand. He slaps
down two dollars. The Operator sighs.

RUCKER

I know, I know. I heard ya.

The Operator hands them both rifles.

Freddy aims his rifle. Rucker does too.

'enjoy your trip to the big city, Freddy?

*Bang.* Freddy misses. *Bang.* Rucker puts one in the center.

'have to make the next five to win.

Freddy turns back to the target, raising the gun to his eye.
*All sound seems to drop away as he squints at the target.*

*Bang.* Center. *Bang.* Center. *Bang.* Center. *Bang.* Center. *Bang.*
*Bull's eye.*

The operator takes a drag on his cigarette and reluctantly hands
Freddy THE PLUSH TURTLE. Rucker sneers, impressed.

CUT TO:

EXT. ALONG MAIN STREET – DAY

Leaning on the side of the Sheriff's office, CINDY BETTS chats with
A PASSERBY. She looks up, noticing –

FREDDY – walking along main street, CARRYING FOIL-WRAPPED
CHICKEN, FLOWERS AND THE TURTLE.

Cindy smiles as he approaches – *assuming the gifts are for her.*
Freddy walks past Cindy, averting his eyes.

EXT. RANDONE HOUSE – LATER AFTERNOON

Freddy stands on the porch, arms full. *He knocks.* Liz peers out a side window; she brightens. The door opens.

> FREDDY
>
> Hello.

> LIZ
>
> Hello, Freddy.

An awkward beat.

> FREDDY
>
> Um. I thought maybe . . . Have you eaten?

CUT TO:

INT. RANDONE HOUSE – LATE AFTERNOON

Freddy follows Liz into the kitchen. She holds her flowers.

> LIZ
>
> Beautiful. And no *condolences.*

Freddy smiles awkwardly. He puts the plush turtle on a chair. Liz notices it.

> Did you win that?

Freddy nods, proudly. Liz smiles, queasy.

> I had to take the other Ollie away from her – he was leaking all over the place.

Liz takes the bottle of wine and pulls out a corkscrew.

> I haven't been very receptive to visitors.

> FREDDY
>
> Well. If you don't feel like company –

> LIZ
>
> No, no. Stay.

Liz pours two glasses of wine.

Caroline's napping – and I was sitting in front of the TV, wondering if my life is over.

Liz hands Freddy a glass.

> FREDDY
> Sounds fun.

Liz turns to the chicken, unwrapping the foil.

> It's probably cold.

> LIZ
> I'll heat it up.

Freddy wanders about the living room, taking it in – like he was considering buying it – *as is*. He squeezes a couch cushion.

Back in the kitchen, Liz slides the chicken into the oven.

> So. All that . . . *hoopla for Joey*. Those ceremonies must give you a headache.

Freddy shrugs, uneasy with this topic.

> I guess you're getting used to it, huh. 'Bury one every two weeks.

Liz crosses into the living room.

> It was like one of the Kennedys died. I thought, here I am, playing *Jackie O*.

Freddy sits down on the couch. He smiles a small tense smile.

> Is this in bad taste? You can tell me, Freddy. It probably is. I'm sorry.

CUT TO:

EXT. RANDONE HOUSE – NIGHT

A GARRISON SQUAD CAR SLOWS. Inside, CINDY looks out at –

FREDDY'S SMASHED SQUAD CAR – *in Liz's driveway.*

AN OLDS DELTA 88 slows as it passes Cindy. It is JACK RUCKER. He smiles at her – following her gaze to –Freddy's car.

CINDY LURCHES HER CAR AWAY BUT – RUCKER THROWS HIS IN REVERSE – BLOCKING HER – staying even with her window. He smiles. TWO COPS SIT IN THE BACK OF RUCKER'S CAR.

> RUCKER
> 'nothing better to do than watch?

> COP #1
> Come on, Jack. We gotta get down there. I want to get this done.

Cindy looks away. Rucker grins at her, intense.

> RUCKER
> We're lookin' for a lost brother. 'Be at the Aces later. 'you get tired of this.

CUT TO:

INT. RANDONE HOUSE – SUNSET

Freddy and Liz sit at the dining-room table, eating. The television plays quietly.

> FREDDY
> – Figs talks like everyone is a car and you can just – change directions like – by turning the wheel. It's not that easy.

> LIZ
> Damn right.

> FREDDY
> Sometimes I feel like a boat. A big boat.

> LIZ
> An ocean liner.

> FREDDY
> Yeah. The *Queen Mary.*

LIZ

The *Titanic.*

FREDDY

Right. Exactly.

(inspired)
And you see this iceberg coming – you know – but
you're so enormous – you can't turn. You have to –
like – you know – in the movies – you gotta alert the
engine room or rudder room or whatever – and it
takes so long and you're so big – you don't turn.
You just hit it.

Freddy looks up from his fevered story, meeting Liz's eyes.

LIZ

I just hope you're not trying to prove anything,
Freddy.

Freddy blinks, taut. Hurt.

I mean, okay – some of them are assholes – 'think
they're high priests or something. But – *why would
they do all this*? – I mean. Maybe they're doing the
right thing?

FREDDY

Liz. I saw pictures of Ray meeting with this guy –
*this mobster.*

LIZ

Says who – *IA*?

FREDDY

And even you said – Joey's death was –

LIZ

Joey fell off a building, Freddy.

FREDDY'S EYES MOVE TO – THE ACADEMY GRADUATION PICTURE
OF JOEY RANDONE on the wall. His medal on his chest. A big grin.

I don't need this, you know – opened up. Maybe
you need this, Freddy. But *I don't.* All Joey wanted

139

was a place for us to live I mean – who are you to
judge? 'Till you've walked in their shoes. (beat)
Maybe that's what you're trying to do with me.

CAROLINE CRIES FROM ANOTHER ROOM. Freddy stiffens.
Liz rises, smiling sadly. She moves upstairs.

Freddy sighs. Dejected, he turns to – THE MUTED TV.

On screen, A 70S COP MOVIE – *à la* 'PRINCE OF THE CITY' – It
plays silently as – a smoking cop talks with a woman at a bar.

Freddy takes the remote, turning up the volume.

> SMOKING COP
> (on TV)
> – Cops are nothing but garbage men. 'pick up the
> trash. 'dump it. Next week, you pick up the same
> trash all over again.

Freddy stares blankly at the screen. *Déjà vu.*

CUT TO:

INT. FREDDY'S SQUAD CAR – NIGHT

FREDDY slams the door, getting behind the wheel. FRANK
LAGONDA sits in the back seat in the moonlight.

> LAGONDA
> What are you gonna do, Freddy? Arrest the whole
> town?

Freddy sits, unmoving. Steady. LaGonda has a gun in his hand.
He cocks it. He leans forward, whispering in Freddy's ear. Freddy
watches him through the rear-view mirror.

> Ray gave you this job. He *made* your sorry ass. So do
> Ray a favor and you tell us where Superboy is.

> FREDDY
> If I knew where he was – he'd be in the city already.

LaGonda smiles. He leans back.

LAGONDA
You're gonna be hurtin', Freddy. You ain't gonna
know when. But you're gonna be hurtin'.
                    (exits)
I'm watching you.

                                        CUT TO:


INT./EXT. FREDDY'S SQUAD CAR – NIGHT

Driving along the water, FREDDY passes – A LINE OF CARS PARKED
ROADSIDE. FLASHLIGHTS SCAN THE BRUSH. A search for Babitch.
DEPUTY BILL watches from squad car. Freddy pulls up to him.

                    BILL
Donlan caught his wife dropping food 'round here.
'So they figure he must be nearby.

Freddy nods, weary.

You know why they call him Superboy?

                    FREDDY
'was a hero.

                    BILL
                (shakes his head)
'Cause he loves Campbell's Chicken and Stars.
*Soup*-erboy. Get it?

Bill smiles. Freddy drives off.

                                        CUT TO:


INT. FREDDY'S HOUSE – NIGHT

Taking off his coat, FREDDY stares at –

AN ENVELOPE lies open on the kitchen table. Addressed to Figs,
it's from STATE FARM INSURANCE, a green check peeking out.

FIGS enters the room, folding clothes, putting them in – HIS NYPD
ATHLETIC BAG. Slightly charred on one corner.

You got your check.

FIGS

Thanks to you, Freddy. 'Filing those papers in such
a timely fashion.

Freddy blinks.

'You with Liz?

Freddy nods, his mind working on something else, staring at Fig's
charred athletic bag. Figs crosses into the bathroom.

FREDDY

Where you going?

FIGS
(off-screen)
My leave came. So I thought I'd look around – for a
new reality, you know? Anyway. You could prob'ly
use the privacy.

Freddy nods, unnerved. He takes his coat and heads back out.
Figs pokes his head out of the bathroom door as – *slam.*

CUT TO:

EXT. CHARRED REMAINS OF FIGS' HOUSE – NIGHT

IN THE MOONLIGHT – THE ROOF BURNT AWAY – THE STARS
SHINE DOWN UPON – a charred toaster. Pot holders on a wall
fragment.

At the center of this box of moonlight – FREDDY HEFLIN sits,
fingering a small charred device. He examines it, tears in his eyes,
with a browning-out flashlight.

FIGS

What's up?

Freddy turns, startled. He smiles, sorrowful.

FREDDY

That lady cop – bomb squad, right? – 'Sold you
these caps and a timer.

Freddy holds up the device.

Figs says nothing. He shakes his head sadly.

> 'Guess you figured – with Superboy – y'figured you
> were covered – if you could just act like *Marlon
> Brando* – keep me busy – ol' Freddy – he's too
> stupid to suspect anything.
>> (needing to understand)
> Y'didn't know she was coming over that night, did
> you?

Figs shakes his head, beginning to weep.

> ### FIGS
> She said she was going to her friend's – to watch
> pay-per-view. The thing – it was on a timer. I didn't
> know she'd be there.
>> (beat)
> She'd still be alive if that *bullshit* tower still held
> water.

> ### FREDDY
> The 'Diagonal Rule' is the bullshit, Gary.

Figs turns and wanders, slumped, back toward his car.

> ### FIGS
> 'till you need it, Freddy. 'till you need it.

> ### FREDDY
> I don't need traffic tips.' *I need help.*

But Figs keeps walking toward his car.

> – I'm gonna bring Superboy in – and – for once –
> we're all gonna tell the truth.

> ### FIGS
> You gotta find him first. Before they do.

Figs shakes his head and opens the door to his car. He lights a
cigarette, looks at the lights of the great city across the river and
back at –

Freddy, alone in the moonlight.

Freddy. I got – in my pocket – a check for two
hundred grand. I got a chance to start my life again.
I do not give a shit about *this town* or –
                    (nodding to NYC)
– *that town* or 'justice'. Being right is not a
bulletproof vest.

Figs gets in his car. *slam.* He starts it up and drives off.

BACK TO – CLOSE ON – FREDDY. He sighs, red-eyed. He looks out
the roof of the charred house into moonlight, staring at –

THE ABANDONED WATER TOWER AGAINST THE SKY.
G A R R I S O N,  N J – it says in fading letters.

Freddy squints. He stands.

                                                    CUT TO:


EXT. GARRISON MEADOWLANDS – THE WATER TOWER – NIGHT

A FIELD OF REEDS surrounds the BASE OF THE WATER TOWER.
There is a path – fresh – trod through the grass.

FREDDY CLIMBS UP THE LONG LADDER. Precarious. Some of the
rungs broken. He is high above the ground. The town lies quietly
below him. Asleep.

                                                    CUT TO:


INT. WATER TOWER – NIGHT

MURRAY 'SUPERBOY' BABITCH OPENS HIS EYES TO SEE – FREDDY
STANDING OVER HIM. Babitch is puffy-faced, unshaven. He wears
sweats. This chamber is a mess – cans of Campbell's Chicken &
Stars soup popped open, all over – clothes scattered.

                          FREDDY
        Let's go.

Babitch blinks, taking this in.

                          BABITCH
        Where?

144

FREDDY

I'm taking you to the city.

Babitch laughs. They are a strange pair – Freddy and Babitch – same age, same build, and the same healing scars on their noses.

Get dressed.

BABITCH

Who are you working with? The Feds?

Freddy shakes his head.

IA?

Freddy shakes his head.

You're *alone*?

Freddy nods. He motions to a pile of clothes.

FREDDY

Get dressed.

CUT TO:

145

INT./EXT. SQUAD CAR – MAIN STREET – NIGHT

FREDDY drives. BABITCH sits in back, staring at his cuffs.
Freddy stiffens. Babitch's eyes widen.

> BABITCH
>
> Oh, Christ.

THROUGH THE WINDSHIELD – RAY DONLAN'S GRAND PRIX AND
OTHER CARS are assembled at THE FOUR ACES. Men mill about,
heading inside.

> FREDDY
>
> Get down.
> (quietly, into his radio)
> Bill . . . You copy?

Babitch slinks down. Freddy snaps off his lights.

> Bill? You out there?

No response. Freddy tosses down the radio. He pulls into the back
of the station house.

CUT TO:

INT. SHERIFF'S OFFICE – NIGHT

FREDDY does not turn the lights on. He escorts BABITCH into the
HOLDING CELL. Babitch flops down on the bench. Sighs.

> BABITCH
>
> You don't know what you're doing, do you?

> FREDDY
>
> Shut up.

Freddy crosses to the dispatch radio. He flicks it on.

> . . . Bill . . . You copy? . . . Bill . . .

The second hand on the clock sticks, then moves on.
It's two thirty.

Freddy crosses to the window. THE STREET IS QUIET.
Everyone's in the bar.

A GARRISON PATROL CAR is parked at the corner. Near the bar.

                    FREDDY
    Shit.

Freddy meets eyes with – THE NEWSPAPER ARTICLE ON THE
WALL. Lit by a streetlamp. *Liz with her beauty queen's crown.*

FREDDY GRABS THE KEYS FROM HIS DESK. He moves to the door.

                    BABITCH
    Hey. Wait a second. You can't leave me alone here.
    Hey. *Hey.*

                                        CUT TO:


EXT. MAIN STREET – NIGHT

Guns at his side, FREDDY HEFLIN walks slowly, steadily, down the
middle of the street, toward THE FOUR ACES. He lights a cig.

Freddy stops in the center of the intersection. He looks about,
taking in the town – the bank clock blinks . . .

                                        CUT TO:


INT. THE FOUR ACES TAVERN – NIGHT

GARRISON REGULARS AT THE BAR. BILL IS DRINKING WITH COP
#I. AT THE BACK TABLE – DONLAN, LAGONDA, CRASKY AND
RUCKER – *With Cindy. They are sitting close.*

FREDDY ENTERS THE TAVERN. All conversations cease. Freddy
moves toward Bill. He pushes out his cigarette.

                    BILL
    It's club soda.

                    FREDDY
    Finish it.

Freddy strides to the back table.

                    DONLAN
                    (smiling)
    Hey, Freddy.

Hey, Ray. Uh. I came to get Bill and Cindy – and I
came to tell you – I found Superboy.

The smile wipes from Donlan's face.

I'm bringing him in. Tomorrow morning. And I
want you to come with me. I owe you that much.

DONLAN

Uh *huh.*

FREDDY

He's a fugitive, Ray. And he's convinced you're
gonna kill him.

Donlan smiles, tense – lights a cigarette, glancing to Rucker.

DONLAN

He's a mixed-up kid. So are you.

FREDDY

There's got to be a way out of this – for everyone. So
I say – we all go in tomorrow. Together. As a
community of law enforcement officers. And we
unravel this. With lawyers or whatever. Together.
Legal. In the city.

There is some laughter. Donlan is getting weary of this.

DONLAN

Just tell me where he is, Freddy. 'You got him at the
station?

Freddy wipes the sweat from his brow.

Bill and Cindy look to Freddy.

Listen to me, Freddy. You know the difference
between *men* and *boys*? Boys bet *everything* on
*everything*. Boys think every hand is a *royal flush*.
You play cards with a man – he knows his limits. He
thinks of his family – back home – before he bets the
house and the car.

**FREDDY**

Ray –

**CRASKY**

Listen to the man, Freddy.

**DONLAN**

Freddy. I invited *men – cops – good men* to live here –
in this town. And these men – to make a living –
they cross that bridge *every day* – to a place where
*everything* is *upside down* – where the *cop* is the *perp*
and the perp is the *victim.* But they play by the rules.
They keep their guns in their holsters and they play
by the rules. The only thing they ever did was get
their families *out* – before *it got to them.* We built
homes – across the river – we made a place where
things make sense and you can walk across the street
– without fear. And tonight – you come to me – your
body pumping with adrenaline – you found my
nephew – you feel powerful with your
acomplishment – so you come to me with a *plan.* A
plan to 'set things right'. Everyone in the city,
holding hands – singing 'We are the World'. It's
very nice. But Freddy – your plan is the plan of a
*boy.* You made it on the back of a match-book –
without thinking – *without looking at the cards.* I look
at the cards – and I see Superboy crucified. I see this
town destroyed. That's not what you want, is it?

**FREDDY**

Ray. I look at this town – And I don't like what I see
any more.

**DONLAN**

What does that mean?

**FREDDY**

There's something sick about this town.

**DONLAN**

*Who the fuck do you think you are?*

> FREDDY

I'm the Sheriff of Garrison, New Jersey.

> DONLAN

Then be the Sheriff. Protect this town. Defend these men.

> LAGONDA

The grass hasn't even taken root above Joey's grave, you fuck.

RUCKER PUTS HIS GUN ON THE TABLE. Playing with it.

> RUCKER

'You feel like a cop now, Freddy, sticking it inside a cop's widow?

Some of the other cops are getting uncomfortable. A few leave.

> COP #1

I'm outta here, Ray.

> COP #2

'Too rich for me.

CINDY AND BILL ARE FROZEN – *Torn* . . . FREDDY'S HAND TOUCHES HIS HOLSTER. Cindy looks away.

> DONLAN

Freddy. You got him at the station?

Freddy says nothing.

> Just drop the keys. Maybe they fell out of your pocket. Or maybe Cindy's. And you *go home* and you sleep. and you wake up – and you guide that traffic through town –

Tears well in Freddy's eyes.

> – and everything will be *the way it was.*

Freddy looks at the clock on the wall.

FREDDY

I'm leaving at six. That's in a few hours.
I'd like you to come with me, Ray.

Bill joins Freddy, hesitant. Donlan wilts.

DONLAN

There's nothing I can say?

Freddy looks up solemnly. Donlan puts his hands in the air.
Crafty.

Okay, then. Six it is. *It's a date.*

Freddy blinks, stunned. Rucker and LaGonda glare at Donlan.

FREDDY

Okay. I'll see you then.

Freddy shuffles, uneasily, toward the door. Bill follows. Freddy
looks to Cindy. She turns to Rucker – *torn.* She shakes her head,
tearful.

Freddy pulls the door shut.

CUT TO:


INT. STATION HOUSE – NIGHT

BABITCH sits in his cell.

TWO SHOTGUNS on the table, FREDDY sits slumped, facing the
windows of the station. BILL paces, on the phone.

BILL

– No, honey. I'm telling you – Because I can't just
leave him here.

Bill hangs up the phone. Slowly.

The second hand on the clock sticks. It is four thirty.

Bill glares out the window. A CAR IDLES OUTSIDE . . .
watching . . .

151

FREDDY
Go home, Bill.

BILL
(tortured)
I mean. I want to be here for you, Freddy. But . . .
Lisa's *nervous*. She's pregnant. I mean. There's a
reason I never applied to the city, *you know*? This is
*your thing.*

FREDDY
So, go on. I'm gonna be fine.
(smiles)
They're not going to kill me.

Babitch mutters in the background. Bill moves to the door.
He turns.

BILL
Why don't you just go now?

FREDDY
I told him I'm leaving at six. Besides. They're out
there already.

BILL
(nodding)
Take care, Freddy.

Freddy nods, weary. Bill exits.

Babitch puts his head in his hands.

CUT TO:

INT. FIGS' CHEVY – NJ TURNPIKE – NIGHT

Driving, music blasting, his car piled with belongings, GARY 'FIGS'
FIGGIS keeps staring at himself in the driver's mirror.

FIGS
Shut the fuck up, would you please?

But Figs looks once more and – with a sigh – hits the brakes.

FIGS' CHEVY screeches to a stop on the deserted turnpike.

CUT TO:

INT. SHERIFF'S OFFICE – DAWN

Birds sing. The mud-yellow sun rises over the distant city.

The second hand sticks, then moves on. *A few minutes to six.*

Freddy wakes with a start. He peers out the window.

The street is empty. Desolate. The car from last night – *gone.*

FREDDY
Oh, well.

He takes A SHOTGUN.
He opens Babitch's cell. Babitch is sitting there, groggy.

Come on. We're going.

CUT TO:

EXT. MAIN STREET – DAWN

The bank clock blinks – 5:58 am, 5:58 am, 5:59 am.

FREDDY and BABITCH exit the station. They round the corner, walking in the alley behind the Sheriff's office toward – FREDDY'S PARKED SQUAD CAR.

Freddy stops in his tracks. The tires have been slashed.

> BABITCH
> Oh God.

A HAND REACHES FROM BEHIND FREDDY, taking his shotgun. He feels the cold press of steel against his head.

> RUCKER
> Get down.

Jack Rucker pushes Freddy down on his knees. LAGONDA takes Babitch. Rucker pushes Freddy's back.

> I said – get down, Freddy.

Color washes from Freddy's face as he gets down on all fours.

> FREDDY
> Jesus. Guys. You don't want to do this.

> LAGONDA
> Don't shit in your pants, Freddy. We ain't gonna kill you.

THE MUZZLE OF A GUN TOUCHES FREDDY'S EAR.

> RUCKER
> This is the good one, right?

Freddy nods. HE CLOSES HIS EYES. HE HEARS THE TUMBLER CLICK. HE HEARS THE HAMMER PULL. *Crack!*

The gun fires, not into Freddy's head, but *into the ground*. Freddy rolls to the pavement, powder burns covering his ear, blood trickling from the canal.

Delirious with pain, Freddy looks up as –

RUCKER AND LAGONDA LOAD BABITCH INTO A CAR.

*Since the gunshot – all we can hear is a ringing sound. A low, distant piano, and Freddy's racing heartbeat.*

THEY ROAR UP THE ROAD, TOWARD THE HOUSING TRACTS ON THE HILL leaving Freddy alone, deaf and bleeding on the roadside. He struggles to stand. He collapses to his knees.

CUT TO:

EXT. ROAD UP THROUGH THE TRACT HOUSES – EARLY MORNING

*The rumble and piano continue to build.*

*Smacked with dawn light, Manhattan glimmers across the river.*

AT A NEATLY KEPT HOUSE – COP #1 – in his robe – takes his morning paper from the stoop. He notices –

Stumbling up the center of the road –
SHERIFF FREDDY HEFLIN, blood trickling from his ear, running down his neck, soaking his shirt. His face is pale and haggard, the powder burn smeared over one side of his head.

SHOTGUN IN ONE HAND, REVOLVER IN THE OTHER, FREDDY LOOKS LIKE A WESTERN GUNFIGHTER, his eyes glazed with anger, his face stone.

*They meet eyes.* The cop closes his door.

Freddy trudges on. Up the steep hill. Past the mailbox that reads: *Randone . . .*

THE DOBERMAN ON THE CHAIN BARKS SILENTLY AT FREDDY . . .

LIZ LOOKS OUT HER BEDROOM WINDOW – SEEING –

Freddy, marching on . . . dazed and bloody . . . moving toward –

CUT TO:

155

EXT. DONLAN'S STREET – GARRISON, NJ – MORNING

IN THE DISTANCE – AT DONLAN'S HOUSE – RUCKER, LAGONDA
AND CRASKY STAND ON DONLAN'S STOOP. GUNS AT THEIR SIDES.
DONLAN EMERGES FROM THE HOUSE WITH BABITCH IN TOW.

FREDDY WALKS TOWARD DONLAN'S HOUSE, SHOTGUN IN HAND.
*We still hear nothing but his heart beating . . . and a distant furious
piano . . .*

IN THE BACKGROUND, LIZ RUNS OUT ONTO HER LAWN,
DESPERATELY YELLING TO FREDDY. UNHEARD – HE KEEPS
WALKING . . .

LAGONDA TURNS, SEEING FREDDY FIRST. HE SHOUTS TO THE
OTHERS. DONLAN TURNS. STUNNED.

FREDDY STRIDES TOWARD THE HOUSE, EMBOLDENED BY THE
SILENCE OF HIS INJURY. He blinks, wiping sweat and blood out
of his eyes.

JACK RUCKER POINTS HIS FINGER AT FREDDY – SAYING
SOMETHING – SCREAMING A BARRAGE OF UNHEARD INSULTS AND
WARNINGS . . .

DONLAN AND CRASKY PULL BABITCH – KICKING AND SCREAMING
– BACK INTO THE HOUSE.

LAGONDA RAISES HIS GUN – SHOUTING SOMETHING AT FREDDY.

BUT FREDDY KEEPS WALKING TOWARD THEM. STEADY. *His
heartbeat increases – tha-thump, tha-thump . . . the piano builds . . .*

THE MUZZLE OF LAGONDA'S GUN FLARES. THE WINDSHIELD OF A
PARKED CAR SILENTLY SHATTERS.

FREDDY DOES NOT BLINK. THE SHOT – SILENT – SEEMS
HARMLESS.

LIZ RUNS BACK TO HER DOOR, WATCHING – TERRIFIED . . .

FREDDY RAISES HIS GUN. HE FIRES. *But there is no sound.*

LAGONDA CRUMPLES TO THE GROUND, clutching his leg.

FREDDY KEEPS WALKING. STEADY.

RUCKER SHOUTS SOMETHING AGAIN, RAISING HIS GUN.
FREDDY AND RUCKER FIRE AT THE SAME TIME. Muzzles flare.

RUCKER FALLS BACKWARD ON THE PAVEMENT. HIT IN THE
CHEST. HIS GUN FLIES FROM HIS HANDS.

BUT FREDDY STANDS. UNSCATHED. AGAIN WALKING STEADILY
TOWARD THE FRONT DOOR OF THE HOUSE.

RUCKER AND LAGONDA LIE ON THE GROUND BENEATH FREDDY,
BLOODY. RUCKER'S EYES ARE WET AND RED. HE SHOUTS
UNHEARD EXPLETIVES.

LEO CRASKY PEERS ROUND THE SIDE OF DONLAN'S HOUSE,
CARRYING A SHOTGUN, AIMING IT AT FREDDY . . .

LIZ SILENTLY SCREAMS AT –

FREDDY, who – OBLIVIOUS, MOVES TOWARD THE FRONT DOOR OF
DONLAN'S HOUSE. SUDDENLY – a spray of blood.

CONFUSED – FREDDY TOUCHES HIS SHOULDER. *He has been hit.*

CRASKY STANDS AT THE SIDE OF DONLAN'S HOUSE, GUN
SMOKING. HE RAISES THE GUN TO FIRE AGAIN – *at Freddy.*

SUDDENLY – A SILENT BLAST RIPS THROUGH CRASKY'S TORSO.
Crasky's gun fires into the air, He falls backward, limp.

FIGS STANDS IN THE CENTER OF THE ROAD, REVOLVER SMOKING.
His Chevy behind him.

LYING ON HIS BACK, LAGONDA FIRES A SHOT AT FREDDY –
MISSING. BUT BEFORE HE CAN FIRE AGAIN . . .

FREDDY RELEASES A SHOT INTO LAGONDA'S CHEST.

FIGS SCREAMS – UNHEARD – RUNNING FORWARD AS –

RAY DONLAN FIRES AT FREDDY FROM HIS CRACKED FRONT DOOR.

DAZED, FREDDY SPINS – RETURNING FIRE – AS DOES FIGS.

THE DOOR SPLINTERS. DONLAN RETREATS INTO THE HOUSE.

CUT TO:

INT. DONLAN'S HOUSE – MORNING

NUMB WITH SILENCE, BLOODY, FREDDY MOVES DOWN THE
HALL. Decorated with medals, citations of heroism, headlines and
photos, there is blood smeared along the wall, and on the cream-
colored carpet leading up the stairs – TO THE BEDROOM . . .

FREDDY FOLLOWS THE TRAIL. CLIMBING THE STAIRS. His eyes
darting left and right, wild . . .

Below, FIGS enters the house, shouting something as Freddy
rounds the banister upstairs, pushing open –

THE BEDROOM DOOR. HIS GUN TRAINED ON – ROSE DONLAN –
HUDDLED ON THE BED – AND BABITCH – HIS LEG STICKING OUT
THE WINDOW AS HE TRIES TO CLIMB ONTO THE ROOF.

A FROZEN MOMENT –
ROSE DONLAN AND BABITCH STARING AT FREDDY . . . *Past
Freddy* . . .

AND IN THIS MOMENT – FREDDY'S EYES FOLLOW –

THE BLOOD TRAIL ON THE CARPET. It makes a loop into the
room, toward the bed, then back around and toward Freddy
under his feet . . . FREDDY SPINS AROUND AND FIRES AS –

RAY DONLAN LEAPS AT FREDDY FROM BEHIND THE DOOR, HIS
FACE CONTORTED FROM THE SHOT TO HIS GUT – WORDS
SILENTLY SPEWING FROM HIS MOUTH.

                         FREDDY
        I can't hear you, Ray.

DONLAN CRUMPLES TO THE GROUND. FIGS ARRIVES AT FREDDY'S
SIDE.

                                            CUT TO:


EXT. DONLAN'S STREET – MORNING

In the golden light, A CROWD OF STUNNED COPS IN ROBES AND
SWEATPANTS. THEIR FAMILIES WATCH FROM THE THEIR FRONT
STOOPS. They are in awe.

CINDY BETTS requests help on her patrol car radio as –

BILL attends to the wounded. They both look up – dull-faced and apprehensive as –

FIGS and FREDDY emerge with BABITCH.

LIZ STANDS AT THE CORNER. HER EYES MEET –

FREDDY'S – AS HE DRAGS BABITCH PAST CINDY – and into the patrol car. Cindy backs away.

CUT TO:

INT./EXT. FREDDY'S PATROL CAR – GW BRIDGE APPROACH – DAY

FREDDY DRIVES, a pool of blood welling in his lap, from the wound to his shoulder. FIGS rips Freddy's shirt, tying a tourniquet. BABITCH lies across the back seat, numb.

> BABITCH
> He's deaf. They shot out his ears, man.

Freddy pulls to a stop at the TOLL BOOTH. Freddy hands THE TOLL-TAKER three bucks. The toll-taker is nonchalant. Oblivious to the blood all over.

> TOLL-TAKER
>
> It's four.

> FREDDY
> (deaf; confused)
>
> Hm?

Figs hands Freddy another single.

> FIGS
> Freddy! *Here!* IT'S FOUR, NOW!

As Freddy pulls the car through the mechanical arm and out onto the bridge, Figs shakes his head in wonder.

> BABITCH
> – watchin' too much 'Gunsmoke', man. He's crazy.
> He *is. He's fuckin' nuts.*

161

Figs turns, meeting Babitch's eyes. Figs smiles.

> FIGS
> No. He's a cop.

Driving across the bridge, oblivious, Freddy glances at Figs.

WIDER – THE GREAT GRAY BRIDGE – MANHATTAN TO THE OTHER SIDE – as Freddy's squad car weaves toward the city, red light spinning.

> CUT TO:

EXT. NYC – CHAMBERS STREET – DAY

FREDDY'S DENTED PATROL CAR JUMPS THE CURB and – LURCHES TO A STOP UNDER MANHATTAN BOROUGH HALL. Twenty yards from POLICE PLAZA.

BABITCH sniggers, his wrists shackled – as he sees –

> BABITCH
> Hey. It's Bobby Doyle.

THEIR CAR IS SURROUNDED BY MEN IN NYPD BLUES, eating hot dogs, Danish, on break, etc. All looking up in wonder at –

THE LOCAL PATROL CAR – AND ITS GRIM OCCUPANTS. Blood running down his shirt – FREDDY emerges.

> PLAZA COP #1
> You can't park there. Buddy. Hey.

Oblivious, Freddy struggles to tow Babitch, in cuffs. FIGS climbs out and tries to help but Freddy shakes him off.

MOE TILDEN WALKS FROM A HOT DOG STAND – EATING A DOG –

> TILDEN
> Holy shit.

Freddy looks up – dazed – as SOME COPS ASSEMBLE AROUND HIM.

> BABITCH
> Hey, hey. Bobby!

PLAZA COP #2 (BOBBY)

Hey, Soups. What the fuck?
'Thought you were dead.

PLAZA COP #1

What the hell is going on?

BABITCH

Crazy shit, man.

Freddy pulls Babitch along. Figs pulls out his badge.

FIGS

We're cool, boys. We're cool.

THE CROWD OF BLUE stands, frozen. Blocking Freddy.

FREDDY

Please move.

THE RING OF BLUE, STONE-FACED. FREDDY'S WEARY EYES
CATCH – TILDEN THROUGH THE CROWD.

TILDEN

Get away from him. Hey. Back off!

CARSON AND OTHER IA DETECTIVES hold up their IDS.

CARSON

It's okay. It's cool.

FREDDY STRUGGLES TO PULL BABITCH TOWARD TILDEN. HE
NEARLY COLLAPSES TO THE PAVEMENT, HOLDING ONTO BABITCH
FOR SUPPORT. THE BLUE THRONG STANDS THERE – SILENT,
CONFUSED.

TILDEN

Call EMS.

Carson nods as he takes off into the building. TILDEN TURNS
TOWARD FREDDY.

FREDDY BLINKS. NUMB. BLOODY. COPS ARE WATCHING.

TILDEN FEELS ALL THE EYES ON HIS BACK. HE TAKES BABITCH by
the other shoulder. HE TURNS TO FREDDY, HIS GREEN EYES
BLAZING.

FREDDY LOOKS AT HIM – DEEPLY – WEARY – PROUD. He wipes
the blood out of his eyes.

TILDEN gestures to the door with a cock of his head.

　　　Come on inside.

THEY WALK – SLOW – UP THE STEPS OF POLICE PLAZA.

　　　　　　　　　　　　　　　　　　　　FADE OUT.

# Heavy

# CREDITS

FADE IN:

EXT. ROAD ALONG HUDSON – PETE AND DOLLY'S TAVERN – DUSK

A RUSTED DODGE DART pulls into the lot.

A MIDDLE AGED WOMAN emerges from the car. Once a country beauty, she has a care-worn face. She wears a blue waitress' uniform. Her name tag reads: *Delores*. She stamps out her cigarette and walks toward the building. Fumbling, she produces a bottle of aspirins from her purse.

Her footsteps stop suddenly. Her eyes fixed sternly upon –

In the window of the tavern, A SIGN: *Help Wanted.*

CUT TO:

INT. PETE AND DOLLY'S TAVERN – DUSK

DELORES hangs up her coat without looking at the rack.

The tavern is empty, dark. There are, however, off-screen voices; an old woman and a young woman talk quietly.

Delores crosses behind the bar where she pops the aspirins and tucks away her purse. Behind her is a FOOD SLOT.

THROUGH THE FOOD SLOT –

A lighted restaurant kitchen; pizza oven, Formica counters, and a rear view of a BIG FLUFFY EASY CHAIR. A white head of permed hair rises over the back of the chair, a pair of dimpled arms weakly gesticulate – an OLD WOMAN sits in this chair. She converses with SOMEONE. From this vantage point however, the view of this other person is also limited; a wisp of shiny hair, an arm, gesturing: A YOUNG WOMAN.

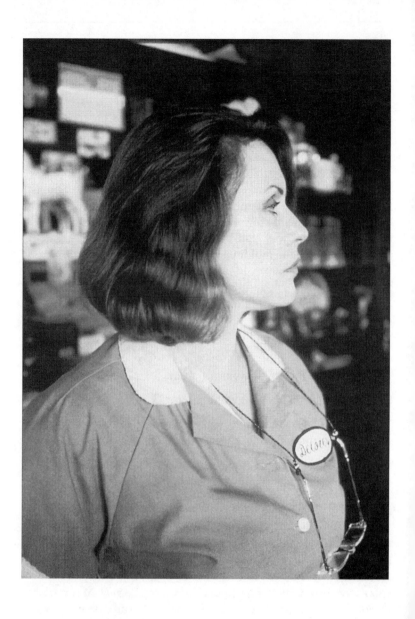

168

                          YOUNG WOMAN
                          (off-screen)
Well, I don't have, working in a real restaurant, I
mean –

                          OLD WOMAN
                          (off-screen)
Experience?

Delores lights a cigarette and flicks a light switch. The bulb does
not light till she slaps the switch with the ball of her hand. She
turns to the register, ringing it ready. She listens to the continuing
conversation, *tense*.

At the far end of the tavern, A FAT MAN IN AN APRON (VICTOR)
backs out of THE MEN'S ROOM DOOR. He drags a garbage bag and
a basket of cleaning liquids. He is very fat. Fat enough to make
you wonder. He has a gentle open face. It is hard to place his age
from his looks; twenty-five, maybe thirty-five.

Delores looks at him quizzically, nodding toward the food slot.

Victor shrugs. He shuffles off into the LADIES' ROOM.

                          YOUNG WOMAN
                          (off-screen)
Actually they're both pretty angry at me right now.

                          OLD WOMAN
                          (off-screen)
Because of school?

                          YOUNG WOMAN
                          (off-screen)
Mm hm.

Delores sighs, blowing smoke. She turns, walks down along the
bar, snapping on the television as she moves past.

                                                    CUT TO:

INT. PETE AND DOLLY'S STOCKROOM – DUSK (CONTINUOUS)
Delores pulls out several beer bottles from open boxes.

                            169

A SIDE DOOR leads straight from the stockroom into the lighted kitchen, revealing a new but still fragmented view of the old woman and the young woman.

> OLD WOMAN
> (off-screen)
> I'm sure they're just worried. There's a lot to worry about in this world.

In the shadows, Delores turns, noticing –

Through a window – A PROPANE TRUCK pulls in. The driver (GAS MAN) holds a nozzle to the spigot of a gas tank.

> CUT TO:

INT. PETE AND DOLLY'S KITCHEN – DUSK (CONTINUOUS)

CLOSE ON – THE OLD WOMAN in the FLUFFY EASY CHAIR. She has a soft warm face; full cheeks that form jowls. A white whisker curls from the tip of her chin. Her embroidered name tag reads: *Dolly.*

> YOUNG WOMAN
> (off-screen)
> – or maybe take a photography course or something at Community.

CLOSE ON – THE YOUNG WOMAN (CALLIE, 19) OPPOSITE DOLLY. She is uncomfortable, self-conscious. Lovely.

– If the hours don't, you know –

> DOLLY
> – conflict?

> CALLIE
> Uh huh.

Callie looks away. There is a hurt in her voice. Her smile tilts at moments toward despair then – just as quickly – crashes back to a tender cheer. She looks at –

A FAT MONGREL LAP DOG sleeps serenely at Dolly's feet.

*clink, clink, clink.* Delores slinks past the kitchen/storeroom doorway, carrying an armful of beer bottles.

> My boyfriend's a musician – I take pictures of him and things, other things. I might also take accounting though. For my dad.

DOLLY
That could be useful.

CALLIE
I guess. Yeah. Definitely.

Dolly winces. She presses her thumb into her neck.

DOLLY
Well. College is not for everyone. Someone's gotta roll up their sleeves, right?

Callie looks up, nodding. Dolly smiles, warm.

> So. When do you want to start?

Off-screen: *smash!*

DELORES
(off-screen)
God dammit!

Callie turns to the sound. She looks back at Dolly. Dolly smirks at Callie, adoring.

DOLLY
When do you want to start? Do you want to start tonight?

*scuff, scuff, scuff . . .*
Delores moves past the food slot, carrying a broom and dust pan.

CALLIE
um. Sure. I mean, you don't have to do this, you know. My mom didn't want –

Dolly gets up, an effort. She moves slowly toward the back room. She waves as THE GAS MAN walks past the back door.

– I mean, if you can use me, I'm a very committed person. Syracuse was a whole different –

                    DOLLY
Your check's in the door, Gary.

                    GAS MAN
'Got it, Doll.

                    CALLIE
– a whole different thing.

                    DOLLY
I think I have an extra blouse back here.

Dolly digs about in a dusty closet. Callie stands, her eyes briefly meeting –

DELORES – THROUGH THE KITCHEN FOOD SLOT.

                                        CUT TO:

INT. PETE AND DOLLY'S TAVERN – AT THE BAR – DUSK

Delores dumps a dustpan of broken glass into the trash.

Dolly shuffles out into the tavern. She holds a powder-blue uniform/blouse in her hands. She snips at an embroidered name patch with a sewing scissors, stepping carefully over the spill.

                    DOLLY
Ooo. Watch your feet.
                    (calling out)
– Victor!

Delores scowls as she takes a rag and crosses back to the spill.

Callie emerges behind Dolly, looking down and about, awkward.

Victor!
                    (to Callie)
That's my son.

Delores wipes up the beer with a rag.

173

DELORES
'doing the bathrooms.

Dolly turns to see Delores.

DOLLY
Oh. Delores. I didn't expect to see you so early.
This is Callie Welles. She's going to be helping us
out, our *waitress-in-training*.

CALLIE
(off-screen)
Hi. How do you do?

Delores eyes the blouse in Dolly's hands as she rips away the
embroidered tag that reads: *Delores*.

CUT TO:


INT. PETE AND DOLLY'S TAVERN – LADIES' ROOM – DUSK
(CONTINUOUS)

CLOSE ON – four red letters – S L U T.

Through a haze of soap suds, the word has been scrawled on a
bathroom mirror with nail polish.

VICTOR (the fat man in the apron) scrubs at the mirror with steel
wool. He sprays more cleanser. His eyes are bright, intense,
thoughtful. He listens to the voices outside.

Out the vent window – THE TOP OF THE GAS TRUCK AS IT PULLS
AWAY.

CUT TO:


INT. PETE AND DOLLY'S TAVERN – AT THE BAR – DUSK

On the wall, the Genesee Cream Ale clock says: 4:45.
The Molson's clock by the register reads: 5:45.

Callie swings nervously on a bar stool, the blue uniform slung on
her shoulder. She picks up a plastic drink stirrer from a bar
dispenser. She plays with it in her fingers.

174

Delores scoops coffee into an auto drip coffee-maker.

Callie shifts in her seat, looking again at the clocks.

> DELORES
> No one knows how to set that one. It's quarter to
> five.

> CALLIE
> Oh.

Callie chews on her plastic stirrer.

> DOLLY
> (off-screen)
> You show her the ropes now, Delores.

In the kitchen, Dolly smiles at Callie as she crosses with a tin of
red peppers. She turns on a slicing machine. *whummmmmmmmm*.

> CALLIE
> Should I go put this on? Or is there something I
> should be doing?

> DELORES
> I don't start until five.

> CALLIE
> Oh. 'Cause Mrs Modino said I start at four-thirty.

> DELORES
> So do I.

Delores smirks. The coffee-maker wheezes.

> CUT TO:

INT. PETE AND DOLLY'S TAVERN – LADIES' ROOM – DUSK

A LIPSTICK-SMUTTED CIGARETTE BUTT floats in a toilet bowl.
*Flush.* The BUTT swirls with the water but does not go down.

VICTOR kneels above the toilet. He holds a bowl brush under his
arm, and a bottle of cleanser. He stares at the butt,
contemplatively. He takes a single piece of toilet paper and lays it
carefully, very carefully, over the floating butt. A shroud? He

reaches for the flush lever when suddenly, there is a sound. Victor looks toward the door, frozen.

CUT TO:

INT. PETE AND DOLLY'S TAVERN – AT THE BAR – DUSK

Delores hangs glasses on the rack above the bar. She looks from CALLIE'S EMPTY STOOL toward –

THE REST ROOM DOOR. It closes.

CUT TO:

INT. PETE AND DOLLY'S TAVERN – LADIES' ROOM – DUSK

CALLIE stands plainly in front of the bathroom mirror. The door swings gently behind her. She pulls off her blouse, laying it on the sink. She wears a simple white lace bra.

Victor stares, frozen in the stall, slightly obscured by the door, his hand upon the flush lever. He looks away, anxious.

Oblivious, Callie adjusts the uniform on her bare shoulders. She buttons it right up to the collar, tucking the tails into her jeans. Then, examining herself carefully . . . *she unbuttons the top button.*

She considers this. She unbuttons another button; again *considering. Then, she notices –*

Fine suds dribbling from the mirror. Callie wipes at them, reading the pale nail polish graffiti: S L U T.

She rebuttons the last button up again.

Victor stares. He does not breathe.

Callie picks up her crumpled blouse and exits.

Victor looks down to –

The paper-shrouded butt in the toilet bowl. *Flush.* The shroud drags the butt down, down into the spiral of water.

CUT TO:

INT. PETE AND DOLLY'S TAVERN – NIGHT – LATER

*Jukebox music plays.*

THICK HANDS make a pizza: flatten the soft dough, spread a velvet red sauce. VICTOR looks up from his work to –

CALLIE, who stands at the KITCHEN FOOD SLOT. She pulls an order slip from the carousel, nervously erasing something. Impatient, DELORES reaches around her –

> DELORES
> Excuse me.

– posting her slip on the carousel and moving off.

CUT TO:

INT. PETE AND DOLLY'S TAVERN – NIGHT

Callie awkwardly carries a tray of empties past the pool table. Intended for no one in particular, a shy smile on her lips.

Two BLUE COLLAR MEN leer.

Standing in front of the KITCHEN FOOD SLOT, VICTOR watches.

CUT TO:

INT. PETE AND DOLLY'S TAVERN – AT THE BAR – NIGHT (CONTINUOUS)

LEO (48) is hunched over at the bar. He wears a tired uniform. He stares at the TV. He sips his bourbon and turns as –

DELORES intercepts Callie behind the bar.

> DELORES
> No, honey. Don't press that. Press reset. See. You
> need to punch in the tax first.

> CALLIE
> Oh. I'm sorry. What do I press?

177

DELORES

Let me do it. You need to punch the tax before you
ring through or else –

CALLIE

It's too late?

Through the cracked kitchen door, VICTOR looks, listens. Behind
him, DOLLY crosses with a smoking dish from the oven.

DOLLY

Victor, what is this? This is burnt to a crisp, here.

Exasperated, Dolly shuffles out into the tavern through the
swinging doors. She is flushed and she fans herself with a menu.

Off-screen: *bark! bark! bark!*

Nanny, hush up.
                    (passing by)
Callie, honey. The parmigiana is up.

Dolly crosses to the front door. She stands, letting it open a crack,
taking in the cold night air. *A car passes by.*

CLOSE ON – CALLIE at the food slot, peering down as –

VICTOR slices and boxes a steaming pie.

CALLIE

'Looks good.

Victor looks up and offers a timid half-smile.

DELORES
(off-screen)

Only pizzas come through the slot.

Callie turns. Delores nods dryly toward the kitchen doors.

CALLIE

Oh. Thanks.

Leo smirks at Delores.

                Maybe Dolly thinks she'll bring in a little more
                business.

Delores shakes her head slowly, pouring a beer.

                            DELORES
                No. I'm being punished.

INT. PETE AND DOLLY'S TAVERN – KITCHEN – NIGHT

Callie struggles to lift A LOADED TRAY. The dishes slide about.
Aware of her struggle, VICTOR stares relentlessly at his work as she
passes by. He glances up as –

The doors swing to and fro in her wake.

INT. PETE AND DOLLY'S TAVERN – NIGHT – LATER

*The television babbles.* The restaurant is nearly empty.

The Genesee Cream Ale clock says: 12:30.

The Molson's clock says: 1:30.

Through the swinging kitchen door, DOLLY asleep in her easy
chair, HER FAT DOG (NANNY) at her feet.

LEO is slumped at the bar. He sips his drink as –

DELORES arrives at the end of the bar, sucking a cigarette.

CALLIE clears off tables. She struggles to stack two beer pitchers
and some mugs onto a small tray. She blows a sigh into her soft
bangs. She looks up, feeling Delores' stare.

Leo also watches Delores. Lovesick. Suddenly Delores turns,
meeting his gaze, *unexcited.*

INT. PETE AND DOLLY'S TAVERN – AT A BOOTH – NIGHT (CONTINUOUS)

A large pan of STEAMING PIZZA sits beside a can of SODA. The pizza is half-eaten. VICTOR holds a folded slice in one hand. With the other hand, he plays a GAME OF SOLITAIRE. Victor watches Callie out of the corner of his eye.

Callie takes a few steps with her tray but the glasses begin to tumble. She unloads some onto an adjacent table.

> CALLIE
> . . . make two trips, stupid . . .
> (turning to Victor; smiles)
> . . . trying to take too much.

Victor stiffens. He nods and turns back to his cards.

> CUT TO:

INT. PETE AND DOLLY'S TAVERN – AT THE BAR – NIGHT – LATER

Rubbing her sleepy face, DOLLY shuffles out from the kitchen. She holds her thumb pressed into the flesh of her neck. It looks like she's taking her own pulse. She sits down at the end of the bar.

NANNY re-settles below Dolly's stool.

*Across the restaurant* – CALLIE wipes off a table. Victor sitting rigidly in the adjacent booth.

> DOLLY
> 'nice to have an extra pair of hands around.

DELORES punches the register keys, hard. She does not reply.

LEO grins, watching Delores. He glances to –

DOLLY who is poking at her neck with her fingers.

> LEO
> 'Heart still beating?

> DOLLY
> I've got to do this, Leo. To keep pressure on my saliva glands.

Doctor's orders, huh?

Dolly nods, her eyes roaming past Leo, toward Callie and Victor.

CUT TO:

INT. PETE AND DOLLY'S TAVERN – AT VICTOR'S BOOTH – NIGHT

Callie wipes off a nearby table. Victor looks up – blank-faced.

CALLIE
Spit? You know, its kind of like solitaire. You know,
'one two three, spit?' There's another name for it.

VICTOR
I know that one.

CALLIE
You know it?

Callie glances at Delores. She tosses the rag back and forth.

You want to play a quick game?

Victor shrugs, nods. He scoops up his cards, reshuffling them.
Callie picks up Victor's pizza pan.

Oh. Shoot.
                    (turning around)
I'm taking away your dinner.

VICTOR
No. I'm done.

Victor is red-faced.

CUT TO:

INT. PETE AND DOLLY'S TAVERN – AT THE BAR – NIGHT – LATER

Leo's head rests at an angle in his hands. Dolly grins, blushing.

DOLLY
– Well, thank you, Leo.

Delores sneers at Leo.

LEO

*What?* It's true, Delores. Dolly has great teeth. What
is she, fifteen years older than me?

Dolly's eyes wander across the tavern toward Callie and Victor.
Delores shakes her head looking at Leo in the bar mirror.

What?

*bing!* Delores pushes shut the register drawer with a pained
expression, opening and closing her hand. She mouths the word
'*dentures*'.

Leo's eyes widen. He slumps.

CUT TO:


INT. PETE AND DOLLY'S – VICTOR'S BOOTH – NIGHT
(CONTINUOUS)

Callie slaps cards down quickly. Victor watches her with wide
eyes. He tries lamely to keep up.

CALLIE

Um . . . I can't do anything with this . . . You ready
for new cards?

VICTOR hesitant, nods.

> CALLIE
> Okay. One two three, *spit.*

Callie lurches into action. Her tongue just touching her top lip, she furiously slaps down cards.

Victor is torn between participating in the game and watching this beautiful girl. She mouths the names of her cards as she jockeys them around. She is plainly kicking his ass.

> Six. Seven. Eight. Uh. Jack. You have a nine you
> can't put down. Ten, Jack. Queen, there.

CLOSE ON – CALLIE. Her eyes dart up and meet –

VICTOR'S EYES. He glances down at his cards. He looks back up.

A GOLD HEART hangs on a chain around Callie's neck. It moves against her skin.

*slap,* ace, *slap,* two, *slap,* ace, *slap,* king.

Callie's lips curl into a smile. She has beaten Victor silly.

> VICTOR
> You're good.

> CALLIE
> Me and my sister – we used to play every day after
> school.

Callie smiles, remembering, shuffling her cards into a pile.

*Through a window* – A DUMPY MUSTANG pulls into the tavern lot. A YOUNG MAN (JEFF, 25) gets out, stands a moment, then reaches back in the driver side window. *Honk. Honnk.*

*bark! bark! bark! bark!* Sitting below Dolly, NANNY yaps toward the door.

Leo has his head flat on the bar, watching TV sideways. He sits up, startled by the noise.

Talking on the bar phone, Delores looks toward –

Through the glass – Jeff paces out in the parking lot, his hands in his pockets.

BACK AT THE BOOTH – Callie places her cards down on the table.

> CALLIE
> That's my boyfriend.
> (turning)
> Um. Mrs Modino . . . Can I – ?

> DOLLY
> Oh. Sure, honey. You can go.

Callie gets up, crossing to her coat on the rack.

Delores pushes the register drawer shut, spinning around. She points at Leo, who's head has sunk back down to the bar.

> DELORES
> You.

> LEO
> (without lifting his head)
> What?

> DELORES
> You better call a cab.

> LEO
> What are you talking about?

> DELORES
> What am I talking about? Look at you.

CLOSE ON – VICTOR looks out through the glass as –

In the parking lot, Callie kisses Jeff. She climbs into the car. Inside, they kiss again, this time hard and long.

*Bark! bark! bark!* – from beneath the bar.

> DELORES
> (off-screen)
> *I'm* not taking you home again.

Leo sits up, glaring at Delores.

What is this, mothers against drunk driving? I don't
need you to take me home.

DELORES (OVERLAP)

Fine. I'll save on gas.

LEO (OVERLAP)

– Maybe you're thinking of one of your boyfriends.
Maybe that trucker.

Delores is incensed. She glances at Dolly, then back to Leo.

DELORES

I'm thinking of the shit-head photo delivery man
sitting in front of me.

LEO

Who's that?

Dolly waves her hand toward Delores and Leo.

DOLLY

Enough, *enough*.

CUT TO:


INT./EXT. VICTOR'S FORD LTD – NIGHT

LEO lies across the back seat, half asleep. VICTOR drives. DOLLY
sits beside him, NANNY on her lap.

DOLLY

That's what they used to call a marrying type.
She doesn't need to be in school.

Victor says nothing.

Did you get the thing off the mirror?

Victor nods.

CUT TO:

EXT. MODINO HOUSE – NIGHT

A squat single story house with a slumped garage. Weeds run amok. Victor's Ford pulls to a stop.

VICTOR gets out and crosses to the passenger door.

As LEO staggers out of the back seat, he notices –

A FIFTIES-STYLE TRUCK RIG sits fat and rusted among the weeds. It's front end is cleaved, split by a deep gash of twisted metal.

> LEO
> Mother of Mary . . .

DOLLY is stiff and groggy. With Victor's help, she emerges from the car, carrying NANNY like a baby. Leo attempts to be of some assistance, taking Dolly's other arm like a clumsy escort. But his eyes soon drift back to –

The truck rig, black, blue and eerie in the moonlight.

Dolly smiles at Leo.

> DOLLY
> My husband saved my life with that truck.

Victor unlocks the front door of the house.

> LEO
> Huh. Oh. Here, let me get that.

Very unsteady, Leo holds open the door.

> DOLLY
> That's how we met, Leo.

> LEO
> You don't say.

The door closes.

CUT TO:


INT. MODINO HOUSE – HALLWAY/KITCHEN – NIGHT

Leo stands disconcerted in a small foyer as Victor, Dolly and Nanny move confidently into the musty dark house.

*A light snaps on* to reveal Victor on the other side of the room standing beside a table lamp. Dolly gathers some sheets and pillows from a linen closet.

CUT TO:

INT. MODINO HOUSE – A BEDROOM – NIGHT

It looks like the room of a twelve-year-old boy. Walls are covered with baseball cards, curling from age. Assorted pennants are strung about. Hanging above the bed, an old poster of Farrah Fawcett, her nipples pushing the skin of her bathing suit.

Leaning precariously on a desk chair, LEO fingers some baseball cards in collectors' plastic wrapers. He notices –

A FRAMED LOCAL NEWSPAPER ARTICLE, yellow with age. *It reads:*

LOCAL GIRL MARRIES HERO
*A knight in six ton armor*

There is a picture of the young newlyweds. Pete and Dolly Modino. Dolly is beautiful. Pete is a burly man, uncomfortable in his suit. Another picture displays the mangled truck rig.

Leo stares, scratching his head. As he turns, he knocks some trinkets (mini NFL helmets) off a shelf. They land on the floor. Leo struggles to pick them up.

VICTOR sets up a flimsy fold-out cot. He watches Leo out of the corner of his eye. Leo turns, feeling his stare.

LEO

Sorry.

In the bedroom doorway, NANNY peers in. Leo kneels.

Here, pooch.

The dog is unresponsive.

DOLLY pokes her head in, smiles, then walks off down the hall, the dog following at her heels.

Leo pulls out a cigarette and struggles to light it. He flops down on the cot. Holding his lit cigarette:

188

Ooo. Shit. You mind?

Pulling off his pants, Victor shakes his head. He climbs beneath his blankets.

Leo takes a slow drag. He looks up at the poster of Farrah.

What's her name? Callie?

Victor says nothing.

Callie.

A pause. Crickets sing.

Hey, Victor.

Victor opens his eyes. Leo stares at him, urgently holding out a wallet of photos.

Victor takes it from him. He opens it. *Inside –*

A COLLECTION OF PRURIENT SNAPSHOTS: *A woman, poolside, with her bikini top pulled, laughing maniacally. A prom queen splayed on the bedspread of a Holiday Inn. A naked man and woman humping from behind, the man holding an instamatic camera pointed into a mirror. A topless biker chick, a big tattoo on her breast . . .*

Victor stares with horror and fascination at the naked parade. Leo whispers, grinning.

It's amazing what people will drop off at the drugstore.

Dolly crosses past the doorway again, her fingers massaging her neck. She wears a natty bathrobe over a nightie.

DOLLY
(off-screen)
Leo – remember – this isn't an everyday thing. You go easy next time.

LEO
Yes, Mam.

In another room, a door closes. A TV clicks on. The babble of a late-night talk show seeps through the walls.

Victor hands the wallet back to Leo, nodding queasily.

Leo looks up again at Farrah on the wall.

> You know, Vick. If you don't use it once in a while.
> It'll fall right off.

Victor rolls over, away from Leo.

*A plane rumbles overhead.* Victor looks out his bedside window.

*Through the window –* PLANE LIGHTS move off into the starry sky.

Victor lies back into his pillow.

Leo takes another drag on his cigarette. He realizes he needs to tip
his long ash. He sits up, looking about, groggy. The collection of
miniature NFL helmets sits, arranged perfectly on a nearby shelf.
Leo grabs a little green NY Jets helmet. He inverts it and tips his
ashes inside. He sinks back into his pillow, taking another drag.
He pushes out his cigarette in the little helmet and rolls over in his
cot. He speaks very quietly.

> There was this guy in the service . . . from
> Mississippi? He'd put his arm underneath himself
> when he fell asleep. Then, he'd wake up, you know,
> in the middle of the night – with his arm all numb.
> And – he'd yank himself off.
> > (whispering even lower)
> Said it felt like someone else was doing it.

Victor rolls deep into his pillow. He stares out into the darkness.

*Through the window* – Barren trees reach into the blue moonlight.
> > (off-screen)
> A big guy like you, though – should probably be
> careful with something like that. 'Could hurt
> yourself. Get gangrene or something.

Victor sighs. He looks up at Farrah. She smiles down on him.

CUT TO:

### INT. JEFF'S APARTMENT – A CONVERTED GARAGE – NIGHT

An unfinished charcoal sketch of Callie is clipped to a drawing board, cocked against the wall. A TV is on, but the sound down.

CALLIE is slumped on the couch. JEFF sits on a stool by the window strumming an unplugged electric guitar. Singing softly, he reads from a crumpled piece of paper on his knee.

> JEFF
> *They call me good for nothing*
> *and they call me a worthless jerk.*
> *They call me in the morning*
> *when I don't show up for work.*

Callie watches Jeff sing. She smiles.

> *I don't think that they understand*
> *I got better things to do.*
> *I'm walking over hot coals,*
> *darling, just for you.*

Callie glances at the television set, noticing something.

*Well some boys they –*
*Well some boys they might fix your car*
*or take you out to eat*
*Some boys they might play guitar and sing*
*you something sweet –* What's wrong?

Callie is staring at the television. She suddenly readjusts.

CALLIE

Keep singing.

JEFF

You're not paying attention.

CALLIE

I am too. I just looked at the television.

JEFF

Whatever. It's cool.

Callie sighs. Jeff pouts, fingering his guitar.

CALLIE

Jeff, this is –

JEFF

It's fine.

CALLIE

– this is the tenth time I heard that song tonight.

JEFF

Third time.

CALLIE

Whatever.

JEFF

It's the third time.

CALLIE

Jeff, look at me.

He glares at her briefly, then looks out the window.

192

                              JEFF
        I am looking at you.

*A plane passes overhead.*

                                                    CUT TO:


INT. DELORES' APARTMENT – NIGHT

The television runs. DELORES sits in a lazy boy recliner. She wears
a velour wraparound.

A PARAKEET sits on the edge of a glass, pecking at some Bourbon
on ice. Delores takes the glass away.

                           DELORES
        That's enough, Max.

The bird jumps to her finger.
*A plane passes overhead.*

                                                    CUT TO:


INT. MODINO HOUSE – VICTOR'S BEDROOM – NIGHT

*Vvvvvrrrmmmmm!* The plane rumbles overhead. With his eyes,
VICTOR follows the sound of the plane across his bedroom ceiling.
Suddenly, in the quiet after the plane, there is a strange sound:
*fruffa fruff, squeak.*

Victor looks over toward LEO.

Lit vaguely in the moonlight. There is movement, quiet moaning.

Victor stares, paralyzed. He reaches slowly, snapping on his NFL
DESK LAMP.

*click.*

Leo is weeping, his eyes red and wet with tears, his pillow clutched
tight to his chest.

                             LEO
        *What?*

                              VICTOR
        What's wrong?

                               LEO
        I don't know.

Victor rolls over.

Leo starts to weep and moan again.

Victor closes his eyes.

                                                          CUT TO:


INT. MODINO HOUSE – VICTOR'S BEDROOM – DAWN

*A door slams.* NANNY *barks.* VICTOR rolls over in bed. He looks out
the window.

In the golden light, LEO trudges down the block, tucking his shirt
in his pants, smoking a cigarette.

Victor closes his eyes, rolling back into his pillow.

                                                          CUT TO:


INT. MODINO HOUSE – KITCHEN – MORNING

In his robe, VICTOR snaps on a TRANSISTOR RADIO that sits on the
windowsill – *talk radio plays.*

                    FEMALE RADIO CALLER
                         (off-screen)
        I mean, I'm not having an affair, but there's
        someone at work –

                         DR VISCOUNT
                         (off-screen)
        And you're attracted to this person?

                            CALLER
                         (off-screen)
        Yes.

DOLLY's bedroom door is half open. She is still asleep. Nanny sits
in the cracked door watching Victor.

                               194

                    DR VISCOUNT
                    (off-screen)
        But you haven't done anything about it?

                      CALLER
                    (off-screen)
        Well, we kissed.

                    DR VISCOUNT
                    (off-screen)
        You kissed. Okay. Once?

                      CALLER
                    (off-screen)
        A couple times. We kissed a couple times. And once
        I – uh, we engaged in oral sex.

Victor sets down a bowl of foods for Nanny. But the dog does not
move from the door.

                                                        CUT TO:


INT./EXT. MODINO HOUSE DRIVE/TWO LANE BRIDGE – DAY

VICTOR back his Ford out of the drive, heading down the road.
The car crosses a TWO-LANE BRIDGE.

                                                        CUT TO:


EXT. CONVENIENCE STORE/DELI – MORNING

VICTOR PULLS HIS WIDE FORD into the small parking lot as –

A JACKED-UP RED PICK-UP TRUCK slides in beside him, very
close. *slam*. The PICK-UP TRUCK DRIVER jumps out of the cab and
heads into the store, oblivious to the fact that –

*tink*. Victor's door can only open a crack before hitting the
polished red body of the pick-up. He tries to squeeze out, to push
himself through the crack like a sausage. He cannot. He clambers
across the front seat, to the passenger side just as –

A DELIVERY VAN backs into the adjacent spot, sealing off the
passenger door.

                        195

*slam.* A DELIVERY WOMAN steps out of the van and crosses into the store, also oblivious.

Victor is entombed. He watches as –

A NIKE-CLAD JOGGER runs along the river, his GOLDEN RETRIEVER keeping perfect stride on a tether.

                                                                CUT TO:


INT. CONVENIENCE STORE/DELI – MORNING (CONTINUOUS)

*Looking through the display glass* – VICTOR, stuck in his sandwiched Ford.

*We are inside* – A 7-Eleven type, everything store. Behind the counter, A CASHIER reads a newspaper. Her name tag reads: *Darlene.*

THE DELIVERY WOMAN wheels a hand truck to the back.

The PICK-UP TRUCK DRIVER steps forward with a cup of coffee.

                              DARLENE
          And a pack of Winston's. Three forty-five.

The pick-up truck driver counts some change into Darlene's hand and exits. He crosses to his truck, revving and pulling out.

Free at last, Victor emerges from his Ford. He enters the store, taking a plastic hand basket.

VICTOR STANDS IN A REFRIGERATED AISLE. He picks up a package of bacon. A carton of eggs. With great consideration, he selects a bottle of juice. He notices –

On the other side of the refrigerator shelves, THE DELIVERY WOMAN is stocking milk cartons. The woman does not see Victor. Her name tag reads: *Maggie.*

THE CANDY AISLE – Victor carries a WRAPPED ICE CREAM SANDWICH. He grabs a BOX OF CHOCOLATE DONUTS, and a package of REESE'S PEANUT BUTTER CUPS.

AT THE COUNTER – A WOMAN STANDS WITH A CHILD. Victor waits behind them with his basket. The child stares at Victor.

Darlene holds out her hand, waving an ENGAGEMENT RING to the woman.

> DARLENE
> Nothing like falling in love to make you think about your weight.

> WOMAN WITH CHILD
> Oh God. It's beautiful.

> DARLENE
> Yeah. He just sprung it on me.

> WOMAN WITH CHILD
> That's great. Alright. Off to Grandma's.

> DARLENE
> Take care.

The woman with child exits. Victor steps forward. Darlene sorts through Victor's groceries, totalling. She sips at her drink. Victor looks closely at her cup: A frothy chocolate-brown liquid. An ULTRA SLIM FAST CANISTER sits beside the cup.

Darlene rings through the register, noticing his curiosity.

> Thirteen fifty-eight.

Victor hands her a bill.

> Out of twenty.

Darlene is a plain woman, but has a tender smile.

> I lost eight pounds on this stuff.

Victor watches as – Darlene puts his groceries in a bag. Her fingernails are painted with sparkling polish.

Victor leans a bit, glancing curiously over the counter – *at Darlene's modest butt – in sweatpants.*

Darlene hands Victor the bag.

> Take care.

Victor heads to the door. As he does, he glances up at the distorted security mirror, and sees *his own very large butt.*

CUT TO:

EXT. TWO-LANE BRIDGE – DAY

*Music plays.* A GROUP OF YOUNG PEOPLE SIT ON THE RAILING OF A TWO-LANE BRIDGE, passing a joint. Among them, CALLIE steps forward, holding a flash camera to her eye as –

JEFF stands on the precarious railing.

Everyone else looks older than Callie, grungier than Callie. Callie snaps a picture as –

Jeff holds his hand out to Callie.

> JEFF
> Here. Come on up. Tony can take our picture.

> CALLIE
> I don't think so . . .

Jeff grins. He pats a bridge support with his palm.

> JEFF
> Come on. You can hold onto this.

Callie looks about, insecure. Everyone beckons Callie to jump on the railing. Tony takes the camera from Callie.

CUT TO:

INT./EXT. CALLIE'S HOUSE/TWO-LANE BRIDGE AND APPROACH – DAY

*Talk radio plays.* VICTOR drives past a strip of middle-class houses. A mailbox says: WELLES: Callie's house. Then further along – JEFF'S MUSTANG parked at the bridge approach.

Victor drives on. He passes:

THE TWO-LANE BRIDGE – THE GROUP OF YOUNG PEOPLE ON THE RAILING. There is a shriek as –

**CALLIE SCREAMS, STOOPED ON THE BRIDGE RAILING, TERRIFIED,** clinging to a steel support. JEFF pulls at her hand, trying to get her upright, further out on the railing.

> CALLIE
>
> No! Jeff! Stop it!

Victor has a hard time keeping his eyes on the road. His eyes drift to the rear-view mirror.

Standing upright, Jeff kisses Callie.

Victor stares until trees obscure the view.

CUT TO:

INT. MODINO HOUSE – MORNING

*Talk radio plays from the transistor radio.*

VICTOR unpacks his sack of groceries. He pulls out a notebook and a pencil. He makes cinnamon toast. He scrambles eggs with a spoonful of mustard and horseradish. He mixes it all in the pan with an egg beater. He mumbles to himself, very seriously. He scoops several spoonfuls of concentrated juice into a blender. Limeade, grape juice, orange juice. Banana chunks. The colors are lovely. He flicks on the blender. It swirls into a strange frothy concoction. He tastes it. He takes some notes in a notebook.

CUT TO:

INT. MODINO HOUSE – MORNING – A LITTLE LATER

VICTOR pours his frothy hybrid juice into two glasses. He neatly arranges two breakfast plates on the kitchen table.

DOLLY sits at the table. She rubs her neck. She wears her bathrobe, her hair in curlers. She looks at her eggs, picking.

> DOLLY
>
> Leo went home?

Victor nods, sitting down. He looks at his mother expectantly.

Mmmmm. Very spicy. This is good.

Dolly takes another forkful. She notices Victor is not eating.

> What?

Victor nods to – *her glass of frothy juice.*

> Oh.

Dolly sips at it, carefully.

> Hmmm.
> > (considering)
> What's in it?

Victor smirks. There is something odd going on between them – almost flirtatious. Dolly takes another sip. She peeks at Victor's notebook.

> This one is very good. Mark this one.

Victor takes the notebook back, closing it.

Dolly starts to eat. Victor follows. And soon the two of them have attained a rhythm, a strange blissful chewing rhythm; forks shoveling, salt and pepper passing back and forth. They smile at one another. *Food is their silent bond.*

> > CUT TO:

EXT. MODINO HOUSE – MORNING

DOLLY locks the door of the house. As she turns, she looks at –

VICTOR, who carries NANNY to the Ford. He wears a nice button-up shirt and tight CORDUROY SLACKS.

> > DOLLY
> Your good pants?

Victor sits in the driver's seat, ready to go.

> > CUT TO:

INT./EXT. MOVING OVER THE TWO-LANE BRIDGE – DAY

Driving with DOLLY, VICTOR stares out at the water. He notices –

The bridge railing. Callie and her friends are gone.

INT. PETE AND DOLLY'S TAVERN – NIGHT (CONTINUOUS)

AT ONE SIDE OF THE RESTAURANT –

TWELVE NOISY KIDS in dirty little league uniforms and A COACH sit at a long table having a post-game party. DELORES nods to them.

> DELORES
> [Your pies are] 'On the way.

She crosses past – AN ELDERLY COUPLE having dinner.

> Everything all right over here?

> OLD LADY
> Just fine. You tell Dolly.

Delores passes an order slip through the slot to VICTOR.

AT THE OTHER SIDE OF THE RESTAURANT –

It is empty, quiet except for CALLIE who stands, folding pizza boxes. She watches as –

Delores intercepts THREE TRUCKERS who enter the tavern, guiding them to a booth on her side of the restaurant. They laugh/flirt with DELORES as she leans on a chair, taking their order.

Leo sits at the bar. He watches television, glancing at Delores.

> CALLIE
> Can I get you something?

> LEO
> Uh. I already told Del. That's okay.

Delores sweeps behind the bar and quickly mixes Leo's drink –

> DELORES
> (putting it down in front of him)
> Chivas and soda.

> LEO
> Thanks, Del.

Callie glares at –

Delores, who fills a beer pitcher. She does not look up.

CUT TO:

INT. PETE AND DOLLY'S TAVERN – MEN'S ROOM – NIGHT

VICTOR UNBUTTONS THE TOP BUTTON OF HIS TIGHT CORDUROY PANTS. The fly springs open from the weight of his belly. He breathes deeply, sighing, from the relief of pressure. He stares in the mirror, his pants hanging open.

CUT TO:

INT. PETER AND DOLLY'S TAVERN – KITCHEN – NIGHT

DOLLY sits in her easy chair. She fans herself with a menu.

CALLIE sits before her on a stool, an INSTAMATIC FLASH CAMERA around her neck. She snaps a picture of Dolly.

> DOLLY
> You know the old theater in Newburgh, on
> Broadway – that shows all the porno now?

> CALLIE
> I think so.

At the other end of the kitchen, VICTOR spreads sauce, cheese, and peppereoni on a pie. He listens to the conversation.

> DOLLY
> Well, it didn't back then. I was coming out of a
> matinee, crossing Broadway. And suddenly I hear all
> this honking and screeching –

Callie looks at Dolly through the viewfinder of her camera. She snaps a few more pictures as Dolly speaks. Dolly is not self-conscious. If anything, the camera makes her livelier. *flash!*

> – and I look up and there's this truck coming at me.

CLOSE ON – VICTOR listens intensely. *flash!*

> A big white Borden's milk truck – out of control.

What did you do?

DOLLY

I tried to move but it was coming straight at me,
Callie. And the next thing I know, glass is flying and
steam and metal – that's where I got this scar right
here (on my forehead) – and I look up and the milk
truck is stopped five feet in front of me. And *another
truck* is smashed into it. Some guy just drove his rig
right into the milk truck – stopping it. Stopping it
five feet from killing me. I fell over from the sound
and my heart was pounding and out of all this
smoke and steam comes Burt Lancaster.

VICTOR turns to –

Callie and Dolly across the room. Dolly's eyes are bright with the
memories.

That was Pete, he looked just like Burt Lancaster,
and he says to me, 'You okay?' And I nod and then
he turns, and he jumps right into that milk truck and
pulls out the driver – who had a heart attack – and
tries to help him.

Victor looks to –

HEIMLICH MANEUVER AND CPR POSTERS hang on the kitchen
wall. 'International' stick figures tangled in life-saving poses.
CLOSER – *a stick figure performs mouth to mouth. flash!*

CALLIE

Wow! He didn't know you or anything?

DOLLY

Pete? He was just passing through – an interstate
trucker. But he gave up his livelihood, just to – *his
truck* – just to save me, to save my life. Out of the
goodness in his heart.

LEO stands in the kitchen doorway. He has been listening in, too.

LEO

Good hearts are good things.

DOLLY

Yes, they are Leo.

LEO

And hard to find.

DOLLY

That too.

*flash!* Callie snaps a picture of Leo. Uncomfortable, Leo makes a face. He speaks as he walks back to the bar.

LEO

Give me the roll when you're done, Callie, I can have it back tomorrow, free of charge.

CALLIE

Really?

LEO

Yeah. I just slip it in the bag.

Victor looks up, concerned.

Dolly touches Callie's knee.

DOLLY
(quietly)

Anyway, Callie. I think you're doing a wonderful job. Delores has had it all to herself here for sixteen years.

*Wrrmmmmmm.* Victor runs the mixer at the other end of the kitchen.

CUT TO:

INT. PETE AND DOLLY'S – BAR – NIGHT

LEO sits at the bar reading the newspaper.

THE THREE TRUCKERS exit in background.

TRUCKER #1
Take care, Leo.

Leo nods, ambivalent.

Across the restaurant, DELORES clears off their table. She finds a worn PeterBuilt baseball hat on the booth.

DELORES
Oh shit. Tommy!

Delores heads outside, waving toward one of the truckers.

DOLLY emerges from the kitchen with a pad in her hand –

DOLLY
(off-screen)
– Del, Victor's making a list for Rykoff –

– but her words trail off as she notices – OUTSIDE –

THROUGH THE GLASS – DELORES RETURNS THE HAT TO ONE OF THE TRUCKERS. He flirts, refusing to release her hand. They laugh.

LEO watches too, exchanging glances with DOLLY.

Delores re-enters the tavern, smiling to herself. Suddenly, her mood deflates as she senses Dolly and Leo's disapproving stares.

CUT TO:


INT. PETE AND DOLLY'S – KITCHEN – NIGHT

Music plays on the jukebox. CALLIE holds her CAMERA, taking flash pictures as –

VICTOR examines an order slip. He pulls out a NEW DOUGH BALL.

CALLIE
Can I touch it?

Victor looks up. He obediently holds out the dough ball for Callie. Callie hands her camera to Victor.

Here.

She takes the mass of dough. She tosses it very delicately. It sticks to her hands.

> Oh, my God. It's falling apart.

                    VICTOR
> Take some flour.

                    CALLIE
> It's so sticky. Like this?

                    VICTOR
> More.

                    CALLIE
> That much?

                    VICTOR
> A little more.

                    CALLIE
> Still?

                    VICTOR
> More.

                    CALLIE
> What if it gets too dry?

Victor smiles.

                    VICTOR
> It won't.

A big slow grin spreads across Callie's face. She tosses the unruly dough ball a few inches into the air. She glances at Victor. There is flour in her hair.

*click flash.*
Victor snaps a picture of her.

STANDING IN THE STOCK ROOM DOOR –

DOLLY watches Callie and Victor, bemused but troubled by their intimacy. She goes unnoticed by –

CALLIE AND VICTOR –

> **CALLIE**
> Here. Victor. Oh, my God. You take it. Please. Take it. It's all lopsided.

Victor takes the dough.

Callie watches as –

Victor spins and works the soft mass into a round wide pizza pie.

> That's amazing.

> **VICTOR**
> Not really.

> **CALLIE**
> Yes it is.

> **VICTOR**
> I hate making pizzas.

> **CALLIE**
> I can't believe that.

> **DOLLY**
> (off-screen; coughing)
> But he loves making breakfast.

Crossing the kitchen, Dolly coughs painfully. She presses her fingers into her neck. The mood is broken.

> **CALLIE**
> You want some water?

Dolly holds her hand in the air, shaking her head – no. She sits down in her easy chair.

> **DOLLY**
> – This boy takes very good care of his mother. He makes a whole buffet. Every day.

Victor's eyes dart to Callie.

What's that cooking school called, that fancy place,
the one across the river – ?

DELORES enters the kitchen, picking up a boxed pizza from atop
the oven. She surveys the scene, perturbed.

You should go there. You could become a great chef
or something.

DELORES
(checking the boxed pie)
He already is.

CALLIE
No. Of course he is. I didn't mean –

DOLLY
– charge us a lot of money to teach him what he
already knows? I don't think so, Callie.

Delores drops the open pizza box in front of Victor.

DELORES
You didn't slice it, chef.

CUT TO:

EXT. PETE AND DOLLY'S TAVERN – PARKING LOT – NIGHT –
LATER

*scuff scuffa scuff scuff.*

CALLIE rushes down the steps of the tavern, pulling a coat on.
Sitting on the hood of his Mustang, JEFF takes the cigarette from
his mouth. They kiss.

*ping*! There is a sound like metal hitting metal. Jeff and Callie look
up from their embrace toward –

Tossing GARBAGE BAGS into a steel dumpster, VICTOR also looks
about for the source of the sound. Making eye contact with Jeff
and Callie, he nods, friendly.

Jeff and Callie both wave back.

Victor turns away, heading toward the back of the restaurant.

Callie takes Jeff's cigarette from his hand. She takes a slow drag.
Jeff says something to her, quiet. She laughs.

Victor stiffens. He stands pressed against the brick exterior of the
tavern. His pants are hanging wide open in the front, the button
popped off. He closes his eyes, the sound of Callie laughing still
hanging in the air as they drive off.

Suddenly, shrill voices rise from inside the tavern . . .

> DELORES
> (off-screen)
> Apologize? Apologize for what? What did I say? Did
> you hear me say anything nasty?

> LEO
> (off-screen)
> Don't drag me into this.

> DOLLY
> (off-screen)
> You have a bad attitude, Delores.

                              DELORES
                            (off-screen)
          What am I supposed to say? 'Gee Sally –

                               DOLLY
                            (off-screen)
          – *Callie* –

                              DELORES
                            (off-screen)
          – I'm really sorry for not saying 'excuse me' when
          you were in my fucking way.

                               DOLLY
                            (off-screen)
          Cursing does not make your argument any more
          persuasive. There comes a time –

                                                        CUT TO:


INT. PETE AND DOLLY'S TAVERN – KITCHEN/STOCKROOM – NIGHT

*Looking through the kitchen doorway – at the bar –* DOLLY *and*
DELORES *squabble.* LEO *sits between them, staring at the TV.*

                               DOLLY
          – There comes a time when you have to think about
          the future.

                              DELORES
          And what is the future? *Her?* How long do you think
          she's gonna hang around this bone orchard?

VICTOR *stands at the back door of the kitchen, holding his pants –*
*watching –*

                               DOLLY
                            (off-screen)
          That's up to my son Victor.

                              DELORES
                            (off-screen)
          Bullshit! Don't talk to me about my attitude. I have
          a job to do and I don't have time to hold her hand.

                                212

Victor crosses to the stockroom.

> **DOLLY**
> (off-screen)
> I don't want any more of this tonight. You have a
> very bad reputation, Delores. It gets you in trouble
> with people –

Dolly retreats into the kitchen crossing toward the rear.

> And that rubs off on my tavern.

Out at the bar – the television prattles on. Delores dumps some
dishes into the sink. She glares at Leo.

In the shadows of the stockroom, Victor finds a safety pin in a
drawer. He fastens his pants, watching in the dark as –

Delores bursts into the kitchen. She crosses toward –

Dolly, who stands over a steaming pot, her hand moving from her
temples to her neck, unwilling to look at Delores.

> **DELORES**
> Someone writes something on the mirror. Who the
> fuck knows who did it?

> **DOLLY**
> I've had enough, Delores. Please.

> **DELORES**
> No. I want to set it straight. Someone writes
> something on the mirror. It could be about *you.*

> **DOLLY**
> (hissing)
> It's not about me, Delores. I didn't take that *trucker*
> home with me.

Dolly crosses to her armchair. Delores follows.

> **DELORES**
> What do you want from me? I'm a block of ice. I'm
> a goddamn celibate. Don't laugh! That goes for Leo
> and *all* the fuck-ups who ever waltzed through here.

Dolly looks up.

> DOLLY
> What about Pete? Were you a block of ice with him?
> What about *my husband*, Delores?

Delores stands silently. Her shoulders fall. She sees Victor
standing in the stockroom doorway – hearing this. They meet
eyes.

Dolly pulls at a thread on her armchair. Delores storms out, the
door swinging behind her.

> DELORES
> (stomping about, getting her coat)
> Fifteen years ago! Jesus Christ! I'm not supposed to
> have a life, is that it? Me and Victor are supposed to
> just tend to you and follow your orders and never
> cross the line –

Leo tries to intercept Delores, offering comfort.

> Get away from me.

Dolly squints. She shouts out to Delores.

> DOLLY
> I've got your number, Delores Kiefer. *You* are a *slut.*

*The door slams.*

Dolly turns away. Sullen. Suddenly she begins to weep. She
covers her face with her hands.

Victor shuffles into the kitchen. He picks up A BOX OF KLEENEX.
He takes it to his mother. Dolly pulls out a tissue and blows her
nose. She takes Victor's hand. She holds it tightly.

> CUT TO:

EXT. PETE AND DOLLY'S TAVERN – PARKING LOT – NIGHT

*vavavavavavavavavavavavava.*

Her face twisted in frustration, her eyes wet from the fight,
DELORES struggles to start her Dodge. But it will not turn over.

Shit!

She digs through her purse frantically producing a cigarette. Still rummaging for matches, Delores looks up, noticing –

Through the sooty windshield, LEO pulls on his coat, crossing to her car. His eyes fixed upon her.

Delores watches him approach with dread, the cigarette hanging on her lip. She finds matches in her purse. But the book's empty.

Leo stands beside her grimy window. He lights a match, cupping the flame just on the other side of the glass.

Delores does not look at him. She tries to start her car again. *vavavavavavavavava*. Nothing.

Leo's match burns out. He lights another, cupping it again.

Delores rolls down her window a bit, guiding the tip of her cigarette into Leo's flame. The cigarette burns. Delores takes the smoke in deep.

Leo crosses and enters her Dodge from the other side. He lights his own cigarette. Delores does not look at him.

The 'Pete and Dolly's Tavern' sign glows red from above.

LEO

What was he like?

DELORES

Who?

LEO

Pete.

DELORES

Sad. Pete was a very sad man.

LEO

Like me?

Delores smiles, dully.

DELORES

No.

Delores tries to start her car again: *vavavava* – nothing.

You gonna take me home?

LEO

Sure.

DELORES

Don't get stupid ideas, Leo.

LEO

What are you talking about?

DELORES

Honey, it's just not there. It's all dried up.

Delores pushes out her cigarette. Leo pouts.

LEO

Why do you have to say things like that?

Delores smiles softly. She shakes her head. Leo looks up, a sad spark in his eye.

CUT TO:

INT. PETE AND DOLLY'S TAVERN – AT THE BAR – DUSK (NEXT DAY)

Rainwater drizzles down the windows of the tavern.
CALLIE sits erect, motionless at the bar.

DOLLY

There.

DOLLY snips a line of thread from a HAND-EMBROIDERED PATCH on Callie's blouse. The patch reads: *Callie.*

*clap clap clap.* At the end of the bar, A CUSTOMER (waiting for pizza) applauds. So does THE GAS MAN (grinning at the bar) and VICTOR, standing at the kitchen door. At the register, DELORES turns, joining in the applause.

INT. PETE AND DOLLY'S TAVERN – LATER – NIGHT (RAIN)

The Genesee Cream Ale clock says: 11:45.
The Molson's clock says: 12:45.

*wwwwWWWWWrrrrrrrmmmmmm.* CALLIE is vacuuming the floor at the far end of the restaurant. She watches Victor anxiously.

Sitting in his booth, VICTOR flips through a STACK OF PICTURES. Before him sits a HALF-EATEN PIZZA and a can of SODA.

*The pictures:* Dolly in her fluffy chair. Leo grinning debonair. Then, some shots of Victor flipping the dough, spreading sauce And among the shots of Victor, *a single picture of Callie grinning, wide and beautiful, flour in her hair.*

Victor pauses on this picture. His eyes full of love. Aware of Callie's intermittent glances, he moves on through the stack.

*The pictures that follow are not from the restaurant:* Jeff and Callie – lakeside. A picture of the two of them, holding each other. Then, night pictures: A camp fire. Jeff's eyes red from the flash.

Uneasy, Victor looks back toward –

Leo, at the bar, who looks back to the television.

Callie's vacuum hose gets tangled with a POOL PLAYER.

> CALLIE
> Sorry.

Victor discreetly returns to the first picture of Callie, flour in her hair. *He removes it from the pack, letting it fall onto the seat beside him.* His eyes riveted upon Callie as she vacuums, he gingerly SLIDES THE PHOTO INTO A FOLDED MENU.

*The vacuum shuts off.* Victor looks up. Suddenly, Callie is above him, kneeling on the next booth, looking down.

> VICTOR
> They're nice.

> CALLIE
> I like the ones of you making pizza.

Victor shakes his head shamefully.

> VICTOR
> I don't know about that.

Flipping through the pack, Victor pulls out a few still-life photos, arty details of the restaurant: a close-up of a neon, empty beer bottles, a row of brandies in a rainbow of colors. He puts them out on the table.

> CALLIE
> I like those, but I thought maybe I was being too,
> you know –

Victor looks up, a fleck of tomato sauce clings to his chin.

> . . . pretentious.

Callie smiles.

> You got something there.

Victor wipes at his chin, frantically removing the fleck.

CUT TO:

INT./EXT. PETE AND DOLLY'S – KITCHEN BACK DOOR – NIGHT
(RAIN)

Victor gathers a pair of garbage bags in the dark. He ties them up,
THE FOLDED MENU TUCKED UNDER HIS ARM.

Delores stands in the doorway of the stockroom. We hear Dolly in
the background: '*I just hope it doesn't freeze over.*'

> DELORES
> What's the menu for?

Victor does not reply, dragging away the garbage bags, the MENU
still tucked under his arm.

CUT TO:

INT. A PARTY AT SOMEONE'S PARENTS' HOUSE – NIGHT

THE YOUNG PEOPLE FROM THE LAKESIDE are gathered, Callie
among them. Jeff sits on the edge of a couch, causally singing.
ANOTHER GUY accompanies him with a second guitar.

> JEFF
> *– could eat twenty hot dogs*
> *Wash it down with two gallons of beer.*
> *Pitchers would pray to the heavens*
> *Whenever Babe stepped to the plate*
> *Mr Ruth would be first to tell you*
> *You gotta be fat to be great.*

On the floor, CALLIE shows her pictures to TWO GIRLFRIENDS
(DONNA AND JEAN).

> DONNA
> Oh, my God. Look how big that guy is.

> JEAN
> Is that who Jeff wrote the song about?

> CALLIE
> No. He never met him.

                        DONNA
He's so big.

                        CALLIE
Jeff doesn't want to go inside 'cause – I don't know
– 'cause he thinks they're all trash or something.

Donna looks at Jean scandalously – *trouble in paradise?*

                        JEFF
*And how about Marlon Brando.*
*He's the best actor around.*
*Did you get to see his latest movie?*
*He must've weighed four hundred pounds.*
*I hear he's got a thing for Haagen Daz*
*Buys his ice cream by the crate*
*Yeah. Okay. Sean Penn might be good*
*But he's gotta be fat to be great.*

CLOSE ON – CALLIE looks at –

A PICTURE OF Victor smiling sweetly. In the pack, Callie finds A
MISFRAMED PICTURE OF JEFF – his head cut off by the edge of the
photo. She places it in front of the shot of Victor, creating a
composite man. *Victor's gentle face atop Jeff's slender body.*

                                            CUT TO:


INT. MODINO HOUSE – BATHROOM – MORNING

VICTOR SITS IN HIS ROBE ON THE TOILET. He gazes at the
STOLEN PHOTO OF CALLIE. Water drips. The sink is cluttered with
prescription bottles, a bottle of Sominex, nail polish and a set of
dentures in a glass.

Victor's reverie is suddenly broken by – *the sound of the dog barking*
– and Dolly chattering – *'Shhh. Hush up, now.'*

Victor slips the photo into his robe pocket. He brushes his teeth,
looking at himself in the mirror. He pulls a bathroom scale out
from under the sink. He stands on it. *Three hundred and four*
*pounds.* Victor takes off his slippers. His bathrobe. He steps on the
scale again: *three hundred and four pounds.*

                        220

INT. MODINO HOUSE – KITCHEN – MORNING

NANNY eats tentatively from her bowl, her eyes upon –

VICTOR, who washes dishes. He wears sweatpants and a sweatshirt which pinches in the pits. *Talk radio plays.*

In a nightie and slippers, DOLLY stands at the end of the hallway. She crosses slowly to the table – where there sits – A BEAUTIFUL BREAKFAST – FOR ONE.

Dolly notices this, taking a bite of toast.

> DOLLY
> – You eat already?

Victor turns. He shakes his head. Dolly smiles.

> Well. You shouldn't skip breakfast – it's the most important –

> VICTOR
> I'm fat, Ma.

This hits hard. Dolly is frozen.

> DOLLY
> – You are not fat. You are not – You're well built – You're husky – *You're macho!*

Victor spins, slamming a pot down.

> VICTOR
> I am fat, Ma!

Dolly is stricken. She steps backward, whimpering . . .

> DOLLY
> (quietly)
> 'There's more of you to love.

CUT TO:

**EXT. CROSSING THE TWO-LANE BRIDGE – MORNING**

In his sweatpants, VICTOR takes NANNY for a walk. Nanny pulls stubbornly at the leash. Suddenly, the fat dog sits down in the middle on the road, right on the double line. A CAR SWERVES, looping around Victor and Nanny. Embarrassed, Victor tries to get Nanny moving, pulling on the leash. But the dog sits there, lazy, unresponsive.

THE NIKE-CLAD JOGGER runs past, his GOLDEN RETRIEVER keeping perfect stride.

                                                    CUT TO:


**INT. CONVENIENCE STORE – MORNING**

LOOKING OUT THROUGH THE GLASS – NANNY whines and pulls, tied to a post.

INSIDE THE STORE – DARLENE (the clerk) reads a newspaper, glum. Smoking.

Victor, in his sweats, picks up a bottle of DIET SALAD DRESSING. A quart of SKIM MILK. He turns, his eye catching –

AN ULTRA SLIM FAST FLOOR DISPLAY. A grinning cardboard Tommy Lasorda holds out a canister.

Darlene totals Victor's groceries.

Victor watches her, anxious for her to make a comment on the Slim Fast. But she is oblivious. Distant. Victor notices –

AN ACE BANDAGE ON DARLENE'S WRIST – as she punches the register keys. Her arm has faint bruises. The ring is gone.

Darlene looks up, dull-eyed. Victor smiles gently, uneasy.

                                                    CUT TO:


**EXT. CONVENIENCE STORE – MORNING**

Holding his sack of groceries, VICTOR stands before –

NANNY'S EMPTY LEASH tied to the post. She has pulled free from her collar and gotten away. Victor walks out into the parking lot, looking about.

CUT TO:

EXT. CROSSING THE TWO-LANE BRIDGE – MORNING

Floating down the river, a branch.

VICTOR stands, his sack of groceries and Nanny's empty leash in his hands. He glances over the railing.

A YOUNG WOMAN lies face down in the rippling water.

VICTOR'S GROCERIES AND THE LEASH DROP TO THE GROUND.

EXT. BENEATH THE TWO-LANE BRIDGE – CLOSE – THE BODY (CONTINUOUS)

VICTOR kneels, turning the woman over. IT IS CALLIE. Her tender skin, rubbery, blue and translucent, mud on her face. Her bright eyes stare upward, watery, dull. A GOLD HEART hangs around her neck.

Victor clumsily moves his hands. He gasps for air. He touches Callie's face, her soft cheek, brushing away the mud. Her clothing clings to her body. He shakes her gently. No response. She is dead. Victor stares, terrified.

VICTOR

> *Oh my God . . .*

Victor leans down, pressing his mouth gingerly against Callie's blue lips. He blows gently (so gentle that all the air squirts out the sides). He looks at her, his eyes wide.

*No response.*

He blows again, this time pressing harder against her mouth. He holds her head firmly in his hands. Kissing/blowing.

Her eyes flutter. He kisses/blows again. Her eyes open weakly, slowly, like Sleeping Beauty. She blinks. She is looking straight up at Victor. Color begins to blossom in her cheeks.

Astonished, Victor leans down and kisses/blows again, gently.

Callie stares upward at him, bleary. She suddenly starts to cough. Victor smiles nervously and leans away.

Callie is breathing on her own.

Victor stands. In awe. Proud.

*A car is approaching. Passes.*

Victor looks back down to Callie.

BUT SHE IS GONE. JUST SOME FROSTED MOSS. NO TRACE.

Just standing there, disconcerted on the bridge, the groceries and the leash still in his arms, VICTOR RISES FROM THE DAYDREAM.

                                                          CUT TO:


EXT. MODINO HOUSE – THE FRONT STOOP – MORNING

Wet with mud and dried grass, NANNY sits on the front steps. She whines eagerly at the door. VICTOR lets her in.

                                                          CUT TO:


INT. MODINO HOUSE – MORNING

His bag of groceries on the kitchen counter, VICTOR holds the can of ULTRA SLIM FAST, scrutinising the instructions. Then, he notices

His mother's place at the table: *There is one clean bite out of his mother's toast. The rest of the breakfast untouched.* Victor looks about, confused. He crosses to his mother's bedroom. It is empty. The bed unmade.

                              VICTOR
     Ma?

Victor looks to –

NANNY sits before the bathroom door, whimpering. Victor pushes it open.

DOLLY is on the floor. Still in her nightie, she lies face down on the tile. She does not move. Her hand clutches her neck.

Victor kneels beside his mother's body. He puts his hand on her back.

Ma?

She is very still. Suddenly, her back rises, then falls. Then after a pause; again. She is breathing.

(whimpering)
Oh my God, oh my God, oh my God . . .

Victor watches her, intense. Nanny watches too, whining nervously.

Dolly's back rises. Her back falls. Her eyes blink open. Suddenly she pulls herself a few inches from the cold tile.

DOLLY
*Ooo.* How did I get down here?

Victor stares at his mother, his eyes filled with fear.

CUT TO:

INT./EXT. VICTOR'S FORD – DRIVING – DAY

A GROUP OF RAGGED MEN congregate outside an OTB* office. Nervous, VICTOR drives through a RUST BELT TOWN.

DOLLY sits, slumped against the back door, her legs up on the seat. She holds her swollen neck. She watches out her window as –

THEIR CAR MOVES ONTO THE NEWBURGH BEACON BRIDGE – Cars pass on the left – *whoooosh*, and right – *whoooooosh*.

Victor speeds the car up. Then, even more . . . He passes a car. He passes a big truck. *whoooooooosh.*

Dolly opens her eyes, suddenly disturbed.

DOLLY
Victor.

* Off Track Betting.

227

Victor does not turn to face his mother. With effort, Dolly leans forward. She stares at the speedometer.

> Victor.

Victor is silent.

> *Victor!*

Victor turns around, glaring. His eyes wide and panicked, his face wet with perspiration. Dolly softens.

> I'm in no rush. We'll just end up waiting anyway.
> It's Sunday. I'm fine.

Victor eases up on the gas. *Woooosh!* The big truck overtakes them.

Dolly sits back against the door. She closes her eyes. She sighs, dabbing her face with the wet towel.

> Men don't feel like they're getting anywhere unless
> they pass other cars. Women look at the scenery.
> They watch the houses and the trees and the
> shopping malls. They watch the world going by, so
> they know they're getting somewhere. Men just
> watch cars.

*Woooosh!* Another car passes.

CUT TO:

INT. UPSTATE HOSPITAL EXAMINATION ROOM – DAY

DOLLY holds VICTOR's hand tightly. The DOCTOR (GRUBER, A BLACK MAN) wears glasses and pokes at Dolly's swollen neck.

> DOLLY
> – to keep pressure on it with my fingers.

> GRUBER
> This was eight weeks ago?

> DOLLY
> Yes.

228

The doctor looks through a manila folder.

> GRUBER
> Uh – do you know what tests were run?

> DOLLY
> I don't think he ran any tests.

> GRUBER
> None?

The doctor looks at Victor through his thick glasses. Victor shrugs.

> CUT TO:

INT. UPSTATE HOSPITAL LOBBY – LATER

VICTOR struggles to sit comfortably on a hot pink plastic chair, much too small for someone of his width. He holds a pack of RED TWIZZLER LICORICE, a single large bite taken out from the top of all twelve licorice sticks. A DESK NURSE stands in front of him.

> DESK NURSE
> . . . She won't wake up until morning. We can call you if – I mean, you don't have to stay, but you can . . . I can get you a pillow. (beat) Would you like to talk to the doctor?

Victor thinks, then shakes his head.

> Are you sure?

Victor nods.

> Okay. Let me know if you need anything.

The desk nurse departs.

Victor gets up, and the hot pink chair comes with him for a moment, stuck on his ass. It drops as he straightens. Victor pulls on his jacket. He presses the elevator button.

> GRUBER
> (off-screen)
> Excuse me, Mr Modino.

Victor turns around. It is DR GRUBER. He pulls Victor to the side, speaking quietly.

> Look, I can't speak for your regular doctor and I don't want to get into that, not now, but I can tell you . . . there was something there, and if it's malignant, and I'm not saying it is . . . but –

A WOMAN WALKS PAST WITH HER SON IN AN ARM CAST. The boy is crying, and the woman is picking something out of his hair.

> – with the time that's gone by undiagnosed, well, there could be some spread. In the glands, it's very fast.

Victor rolls his tongue over his teeth, looking at the floor.

> I just want you to understand what we could be facing here.

Victor nods.

*bing!* The elevator door opens. Victor steps inside.

CUT TO:

INT./EXT. DRIVING HOME – LATE AFTERNOON

VICTOR drives.

*Out the side window –* A LONE FIGURE, WALKING ALONG THE SHOULDER. A MAN IN A BIG WHITE CHEF'S HAT walking along the road.

A SIGN READS: *The Culinary Institute.* An IVY-COVERED CAMPUS.

Victor drives on, his eyes darting to the rear view mirror.

CUT TO:

INT./EXT. DRIVING HOME – BRIDGE – LATE AFTERNOON

VICTOR drives across the bridge. *The radio plays.*

RADIO FINANCIAL ADVISOR
(off-screen)
– going to read the business section. You're looking
for the best rate on short-term –

MABEL
(off-screen)
– homeowner's loans, uh huh.

Victor's Ford moves up alongside –

A STATION WAGON. Inside, A MAN is yelling and screaming and
gesticulating wildly in the direction of HIS WIFE. A LITTLE BOY
sits in the back, obliviously punching the keys on a Gameboy.

RADIO ADVISER
(off-screen)
– and then you'll have one monthly payment. You
know what else you're going to do?

MABEL
(off-screen)
Cut up the cards – ?

Victor exits onto a two-lane road. It leads along the river.

CUT TO:

INT. PETE AND DOLLY'S TAVERN – AT THE BAR – NIGHT

CALLIE taps on the light switch, restoring the bar light. She holds a
paper bag.

DELORES stands beside her examining TWO GREETING CARDS. She
closes the first card, expressionless. She fingers the second one
open, reading the sentiments. Unimpressed, she hands them both
back to Callie.

LEO sits at the end of the bar. He holds out his hand.

LEO
Can I see?

Leo fumbles with them, glancing at Delores.

231

DELORES

I don't know, Callie. These are like she's dying or
something.

Delores moves off toward a table. Leo stares at the cards, rubbing
his chin.

LEO

I got a card once from the girls over at Caldor's – I
was out for two weeks, with mono – no comments
please – and it was, this card, it had this little guy
with a pot belly and it looked like he was sick in bed,
you know? But when you opened it up, he was
actually in bed with a bunch of very well endowed
women.
(he smiles, remembering)
What did – *Shit.* I forgot what it said, but it was
funny. I mean these are sweet and everything. But
funny cards –

Callie looks over toward the food slot.
(off-screen)
They cheer you up.

She finds – VICTOR staring at her. Callie turns back around and
takes the two cards from Leo. She pivots back toward the slot, but
Victor is gone.

CALLIE

Victor?

Callie leans in the food slot. Victor is not there. Leo smiles at
Callie, sly. Delores has moved to the register, punching in her
paid check.

(to Delores)
I wanted to show him the cards.

Delores doesn't respond.

(through the slot again)
Victor?

232

Honey. You can't work him into a lather every
goddamn night of the week.

*Ding!* Delores pushes shut the register drawer, turns around and
moves through the swinging doors into the kitchen.

CALLIE
What is that supposed to mean?

Leo laughs through his nose.

CUT TO:

INT. MODINO HOUSE – KITCHEN – DAY

The sink is cluttered with dirty dishes. Dolly's unfinished
breakfast plate sits on the table exactly as it was left the day Dolly
fell ill. *Talk radio plays.*

VICTOR puts down a bowl of dog food. NANNY growls, sitting
rebelliously in the doorway of Dolly's bedroom. She lies down,
watching Victor closely.

CUT TO:

Victor sits at his place at the table. He stirs a SLIM FAST SHAKE as
he reads a folded section of the newspaper.

*The folded newspaper* – AN ARTICLE – about an ice carver at the
Culinary Institute of Poughkeepsie. A PICTURE shows the ice
carver at work with a chisel on a giant SWAN.

Victor sips his shake. *There is a sound.* He looks up from the article.

ACROSS FROM HIM – CALLIE ('WET CALLIE') soaking wet, exactly
as she was when 'rescued', eating one of Victor's breakfasts. She
bites a piece of toast.

WET CALLIE
Mmmm. Cinnamon.

Wet Callie looks up at Victor. She beams. Victor smiles back.

CUT TO:

233

EXT. 24-HOUR GAS AND CIGS – NIGHT

JEFF stands in a glass booth. He runs a credit card purchase through for a MAN IN SOILED WORK CLOTHES.

INSIDE A LIGHTED VAN at the pump, A SHIRTLESS MAN pulls on a fresh shirt, throwing a crumpled sweaty one into the back. He is well built, strong. He notices –

CALLIE, behind Jeff, in the shadows. She sits on a crate of motor oil. She is checking herself in a clip-on visor mirror that hangs upon a RACK OF AUTO ACCESSORIES.

The man in the van stares at Callie. Callie nervously returns the glance. His partner joins him in the van and they depart. Jeff turns around. He sighs.

                    JEFF
          Whatever.

                    CALLIE
          I have Mondays and Tuesdays off. I mean, here I
          am.

                    JEFF
          Nothing's ever happening on Mondays and
          Tuesdays.

Jeff crosses to Callie.

                    CALLIE
          At least I'm not up at school.

Jeff kisses her. She wraps her legs around him, taking his kiss deeper. She runs her hand up his shirt.

                    JEFF
          I missed you so much. I still miss you.

He kisses her neck. He unbuttons the first button of her sweater, moving lower, pawing her blouse. She kisses his hair.

                    CALLIE
          Mmm.

234

Intertwined, they move into the shadows behind the crates. Callie pulls off her sweater and spreads it down, lying back on the floor in a loose v-neck. Jeff kneels over her.

— what if someone — ?

                    JEFF
We're invisible.

Jeff kisses her lips, her neck, moving down to her soft belly. He unzips her jeans, pulling them inside out, off her legs. Callie smiles. Jeff lowers into the darkness.

They kiss. Callie helps Jeff find her. He kisses her ear, her neck, moving faster. Callie looks about the dark chamber, suddenly distant. Her eyes come upon —

A POSTER OF A PENN STATE MOTOR OIL GIRL.

THE STREET LIGHTS GLOW ON THE CEILING. A roll of fly paper hangs down, encrusted with dead flies. A DISPLAY RACK OF ASPIRINS . . . AND CONDOMS.

Callie stares, ashen-faced. Jeff arches, holding Callie tight.

                                        CUT TO:


INT. UPSTATE HOSPITAL ROOM — LATE AFTERNOON

*A football game on a small TV.*

CALLIE'S GET WELL CARD sits on a bedside table beside a water glass and a box of Polygrip.

DOLLY sits upright in a hospital bed, the pink Samsonite case open at her feet. There are bandages around her shoulder and neck. Her face is weary. She strains to read a section of a folded newspaper (the ice-carving article)

A WRINKLY OLD PAIR OF FEET stick out from an adjacent bed, their owner obscured by a yellow divider curtain.

VICTOR picks at the peeling arm of his vinyl chair.

                    DOLLY
The runaway expansion is going to go through, you

know that, and then boom. The restaurant could be
a gold mine.

                    VICTOR
That could be years.

                    DOLLY
I worry, that's all.
                    (looking at the newspaper)
Fondu, sushi . . . I don't know. I mean, what about
the business? (beat) The restaurant is going to be
yours. That might be sooner than later.

Victor glares at the television.

On the TV, AN AD FOR ULTRA SLIM FAST DIET DRINK. Before and
after pictures are flashed over and over. TWO NURSES pass by the
curtain, laughing.

They're the ones who should go to cooking school.
They feed me baby food – cold carrots – in a dixie
cup. That's my dinner.

                                                    CUT TO:


SLOW TRANSITION: WINTER/SPRING MONTAGE

Buds forming. Water dripping. Purplish trees along the thawing
lake.

*At the road's shoulder,* A SNAPPING TURTLE pushes through the
dried grass, moving out onto the wet asphalt. The turtle makes its
way across the double yellow as – *Whhoosh!*

A CAR RIPS PAST, just missing it. It continues its steady progress as
ANOTHER CAR ROARS RIGHT OVER, both tires missing. It pops its
head out of the shell. Resolute, it continues its progress toward the
churning river. It moves off the asphalt, shuffling past A
FLATTENED RACCOON CARCASS, advancing onto the mossy
shoulder of the riverside.

*plop.*

                                                    CUT TO:

INT. PETE AND DOLLY'S TAVERN – STOCKROOM – LATE
AFTERNOON

A BOWL OF HALF-EATEN SALAD drops to the floor. Among cans of
tomato purée and twenty-pound bags of semolina flour, VICTOR
sleeps in the shadows.

DELORES stands in the doorway.

> DELORES
> Knock, knock?

Victor looks up, startled.

Delores sits down on a crate beside Victor. She reaches in her
purse and pulls out a cigarette.

> I have something for you. It might be a little melted.
> I had my purse next to the radiator.

Delores holds out a MOUNDS BAR. Victor takes it.

> VICTOR
> Thanks.

*Through the stockroom door –*

CALLIE joyfully greets THREE FRIENDS: a young woman (DONNA),
and two guys: JEFF and TONY (Donna's boyfriend).

Victor watches as – Callie seats them at a booth. Delores pulls a
lighter from her purse, lights her cigarette.

*Through the stockroom door –* Jeff plays music on the jukebox. He
walks back to their booth, glancing to the shadowed doorway –

Where Victor sits, watching.

> DELORES
> Eat it. I was on line at Shop Rite and I remembered
> how much you loved coconut when you were a kid.

> VICTOR
> I'll save it for later.

*A plane whines overhead.*

Delores takes a drag on her cigarette. She stares at the ceiling, following the sound of the plane with her eyes.

> DELORES
>
> Sometime I want to take you to this spot I found, off 9w – near the back entrance to Stewart. It's a dirt road. And you can park, right next to the runway. By the fence.

Victor is oblivious to Delores, still staring out at –

Donna and Tony are laughing as Callie plays waitress, 'taking their order', holding out her waitress pad and pulling a pencil from her ear, she sashays about (like Delores) leaning on a chair, her hip jutting out.

Standing at the pool table, Jeff is not amused by the 'act'. He rolls the cue ball around the table. He looks up. He notices –

Victor, still looking at him/them/Callie through the doorway.

> I go there some nights after work. And I watch the planes. You look up and they're coming in, coming over you with this sound – you think they're going to rip the roof right off. Right on top of you.

Victor continues to stare at Callie and her friends.

> (off-screen)
> Victor.

Jeff looks up again, *again meeting Victor's eyes.*

> (on-screen)
> Victor.

Victor turns, blank-faced. Delores glares. But when she traces the line from Victor's eyes through the doorway to Callie, laughing with her friends, Delores softens.

> Go home.

> VICTOR
> It's seven o'clock.

DELORES

Go home and get some sleep. You don't need this –
to be watching this.

VICTOR

What about the pies?

DELORES

We ran out of gas.

Victor smiles wearily.

CUT TO:

INT. MODINO HOUSE – VICTOR'S BEDROOM – NIGHT

It is dark. Clothes are strewn about. The DIGITAL CLOCK reads
7:22. THE HALF-EATEN MOUNDS BAR sits beside an OPEN BOTTLE
OF SOMINEX and A CAN OF SODA on Victor's bedside table.
A television drones in the living room.

VICTOR lies face-up in bed, rigid – wide awake, fully dressed. He
reads the side of the sleeping pill bottle. He pops another sleeping
pill. He closes his eyes as a plane passes overhead. Suddenly, he
opens them looking at –

*In the darkness* – the Farrah poster on the wall. But Farrah is gone
*– there is just an empty background. A wet spot on the mat where her
ass was.*

Victor is alarmed. He sits up.

*creak, shuffle.* The dog barks.

Somebody is walking down the hall. Victor jumps from bed,
peering down the hall.

*nothing. a breeze blows.*

Suddenly: *the phone rings.*

CUT TO:

Victor picks it up.

> VICTOR

Hello?

> DOLLY
> (off-screen)

Sweetheart, do me a favor. I need my nail kit. It's
under the bathroom sink.

Dolly speaks in a depressed whisper.

Farrah has re-appeared in her poster, smiling down on Victor.

> VICTOR

I'll bring it tomorrow.

Dolly sighs – it makes a strange hollow sound on the phone.

> DOLLY
> (off-screen)

Oh well. I guess it's too late – are you alright? I
called the restaurant.

WET CALLIE stands in the door of Victor's bedroom, her hair
back-lit by the throbbing television. She looks like an angel.

> It's very quiet here.
> (sighing)
> You get your rest. I don't need to see you every day.
> Are you alright?

CUT TO:

INT. MODINO HOUSE – BATHROOM – NIGHT

Victor slaps water on his face. He opens the medicine chest. He
loads A BAG with Dolly's toiletries. Fumbling, he produces A
BOTTLE OF RED NAIL POLISH. He pauses, examining the bottle.
He opens it. He smears a line on the mirror.

Bright red enamel – *the same color as the graffiti on the restaurant
mirror.*

CUT TO:

INT. HOSPITAL ROOM – LATER – NIGHT

A nail file and the bottle of polish sit on her bed tray. DOLLY pulls at a plastic IV BAG, her fingernails painted red.

> DOLLY
> Remember when we left you all alone on Saint Patty's Day – how you filled up all those baggies with colored water? How old were you? Ten? All over the house. Every color in the rainbow. Your father threw a fit.

VICTOR nods, exhausted (fighting the sleeping pills). He sits slumped in the vinyl chair. He smiles weakly at his mother.

Dolly sighs weakly. She closes her eyes.

> How we doing on those veal patties I made up?

Victor does not reply, his groggy eyes glued to the throbbing light of the television.

> Victor

> VICTOR
> Fine.

> DOLLY
> 'You've been feeding Nanny from the yellow cans?

Victor vaguely nods as his head rocks backward.

> (off-screen)
> No. I'm not sure we should keep Callie any more.

About to fall asleep, Victor suddenly sits up, rubbing his face. He looks to his mother, sleeping.

> CUT TO:

INT. HOSPITAL CORRIDOR – NIGHT

A thick strand of fluorescent tape cordons off the elevator. VICTOR stands a moment, groggy and perplexed, then steps awkwardly over the ribbon. He presses the 'down' button.

At a nearby desk, AN INTERN speaks in a hush to a DESK NURSE.

> INTERN
> . . . no, no . . . obstructive jaundice.

> DESK NURSE
> Where are they putting him?

> INTERN
> On the third floor.

> DESK NURSE
> Oh, good.

Victor presses the elevator button again. He rubs his face.

> INTERN
> They booked the whole wing for the police
> entourage or whatever. Witness protection. (beat) If
> you ask me they should make assholes like that stand
> trial – as is. *Fuck 'em.*

THE ELEVATOR DOOR SLIDES OPEN. Victor is about to step inside, but realizes –

THERE IS NO ELEVATOR. It is just an open shaft, leading downward into darkness.

The nurse and intern babble on, oblivious to Victor. Victor backs away from the open shaft. Victor carefully side-steps back over the yellow ribbon. A sign reads: *Out of Order.* He heads down the hall toward a door marked *Exit.*

CUT TO:


INT. HOSPITAL – VENDING MACHINES AREA – NIGHT

*Gummi Bears. Mounds. Snickers. Twinkies. Sweet Tarts. Ding Dongs.*

VICTOR stares hazily at all the alternatives.

A POST-IT NOTE reads: *Out of Order.*

CUT TO:

242

Two styrene tanks flush with vivid orange and purple syrup. Franks spin on greasy rollers.

VICTOR stands at the counter, looking over the backlit menu. At the far end, A MIDDLE-AGED WAITRESS in heavy mascara sits motionless on a stool, lost in a romance novel. Her name tag reads: *Blanche*.

> VICTOR

Hello?

She doesn't notice Victor. Victors stand there. Patient.

> MAN
> (off-screen)
> Take whatever you want. She don't care.

Victor turns.

Hunched at a booth, A MAN. He is drawn, his skin the grayfish yellow of a non-stop smoker. He wears a hospital gown. He stops eating his hot dog. He has one more on a plate.

> Buns are right under the counter. (beat) You want
> me to get you one?

Victor shakes his head.

> VICTOR
> (again, to the waitress)

Hello?

The waitress does not look up. Victor shifts, uncomfortable.

The man notices Victor's Yankee jacket.

> MAN
> You a fan or you just bought the jacket?

> VICTOR

Fan.

> MAN
> I bet you're a Thurman Munson man. Seventy-nine.
> Am I right?

Victor nods. He looks to the frozen waitress.

> Me too. (beat) Hey. Bud. Look.

The man takes his silverware and drops it on the floor. It clatters loudly. The waitress does not react.

> The invisible fucking man. That's me, baby. It's rubbing off. Just take one.

Victor stands, unsure. He watches the waitress intensely.

> Go on.

Victor tentatively crosses around the counter. The waitress does not look up.

Victor finds the buns. HE TONGS A HOT DOG and quickly crosses around to an adjacent booth. The man turns, grinning.

> Big as an ox but no one sees you. I got the same thing only I ain't big. I just talk a lot. And no one hears me. Then a funny thing happens. I start whispering. Suddenly, everyone hears me.

Victor takes a bite of the hot dog.

> You're not sick, are you?

Victor shakes his head.

> Your mother?

Victor nods.

> That's tough. That's the toughest one. Except for losing a kid. Watching a kid die. That is *it*. That's the toughest one.

#### VICTOR
Are you sick?

#### MAN
Oh. They say I'm getting better, but I don't buy green bananas any more. (beat) They just want me out of here.

Victor turns, noticing –

AT THE COUNTER – THE WAITRESS serves coffee to A DOCTOR. They chat.

The man grins.

> Munson's our type. 'Didn't need a plane crash to
> get my attention. But that's what he did, you know?
> He crashed that plane right on purpose – 'cause he
> got sick of it, losing all the limelight to Reggie.

The man turns away, sucking on his cigarette. His back to Victor.

> – Now Reggie gets fat – and Thurmon, he's the
> goddamn patron saint of baseball.

                                                    CUT TO:


INT. DOLLY'S HOSPITAL ROOM – NIGHT

Rubbing his face, VICTOR turns the corner into Dolly's room. Yellow curtains are drawn around Dolly's bed.

                         VICTOR
> Ma?

No response. Victor pulls open the curtains. The bed is empty. The mattress bare. New bedding sits at the foot. Victor backs away.

In the adjacent bed, THE PAIR OF WRINKLY FEET stick out from the sheets.

As Victor backs toward the door –

The ADJACENT PATIENT becomes visible. It is a VERY WRINKLY OLD WOMAN. She is watching a TV. She looks at Victor. She smiles sadly.

                                                    CUT TO:


INT. HOSPITAL LOBBY/CORRIDOR – NIGHT

Victor stands in the hallway, frozen. He approaches a counter.

The desk nurse is not there. *There is a noise:* down the hall, THE DESK NURSE WORKS WITH THE INTERN, moving some equipment into a room, dealing with an emergency.

On the other side of the counter sits DOLLY'S PINK SAMSONITE CASE and beside it, A SEALED PLASTIC BAG. *Inside:* DOLLY'S DENTURES, NAIL POLISH AND PERSONAL AFFECTS.

Victor stares, blank-faced.

CUT TO:

INT./EXT. VICTOR'S FORD – NIGHT (RAIN) – LATER

*Ffftzick. Ffftzick.*

The windshield wipers on Victor's Ford smear the sooty water to and fro. VICTOR drives, squinting against opposing headlights.

*On the car radio: call-in therapy.*

>              RADIO CALLER (MONTY)
>                   (off-screen)
> Uh. I have a question I've been thinking about. Uh –

>                   DR VISCOUNT
>                   (off-screen)
> Yes?

Victor stares out at the road, listening.

>                      MONTY
>                   (off-screen)
> Do you think . . . that people's lives have different
> like, shapes?

Victor stops at a red light.

>                   DR VISCOUNT
>                   (off-screen)
> Hmm. That's an interesting question, Monty. What
> exactly do you mean?

*Vavavavavava gug uga* . . . Victor's Ford gurgles loudly. Victor shifts it to neutral. The car immediately stalls out. He starts it up again and revs the engine. *vvvvVVVVRRRM!*

> MONTY
> (off-screen)
> Well, the way you talk sometimes – I mean, it seems
> like you think if people just do what you say, that
> everything is going to go great, everything's going to
> come up roses.

A CAR PULLS UP alongside. Inside, THREE GIDDY HIGH SCHOOL
GIRLS in satin dresses, each wearing a great deal of eye shadow.
Two of the girls look across at Victor.

Victor stares back.

The girls suddenly break out *laughing* hysterically, like hyenas.

> DR VISCOUNT
> (off-screen)
> Well, no, that's not entirely true, Monty. I just try to
> help people understand themselves better,
> understand the choices that they have. Do you have
> a car, Monty?

> MONTY
> (off-screen)
> Yeah.

The light turns green. The 'Homecoming' car roars ahead.
Victor presses on the gas and follows.

> DR VISCOUNT
> (off-screen)
> I try to help people get their personal cars tuned up,
> you know what I mean? Sometimes people neglect
> their personal cars and stop believing they can drive
> them where they want to go.

The 'Homecoming' car disappears around a bend.

> MONTY
> (off-screen)
> But. See, my point is, don't some people's lives,
> aren't some people . . . I mean don't some people

have a shape to their lives that isn't like, necessarily up, upward?

> DR VISCOUNT
> (off-screen)
> I guess you mean down. Is that what you mean, Monty? Do some people's lives go down?

Victor furrows thoughtfully.

> MONTY
> (off-screen)
> Kind of, yeah. I mean, in economics you'd call it a downward trend.

Victor's Ford struggles to mount a STEEP HILL. Victor gases it but it still labors. From behind A PICK-UP TRUCK FLASHES ITS BRIGHTS.

> DR VISCOUNT
> (off-screen)
> Is your life in a downward trend, Monty?

> MONTY
> (off-screen)
> I knew you'd do that.

> DR VISCOUNT
> (off-screen)
> Is it?

> MONTY
> (off-screen)
> Well . . . I definitely feel like the high points of my life are behind me.

> DR VISCOUNT
> (off-screen)
> What a terrible way to feel.

> MONTY
> (off-screen)
> It's not so bad. It's realistic. I mean, everybody can't be a somebody in the world and, uh, I think that

248

right there is the problem with the advice that you give. It's all pie in the sky. I mean, some cars are just lemons. I mean, on some cars a tune-up ain't gonna make no difference.

At the top of the hill, the pick-up pulls into the opposing lane and roars ahead.

*Honnnnnnnk! An oncoming car nearly hits the Pick-up.*

> DR VISCOUNT
> (off-screen)
> You're losing me, Monty. What do you want me to say to all this?

Victor pulls off the road, into the small parking lot in front of PETE AND DOLLY'S.

> Do you want me to say that you'll never do anything with your life? Fine. With the attitude you've got, Monty, you're not going anywhere. Is that what you wanted to hear?

> MONTY
> (off-screen)
> Yeah.

CLOSE ON – VICTOR intense, as he sits, looking at the lighted tavern. He shuts off the car. Rain is pouring down now. Over the windows. The mirrors. *Ka-boom*, thunder cracks.

> CUT TO:

INT. PETE AND DOLLY'S TAVERN – NIGHT

VICTOR stands in the door, rain falling down behind him. The tavern is busy, music plays from the jukebox. LEO sits at the bar, talking with ANOTHER MAN in work clothes.

CALLIE struggles to scribble down an ever-changing drink order from a group of MIDDLE-AGED MEN (ELKS CLUB) around the pool table.

DELORES moves through the swinging doors, sashaying, carrying a pitcher of beer toward TWO COUPLES at a booth.

249

No one notices Victor as he walks slowly to the back. *It is as if he is on a ride at Disneyland, everyone in the restaurant moving about obliviously, like audio animatronic dummies.*

CUT TO:

INT. PETE AND DOLLY'S – STOCKROOM – NIGHT

Sitting in the shadows, watching the activity through the stockroom door, VICTOR inhales the STASHED MOUNDS BAR. *Not enough . . .*

He reaches deep into a shelf producing a BOX OF CHOCOLATE COVERED DONUTS. He opens the box and bites into a donut voraciously, tears in his eyes –

CALLIE brings a round of beers to the MEN AT THE POOL TABLE. LEO crosses past the stockroom doorway, checking his fly. *No one has noticed Victor since he entered the tavern.*

CUT TO:

INT. PETE AND DOLLY'S TAVERN – KITCHEN – NIGHT

VICTOR pulls on an apron. He opens the oven door. He slaps his hand in the oven. He withdraws it quickly, burnt.

DELORES pokes her head through the slot. Her voice startling.

DELORES
Sorry. It's still on.

Victor crosses to the sink, running his hand under cold water.

What are you doing here? You okay?

Victor nods.

How's Dolly?

VICTOR
Fine.

Victor looks up, smiling weakly.

CUT TO:

INT. MODINO HOUSE – DAY

*A radio plays.* Water drips onto dishes piled in the sink.
NANNY knocks over a bag of dry dog food. She eats from the spill.

Farrah Fawcett stares down from her poster at –

VICTOR, lying face-up in bed. *Hisssssss:* the sound of hydraulic
brakes. Victor turns, peering out his bedside window.

Outside, A SCHOOLBUS comes to a stop, letting off *several kids.*
Among them, A PUDGY BOY who trails behind the rest. Alone.

                                                    CUT TO:

INT. PETE AND DOLLY'S TAVERN – KITCHEN – NIGHT

CALLIE converses with A HANDSOME GUY IN AN ATHLETIC
JACKET.

                          CALLIE
          I don't know. I just got sick of it – you know? The
          people there – not you –

                        COLLEGE GUY
          I hear ya. I hear ya.

VICTOR turns, pulling a pie from the oven, slicing it, his eyes
riveted through the slot.

          Greg was talking about you the other day.

                          CALLIE
          Greg Shuler?

                        COLLEGE GUY
          'Said he missed you.

                          CALLIE
          He did not.

                        COLLEGE GUY
          Yes, he did. We crashed this frat thing over at
          Bangers. It was crazy. And Greg was talking about
          some party that you two – that you two had a really
          good time.

                            251

CALLIE
What party? What did he say?

                COLLEGE GUY
He wasn't saying nothing bad, Callie. He was just
remembering some good times.

Victor pushes a pie out through the slot. Callie hands it to the
college guy.

                    CALLIE
Here you go, Joey. Say hi to everyone when you
head back up.

                COLLEGE GUY
I will, I will indeed.
                    (turning back)
Hey, Callie. What would happen if I called you this
weekend?

                    CALLIE
What do you mean?

                COLLEGE GUY
You want to go to Garfield's?

                    CALLIE
I'm working.

                COLLEGE GUY
After.

The College Guy grins, charming.

                    CALLIE
Oh. Uh. I don't know – *Sure.*

                COLLEGE GUY
Okay. I'll call you.

As the guy departs, Callie turns around, sighing.

VICTOR WATCHES HER.

                                        CUT TO:

INT. PETE AND DOLLY'S TAVERN – NIGHT – LATER

The restaurant is quiet except for the TV. DELORES and LEO sit at the bar, smoking cigarettes, staring at the television. CALLIE clears off tables. She looks glum. VICTOR sits at his booth, eating the last of a big salad. He sips his Tab, watching Callie.

> DELORES
> Hey, Mr Nutri-system!

Leo laughs.

> Get your butt over here and make me one of your specials.

Victor turns. Callie looks up.

> CUT TO:

INT. PETE AND DOLLY'S TAVERN – AT THE BAR – NIGHT

VICTOR mixes different liquors and flavorings. A symphony of colored liquids pouring over ice. Victor is adept with the shakers and has a confident air. He places two filled hi-ball glasses onto the bar. He stirs them.

DELORES takes hers, sipping it.

> DELORES
> Excellent.

LEO sips his hi-ball, nodding approval.

CALLIE sits down at the bar. She smiles, coy, looking at Victor.

> CALLIE
> How about one for me, bartender?

Victor hesitates.

> DELORES
> Make the girl a drink, Victor.

> LEO
> Go on, Vick. I'll bring you an extra celery stick tomorrow.

Everyone snickers. Victor smirks.

CUT TO:

VICTOR MIXES ANOTHER HI-BALL. He places it in front of Callie.

Callie sips it at first. Then suddenly, she lifts the glass and quaffs down the entire drink, chug-a-lug style.

Victor watches her, wide eyed. Delores and Leo chuckle.

> LEO
> I'm impressed, Callie. I'm very impressed.

Callie grins, wiping her chin.

CUT TO:


INT. MODINO HOUSE – KITCHEN/BEDROOM – MORNING

*Talk radio plays from the transistor radio on the windowsill.*
Dishes have piled up higher in the sink.

In his bathrobe, VICTOR measures two scoops of ULTRA SLIM FAST into a cup. He fills it with milk. He stirs it.

THE DOOR TO DOLLY'S BEDROOM is half open. Inside, WET CALLIE lies in Dolly's bed, the covers pulled up around her, her skin still as pale as moments after her 'rescue', her hair still stringy and moist with the lake.

*knock, knock, knock.* Someone at the door. *knock, knock, knock.*

CUT TO:


INT. MODINO HOUSE – AT THE DOOR – MORNING

*Victor opens the door upon –*

A UPS MAN walking away, to his truck, a package under his arm. A 'while you were out' Post-it note hangs on the door. VICTOR pulls it off. He looks up at the UPS man.

> VICTOR
> Hello.
> (louder)
> *Hello?*

The UPS man stops and turns around.

> UPS MAN
>
> Oh.

The UPS man hands Victor the package, a clip-board balanced on
top of it. He pulls a pen from his pocket, clicking it.

> Sign on twelve.

Victor signs the clipboard.

> I'm glad you were here. I hate keeping fruit on the
> truck.

Victor nods. The UPS man takes his clipboard and heads off
toward his truck.

> Take care.

Victor closes the door. He puts the package down on the table.
Beside it sits THE STOLEN PICTURE OF CALLIE, flour in her hair.

*Your box of Florida Sunshine!* The shipping label is addressed to
Dolly.

Victor opens the box. It is filled with a brightly colored assortment
of fruit: oranges, grapefruits, tangerines, lemons. And a mango.
Victor picks up the mango. It is wet and sticky.

> CUT TO:

INT. CONVENIENCE STORE – DAY

'Happy Valentine's Day!' proclaims a display.

Toting a basket, VICTOR shuffles down an aisle. He picks up a
bottle of ONE A DAY vitamins. He examines the bottle. There is
also ONE A DAY FOR WOMEN (PLUS IRON) on the shelf. He grabs
these (putting back the plain ones).

> DARLENE
> (off-screen)
> No. I'm not saying it was my *fault* – I'm not saying
> *that* – but there was two of us there.

At the counter, DARLENE, grim and self-absorbed, breaks a coin
roll. There is a phone propped on her shoulder.
> (on phone)
> You know. You're really starting to piss me off.
> 'He's an asshole, Darlene.' I mean – you're
> supposed to be *supportive.*

Victor, turns away. His eyes fall upon –

A BAG OF CANDY HEARTS. A CANISTER OF Ginseng Lift.

> Well, I am *happy*!

CUT TO:


INT. MODINO HOUSE – DAY

The door to Dolly's bedroom is closed and NANNY whimpers
as –

In the kitchen, VICTOR feverishly mixes AN ELIXIR. (A LOVE
POTION?) He grinds up the vitamins, and valentine hearts into a
fine powder. He mixes them in a blender with sweetened
condensed milk and brilliant orange mango flesh. He marks things
in his notebook. He flips to other pages for reference. He places a
paper doily on a small tarnished silver tray. Upon the tray, he
places a GLASS TUMBLER FILLED TO THE BRIM WITH THICK
ORANGE ELIXIR.

*rinnng. rinnng*: the telephone. Victor does not move. He stares at
the phone on the wall. *rinnng. rinnng.* Nothing. It stops.

CUT TO:


INT. PETE AND DOLLY'S TAVERN – LATE AFTERNOON

The restaurant is empty. VICTOR turns on the lights. He slides the
TRAY AND TUMBLER CONTAINING THE THICK ELIXIR into the
BAR FRIDGE. It is wrapped in Saran wrap.

DELORES comes in the front door. She hangs up her coat, crosses
and tucks her bag in the bar nook.

Victor shuts the refrigerator door.

Delores looks at the wrapped tumbler through the glass door.

> DELORES
>
> What's that?

> VICTOR
>
> Nothing.

Delores crosses toward the ladies room. She looks back once more. Victor watches her suspiciously.

> CUT TO:

INT. PETE AND DOLLY'S TAVERN – KITCHEN – LATE AFTERNOON

VICTOR MOVES THE TRAY AND TUMBLER into the KITCHEN REFRIGERATOR.

> DELORES
> (off-screen)
>
> Victor?

DELORES sticks her head in through the food slot.

Victor casually pushes the tumbler behind the bricks of cheese as he turns.

> How's Dolly?

> VICTOR
>
> Fine.

Victor crosses. He pats his hand in the mouth of the pizza oven. He lights a match, sticks it on a prod, and ignites the burners.

> DELORES
>
> Can you be more specific?

Victor turns stiffly.

> VICTOR
>
> They took the thing out of her neck.

Delores tilts her head.

                              DELORES
And that's the end of it? They got it all out or
whatever? She didn't sound very good when she
called.

                              VICTOR
They're running tests.

Victor shrugs and heads to the stockroom to grab a flour sack.

                              DELORES
I'm gonna need a lift tonight. My car's dead.

Knocking on the back door, THE GAS MAN enters the kitchen,
holding a blue slip of paper. HIS PROPANE TRUCK IDLES OUTSIDE.

                              GAS MAN
Hello.

Victor puts down the sack of flour, suddenly looking about for the
checkbook, opening drawers beside his mother's easy chair.

It's ninety-four even. (beat) How's Dolly doing?

                              VICTOR
She's fine.

Victor nods crossing into the tavern.

                                             CUT TO:


INT. PETE AND DOLLY'S TAVERN – AT THE BAR (CONTINUOUS)

VICTOR approaches DELORES at the bar. Her back is to him as she
pokes through the bar refrigerator (looking for the tumbler).

                              VICTOR
I need the checkbook.

Delores turns, startled. She smiles, guilty, shrugs.

                              DELORES
Hm? – we could give him cash.

The GAS MAN slaps the blue receipt down on the bar.

                              GAS MAN
        I'll get you next time.

Turning to leave, THE GAS MAN pauses. He holds the door open
for CALLIE, HER PURSE clutched under her arm.

                              CALLIE
        Sorry.

                              GAS MAN
        My pleasure.

                                                    CUT TO:


INT. PETE AND DOLLY'S TAVERN – NIGHT – LATER

VICTOR slides a STEAMING MEATBALL DINNER through the slot.

CALLIE takes it, glancing toward DELORES.

Delores rises from a table with FOUR MEN who share two pitchers
of beer. She is laughing. She crosses toward the register.

                              CALLIE
        I thought only pizzas came through here.

Victor shrugs, smiling. Callie grabs some napkins, silverware and a
Parmesan shaker – *thunk* – Callie glances stiffly at –

Delores, who rings through a check.

CALLIE'S PURSE has fallen to the floor.

                              DELORES
        Oops. Sorry.

                              CALLIE
        Let me get that out of your way.

Callie gathers her purse and passes it to Victor.

        Can you keep this back there for me?

                              VICTOR
        Sure. (beat) You know. I have something for you.

But Callie has moved off with the tray, oblivious.


                                259

Victor looks down to the purse. It is cracked open, in a jumble. Sticking up from inside, an over-the-counter home pregnancy test.

CUT TO:

INT. PETE AND DOLLY'S TAVERN – VICTOR'S BOOTH – NIGHT – LATER

VICTOR plays solitaire. CALLIE sits opposite him, watching. She tilts her head.

CALLIE

> The king.

Victor plays the king.

> Sorry. They don't call it solitaire for nothing, right? (beat) You must wonder about me – what I'm doing with my life. I know I'm a lousy waitress. I'm a lousy student. I'm a lousy girlfriend. I'm a mess.

VICTOR

> No you're not.

Callie shrugs. she stares down at Victor's cards. She speaks softly.

CALLIE

> Well. Thanks. The ten – *sorry*.

Callie sips Victor's coffee. Victor looks up.

> Oh God. Look at me. (I'm drinking your coffee.)

VICTOR

> You can have it.

Callie holds the sugar dispenser inverted, pouring a mound of white into the coffee cup.

Victor smiles urgently.

> – I could make you one of my specials.

CALLIE

> What? No, this is fine. So. How's your mom?

260

>                         VICTOR
> . . . Fine.

>                        CALLIE
> When are you going to see her next?

Victor is stiff. A pause.

>                         VICTOR
> Tomorrow . . . *maybe.*

>                        CALLIE
> Maybe I can come with you. (beat) Do you think
> she'd write me a letter of recommendation?

Victor looks up from his cards, concerned.

>                         VICTOR
> What do you need a letter for?

>                        CALLIE
> Well. I mean. I can't work here forever.

Victor takes this in, hurt. From over at the bar, DELORES watches
them.

> You can put the four over here.

Through the window – JEFF'S DUMPY MUSTANG idles in the lot,
its headlights spraying into the tavern. *Honk. Honnk.*

>                                              CUT TO:


INT. PETE AND DOLLY'S TAVERN – KITCHEN – NIGHT

VICTOR opens the kitchen refrigerator door. Behind bricks of
cheese, sits THE TRAY, EMPTY: a moist ring on the paper doily.
DELORES stands with the glass in her hand. She wipes her chin.

>                        DELORES
> Excellent.

There is a strange look in her eyes.

>                                              CUT TO:

INT./EXT. VICTOR'S FORD – NIGHT – LATER

VICTOR drives DELORES home. It is a bright moonlit night.

> DELORES
> Turn left here. Turn left.

Victor looks confused. He turns left.

> Relax, Victor.

Delores grins. Victor stiffens.

CUT TO:

INT./EXT. VICTOR'S FORD/AIRPORT ACCESS ROAD – NIGHT

Sitting in the front seat of Victor's Ford, VICTOR and DELORES.

*Vaaaarrroooooommm!* A gigantic transport plane passes right overhead with a thundering roar. You can clearly see each rivet on the underbelly of the aircraft. It feels like you could reach up and touch it. It is exhilarating.

Victor's eyes widen.

The fat plane screams off into the night sky.

Victor giggles, his eyes still riveted skyward.

Delores smiles, pleased with Victor's reaction. She leans forward, touching his arm.

> DELORES
> Great, huh?

Victor looks at his arm where Delores has touched him. He turns away toward the rising sound, looking to the sky again. Another plane approaches in the distance.

Delores sits there, staring at Victor. Feeling this, Victor turns back around to face Delores. Delores leans forward. She smiles softly. She raises her hand.

*Putta putta puttapputaa!* A small propeller plane crosses their windshield and touches down on the runway.

Rigid, Victor's eyes leave the plane to follow the slow gentle trajectory of Delores' hand as – she touches his cheek. She scrunches closer on the vinyl seat. She kisses his cheek. Victor receives the kiss, unmoving, tense. Suddenly, he reaches in his pocket, producing a roll of candy. He pops a little candy tablet into his mouth. Delores sits back.

DELORES
What's that?

Victor shows her the roll. Delores smiles. She moves closer. She strokes Victor's leg.

Can I have one?

Victor looks at Delores, his eyes wide and curious. He passes her a breath mint.

Delores takes his hand. She removes the breath mint from his palm and pops it into her mouth. She chews it up and swallows it. She pulls Victor's empty hand to her lips. She kisses Victor's hand, his fingers.

Victor just watches her, his eyes wide, sucking on his mint. Delores releases his hand. Victor is rigid. He blinks. He bites on his candy, chewing it up.

*VvvvvvvRRRRRRMMMMM!* Another plane flies overhead.

Delores leans closer. She smiles. She kisses Victor on the lips. Victor just receives. Delores begins to back away. Suddenly, Victor leans forward, perpetuating the kiss, very gently. For a moment he opens his eyes and sees – *Callie.*

Delores reaches her arms around Victor's neck, his head, pulling him to her, harder.

VICTOR PULLS BACK. He puts his hand to his face. Delores is hurt. She smiles sadly. She lights a cigarette.

Saving yourself for someone special?

The car sits there as a cargo plane screams overhead.

CUT TO:

INT. MODINO HOUSE – MORNING

*Talk radio squawks in the background.*

VICTOR lies face up in bed. He stares at –

Farrah Fawcett. She looks down at him.

*rinnng. rinnng. rinng.* – the telephone. Victor sits up. *rinnng. rinnng.*
He picks up the phone.

> VICTOR
> . . . Hello?

CUT TO:

INT. HOSPITAL LOBBY – DAY

VICTOR stands at a counter. He wears a tie and sport coat. The
sport coat could not possibly button around him and so each side
sticks out straight like fenders. It cinches him tightly in the
armpits. Under one arm are the PINK SAMSONITE CASE AND THE
PLASTIC BAG OF PERSONAL EFFECTS. He reads some papers on a
clipboard. He looks up, pointing at a spot on a form.

THE DESK NURSE looks up from her work.

> DESK NURSE
> Just don't put anything for now.

DR GRUBER stands in the hallway, watching Victor. He nods to
him, encouraging Victor to come talk to him. Victor obliges.
Gruber speaks urgently, quietly.

> GRUBER
> Look. I know this is a rough time to – but – if you
> need someone – *I don't usually do this* – but it was
> clearly – it was clearly negligent – they should have
> done the biopsy when it began. Months ago.
> Anyway. Your lawyer can call me. You have a
> definite case.

Victor looks blank-faced. Over Gruber's shoulder, THE GRAY-
SKINNED MAN – now in a suit – moves to an elevator, led by
several POLICEMEN. The Gray Man nods respectfully to Victor.

264

CUT TO:

INT./EXT. VICTOR'S FORD – DAY

VICTOR drives. He loosens his tie. He slows down the Ford as he drives by the CULINARY INSTITUTE. Suddenly, he pulls over on the shoulder of the road. He backs the car up. He turns into a winding service road which spills into the campus parking lot.

CUT TO:

INT. CULINARY INSTITUTE – DAY

VICTOR stands silently in the lobby looking at mounted publicity pictures of the institute. A GROUP IS FORMING on the other side of the lobby. A GUIDE ARRIVES, taking charge.

> GUIDE
> – And how many here are potential students?

A PAIR OF TEENAGERS raise their hands, each accompanied by PARENTS. Victor shuffles over toward the tour group, infiltrating unnoticed.

CUT TO:

INT. CULINARY INSTITUTE – TOUR – DAY

*The Tour Group are shown the facilities by the Guide:*

VICTOR separates from the group, the guide oblivious, prattling on with her well-rehearsed patter. Victor wanders *unnoticed* through large cooking rooms, students at work in them. Long shelves contain hundreds of spices and flavorings. In another room they bake pasteries, cakes, breads. In a room at the end of the hall, there is music playing.

Victor peers in the doorway –

A YOUNG MAN in a coat IS CARVING AN ICE SCULPTURE with an electric hedge trimmer. A big service door is open, cold air blowing in. THE ICE SCULPTURE is a dazzling rendering of a GIANT SWAN, its head raised high in the air.

Victor stares. He steps farther inside the room. He is in awe. The ice carver turns off the trimmer. He pulls out a chisel and hammer. *Tap tap, tappa.* He turns.

Victor is gone.

CUT TO:

INT./EXT. VICTOR'S FORD/PETE AND DOLLY'S TAVERN – NIGHT

Pulling into the lot. Through the windshield, VICTOR notices –

CALLIE stands, speaking into the corner pay phone. Victor steps out of his car.

*A plane roars overhead.* It screeches loudly, it is low, obviously pulling in for a landing. Victor moves toward the tavern. But he walks slowly, straining to listen to . . . *Callie's voice.* He glances toward the pay phone.

> CALLIE
> No. But – Jeff. I can't. *Because.* I can't just quit on her. She's in the hospital.

Callie's eyes are wet. Hunched, she twists her hair on her finger.

> Well that's what I – *right*. What I promised.
> (she sobs)
> Jeff. Please don't. Please? 'Cause I can't deal with all this. I'm gonna freak out. I told you (he's) from school. I don't know. *No*. Just dancing.

CUT TO:

INT. PETE AND DOLLY'S TAVERN – NIGHT

VICTOR enters.

DELORES kneels before a pile of broken beer bottles. She looks up at Victor. (*This is the first time they have seen each other since they 'parked' last night.*)

> DELORES
> I told her she was gonna drop them. I told her to make two trips.

266

LEO and a FRIEND (SONNY) sit at the bar.

> LEO

Hey, Vick.

Victor nods and heads into the kitchen.

> CUT TO:

INT. PETE AND DOLLY'S KITCHEN – NIGHT

VICTOR reads an order slip and begins to make a pizza.

*Through the food slot – past* DELORES *– Victor can see –*

CALLIE re-enters the building. She wipes her eyes on her sleeve. She shuffles across the tavern and through the swinging doors entering the kitchen. She flops down in Dolly's easy chair. Suddenly, Callie begins to cry again.

Victor stands there, awkward. He picks up a box of Kleenex on the counter. He approaches Callie. He stands behind the chair. Her hair glistens with the soft light. A tear runs down her cheek. It drops, falling on her breastbone. Tender, Victor touches Callie's hair, her cheek. She does not respond. (Is she even aware?)

Suddenly, Callie takes a tissue from the box in Victor's hand. Callie blows her nose. She looks up at Victor with red teary eyes. She takes Victor's hand in hers, holding it tight to her chest as she cries through another wave of tears. Victor pats her head, her soft silky hair. Callie regains composure. She releases Victor's hand.

> CALLIE
> (nodding toward the front of the restaurant)
> What did she tell you?

> VICTOR

Nothing.

Callie sighs.

> CALLIE
> I'm gone, I'm out of here.

267

Victor takes this in, devastated. Callie glances up at Victor. She crumples the tissue in her hands. She sighs.

– I'll wait till she's back from the hospital, okay?

Victor is dull-eyed.

Okay?

Victor nods.

Delores leans in through the slot. She sticks another order slip on the spring holder, smiles, and moves off.

Callie glares.

She's a fucking witch.

CUT TO:

INT. PETE AND DOLLY'S TAVERN – NIGHT – LATER

As VICTOR crosses from the refrigerator, he sees –

CALLIE stands in the front doorway of the tavern, facing JEFF. Jeff stands outside. They squabble in hushed tones.

> CALLIE
> Jeff, I can't talk now.

> JEFF
> The fuckin' place is empty, Callie. What? Who is this guy? Tell me.

DELORES listens in as she moves dishes to the bar sink.

Callie glances over her shoulder, briefly meeting Delores' stare. Her eyes are welling with tears again.

> CALLIE
> Jeff . . . *please*. I can't talk now.

> JEFF
> Whatever.

Jeff walks off, leaving Callie standing in the doorway.

                              CALLIE
    Jeff!

Jeff slams the door to his Mustang and – *screeeeech* – roars out of
the parking lot.

Delores passes by Callie, clearing off another table.

                              DELORES
    Lovers' spat?

                              CALLIE
    Fuck you.

Delores drops more dishes in the sink. She holds a fistful of
silverware.

                              DELORES
    Excuse me?

Callie thinks a moment – then, bluntly.

                              CALLIE
    Fuck. You.

Callie moves quickly toward the kitchen door but – Delores
lurches forward, throwing down the silverware, blocking her way.

                              DELORES
    Little cock tease . . . you have a big –

                              CALLIE
    Get out of my way!

Victor stands to the other side of the kitchen door, his eyes wide.
He watches, paralyzed.

                              DELORES
    – You have a very big mouth.

                              CALLIE
    Well, I guess I do then, don't I?

LEO stands up.

                           LEO
        Hey, hey. Girls. Please!

Callie pivots, crossing to the ladies' room.

                          CALLIE
        'dried up bitch.

Callie disappears into the bathroom. Delores is livid, red-faced.
She struts past Leo to her purse.

At the bar, Leo looks at SONNY. Sonny looks to –

Victor, who emerges from the kitchen. He says nothing.

                                                   CUT TO:


INT. PETE AND DOLLY'S TAVERN – STOCKROOM – NIGHT

DELORES sits in the dark stockroom, smoking. She plays with the
'Help Wanted' sign (from Scene I). VICTOR stands in the
doorway.

                          DELORES
        She's not ready for this world. Ma and Pa must treat
        her like a goddamn little princess.

Victor approaches the window, looking out. Delores touches him.
Victor pulls away.

        Whoa.

                          VICTOR
        Can't you be nicer to her?

                          DELORES
        Nice? Did you hear what she said to me?

                          VICTOR
        You don't have to be nice. Just nicer.

                          DELORES
        Or what, Victor?

                          VICTOR
        I'll fire you.


                           270

Delores is stunned. Victor storms off.

> **DELORES**
> Last I heard, your mother still ran this place.

CUT TO:

EXT. PETE AND DOLLY'S TAVERN – NIGHT – LATER

Out on the corner, CALLIE stands by the pay phone, waiting.

VICTOR stares at her as he crosses toward his car.

LEO and SONNY are leaning on Victor's Ford. Leo is shit-faced. He slurs his words.

> **LEO**
> Don't you think – I don't know – I think – you know
> – it wasn't very polite, Vick.

Leo is drunk enough to be scary. Victor nods, stiff.

> I guess . . . you know . . .
> (nodding toward Callie over at the payphone)
> someone should talk to that girl . . . Del don't need
> that shit, you know? I mean she said some nasty
> things.

Victor nods again, sheepishly. He says nothing as he shuffles back against the side of his Ford. Sonny snorts, laughing.

> Someone should talk to the girl . . . But what does
> he do, Sonny? He goes, he goes to Del – she's
> innocent for Christ's sake – worked in this dump for
> fifteen years – innocent as driven snow – and he tells
> her –

Victor shakes his head.

> Oh, you didn't.

LEO SLAPS VICTOR'S FACE WITH THE BACK OF HIS HAND. Sonny sneers.

> Oh. I'm glad you didn't. 'Cause I – then I would
> have to fuck you up.

**FROM OVER BY THE PAY PHONE – CALLIE WATCHES AS –**

Victor tries to pull Leo's hand from his jacket.
> (in Victor's face)
> Delores is a real fine lady friend of mine, Victor.
> And I . . . I –

Victor breaks away, walking quickly around his car.

> I'm not done talking to . . . Hey. Come back here,
> fat boy! Hey!

Leo follows. He lunges, taking a swing at the back of Victor's head. *Whap*. Victor turns receiving a second slap to the face. *Slap*. Victor just looks glumly at Leo. For a moment, there is a twinge of fear in Leo's eyes. Victor climbs into his car. Sonny sneers.

> Just cause your mummy is sick don't mean you can
> treat people like shit, you fat fuck.

Victor rolls up his window. Victor sits there.

Leo and Sonny climb into a van –
**HUDSON PHOTO FINISHING** *it says on the side* – and peel out.

*tap tap.*

**CALLIE PEERS IN VICTOR'S PASSENGER SIDE WINDOW.**

> **CALLIE**
> Can you give me a ride home?

> CUT TO:

**INT./EXT. VICTOR'S FORD – NIGHT**

**VICTOR** drives. **CALLIE** sits, her head leaning against the glass. She reaches in her purse, producing a little squeeze bottle. She squirts some liquid into her mouth. Victor watches her.

> **CALLIE**
> Southern Comfort. You want some?

Victor shakes his head, no.

> Did you go to the hospital today?

Victor shakes his head again.

> Are you going to the hospital tomorrow?

VICTOR
> Maybe. Very early.

CALLIE
> Would you take me? Can I go with you?

Victor is hesitant.

> Please? I need to talk with Dolly. A lot of things are
> happening.

Callie smiles hopefully . . . sadly. Victor shrugs. Callie swallows
more Southern Comfort.

> My dad says that if I was a car, I'd have five gears in
> reverse.

Victor smiles back weakly. He looks out to the road, making a left
turn.

CUT TO:

INT./EXT. VICTOR'S FORD/AIRPORT ACCESS ROAD – NIGHT

Victor pulls his Ford up alongside the airport runway. Callie lifts
her head. She looks around.

CALLIE
> Why'd you stop?

Victor points skyward.

*WHHHHHOOOOOMMMMMM!* A big plane slides overhead.

> Holy shit! That's amazing.

Victor smiles. He pulls out his breath mints, popping one. He
offers one to Callie. She takes it from his hand.

> Thanks.

Victor sits there. Callie looks at him. She chews her breath mint,
her eyes drifting back to the sky. Victor chews his breath mint.

*Wrummmmmmmmmm!* Another plane. A big fat one.

Wow.

The plane rumbles off into the sky. Callie smiles, big and broad, the dark clouds suddenly lifted.

You're a real cool person, you know that? Cooler than someone would think.

Victor stares at Callie lovingly. Her skin glows with the blinking lights of the airport perimeter. Crickets sing. Victor turns away.

Just more of you to love, right?

Victor leans, cautiously reaching out his thick hand, timidly moving toward Callie's soft radiant cheek.

As the plane disappears, Callie turns, meeting Victor's big moist eyes. He looks handsome in the blue light. Victor's fingers make contact with her cheek and, trembling, move gently, pushing a lock of hair back, over Callie's ear.

Callie smiles a small sad nervous smile, her rigidity melting with her sense of Victor's tenderness. She moves her fingers, cautiously gesturing bashful Victor closer.

Hesitant, Victor leans halfway, *the vinyl seat scrunching.* Callie turns. She leans halfway, *the vinyl seat scrunching.* She gently kisses Victor's cheek.

Victor awkwardly kisses Callie's cheek, closing his eyes. He holds the tender kiss against her sweet skin. Suddenly, Callie turns to face Victor, her face only an inch from his.

What am I doing with my life? I don't know anything any more.

Callie puts her hand to Victor's cheek.

Tears drop from Victor's eyes onto Callie's fingers.

*A plane roars overhead.*

For a moment, their lips inches apart, it appears they might kiss.

There is a pause, the possibility hanging in the air. Suddenly, Callie breaks, looking out the windshield as –

A ROARING JUMBO JET descends from above, touching down.

Victor blinks. His eyes misty and wide, his cheeks wet.
*The vinyl scrunches* as Callie leans back against the door.

>We should go home now. We gotta get up early.

Victor nods, hesitant.

CUT TO:

INT. MODINO HOUSE – BATHROOM – MORNING

Victor stands on the bathroom scale. THE NUMBERS SETTLE AT – TWO HUNDRED NINETY NINE pounds.

VICTOR looks in the mirror. He cocks his head, staring at himself. He flexes a muscle in his thick arm. It is big. He flexes both muscles up over his head, Charles Atlas-style. He smiles, suave.

CUT TO:

EXT. ALONG THE WATER – LATE MORNING

In his sweats, VICTOR walks NANNY. A TATTERED BASEBALL sits on the edge of the road. Victor picks it up. He waves it before Nanny, trying to interest her in fetching it.

VICTOR
Nanny.

Nanny watches tepidly. Disinterested. Victor tosses the ball away. The ball lands on the rushing river, floating away.

Suddenly, Nanny awakens from her stupor. She tugs at her leash, looking back at the ball out on the frozen lake. Victor pulls her along, but she continues to resist, looking out at the ball.

CUT TO:

INT. MODINO HOUSE – LATE MORNING

Lights sprays in through the windows. The house is a mess. Dishes rise high out of the sink. *Talk radio plays.*

The box of Florida citrus fruit lies open on the table, some of it rotting. Beside it, Dolly's breakfast sits on the table, still unmoved, untouched from the day she fell ill.

In his bathrobe, VICTOR stands at the kitchen counter, mixing a Slim Fast shake. He sits down at the table, sipping his shake. He looks across to –

WET CALLIE wears Dolly's robe and slippers. She crosses from the bathroom and sits. She nibbles weakly at a steaming breakfast plate of eggs and toast. Victor watches the apparition intently.

Wet Callie looks up, meeting Victor's stare. She reaches slowly across the table, taking Victor's hand.

Suddenly: *knock, knock, knock, knock*. Someone at the door.

Victor peers out the window. It is CALLIE (real, dry Callie). She stands at the door, holding a box in her hand.

                                                            CUT TO:

INT./EXT. MODINO HOUSE – LATE MORNING

VICTOR opens the door onto CALLIE. She smiles, tilting her head. She holds a box of candy.

                          CALLIE
        Good morning.

                          VICTOR
        Good morning.

Victor steps backward, checking his ratty bathrobe. Callie steps inside. She looks about at the messy house.

                          CALLIE
        I got your mom some candy. You said early, so I –
        you want me to come back in an hour or something?

Victor shakes his head. Nanny barks frantically from inside.

                                                            CUT TO:

INT. MODINO HOUSE – LATE MORNING

VICTOR dresses, watching through a crack in his door as –

CALLIE waits, awkwardly looking about the messy house.

SUDDENLY, VICTOR NOTICES –

THE STOLEN PICTURE OF CALLIE SITTING ON THE KITCHEN TABLE. Victor steps into the room. HE PALMS THE PICTURE AS –

CALLIE APPROACHES HIM, HOLDING OUT THE BOX OF CANDY.

CALLIE

> Do you think she'd like these?

VICTOR TAKES THE BOX IN HIS ONE FREE HAND, HIS OTHER HAND, THE ONE WITH THE PICTURE IN IT, DANGLING AT HIS SIDE.

> Open it up.

VICTOR DROPS THE PICTURE TO THE FLOOR. He opens the box. Chocolate-covered cherries.

> Where'd you get this?

Callie kneels, picking up the picture of herself.

VICTOR

> Cleaning up. I found it behind the booth. I was
> gonna show it to Ma.

Callie examines the picture. She shrugs, puts it face up in the box of chocolates, and replaces the cover.

CUT TO:


EXT. MODINO HOUSE – DAY

NANNY is tied to a pulley-chain. She watches, whining and pulling as –

VICTOR'S FORD backs out of the drive.

CUT TO:

INT./EXT. VICTOR'S FORD – DRIVING – DAY

A crisp spring day on the parkway. VICTOR looks at CALLIE.
She rolls her window down halfway. Her hair blows.

> CALLIE
> Did you get picked on in school?

Victor shrugs. Callie smiles gently.

> I did. On a field trip, this pom-pom girl stuck me
> with a pencil – in my chest. I still have a blue dot –
> see?

Callie pulls her collar down a bit, pointing to her chest.
Victor nods, bashful.

> VICTOR
> Nobody did anything to me. Except this one guy –
> would kick me.

> CALLIE
> In the balls?

Victor nods, grinning at Callie's bluntness.

> Ouch. (beat) Have you always been . . . heavy,
> heavy set?

Victor shrugs, nods. Callie smiles at Victor. Victor relaxes.
Callie turns on the car radio: *of course, a talk show plays.*

> You mind if I change the – ?

Victor shakes his head.

Callie turns the radio dial, tuning in an FM rock station. Music
plays as they drive. Callie smiles at Victor again. Bigger. Victor
smiles back. He presses a little harder on the gas. Callie's hair
blows harder. She pins it back, her head moving to the music.
She mouths the words of the song.

> You like this song? I love these guys. They're real,
> you know? They're not just pretty-boys.

Victor nods. He taps his thumb against the wheel.

INT./EXT. VICTOR'S FORD – DRIVING – DAY

*Obnoxious FM radio ads play.* Tense, VICTOR turns the Ford onto a narrow road. A steady parade of gravestones moves past CALLIE's window. Victor drives slowly. He glances at Callie, stiff. Callie notices the rows and rows of markers.

> CALLIE
> Where is this place, in the middle of a cemetery?

Callie snaps off the radio.

> Pretty morbid.

Victor pulls the Ford into a small parking area. He glances at Callie, smiling uneasily, then climbs out. Callie sits there a moment. She looks about, confused.

Victor walks off, heading along a path that leads into the cemetery.

Callie gets out of the car. She stands at the door, hesitant. There are grave markers everywhere, on all sides, as far as the eye can see. They are parked at the center of a great cemetery. Callie's confused expression becomes a pale look of horror.

> *Oh, my God.* Oh, my God.

Callie starts walking, following Victor along the winding path, the box of candy in her hands.

CUT TO:

EXT. GRAVEYARD – DAY

CALLIE comes upon a FRESH GRAVE SITE. VICTOR lays a flower on the BROWN MOUND of dirt. There is no stone, just a yellow plastic flag that reads – *D. Modino.*

> CALLIE
> Jesus Christ, Victor.

Victor turns. Callie is terribly shaken, unsteady.

> Dolly's dead.

Victor nods. Callie stands there, motionless. She is overwhelmed, in tears.

　　　　Your mother is dead.

Victor nods again calmly. He smiles at Callie. It is a strange, sad, guilty smile.

　　　　When did it happen?

Victor says nothing.

　　　　Victor? When did she – when did this – ?

Victor stares down at the mound of earth.

　　　　Victor!

Victor looks up, visibly frightened by her tone.

　　　　　　　　　VICTOR
　　　　Two weeks ago.

Callie stares, mystified, shaken.

　　　　　　　　　CALLIE
　　　　You say anything?

Victor shrugs.

　　　　You didn't tell anybody?

Victor says nothing.

　　　　　　　　　CALLIE
　　　　Victor!

　　　　　　　　　VICTOR
　　　　No.

　　　　　　　　　CALLIE
　　　　Why?

　　　　　　　　　VICTOR
　　　　I don't know.

Callie looks down to the gift box of candy in her hands. Victor smiles at her sadly.

Callie looks up, her eyes dripping with tears. Flushed, Callie turns and starts running back toward the car.

> I didn't want anything to change.

CUT TO:

INT./EXT. VICTOR'S FORD – DRIVING BACK – DAY

Silent. Sullen. CALLIE stares out the window at the passing scenery. She holds her hand at the side of her face like a partition between her and VICTOR.

Victor is rigid as he drives. He turns, glancing at Callie. Callie feels his eyes. She does not look up.

Victor turns on the radio. *Rock music plays.*

Callie re-adjusts herself in the front seat. She reaches over and snaps the radio off.

CUT TO:

INT. PETE AND DOLLY'S TAVERN – LATER – TWILIGHT

LEO stands on a stool. He has the Molson's clock off the wall, its opened up.

A PIZZA CUSTOMER puts some money down and heads to the door with his pie. DELORES rings it through.

VICTOR emerges from the kitchen, stiff, his apron on. Delores puts out her cigarette.

> LEO
> Where's Callie?

> DELORES
> It's getting pretty late. You want me to call her.

Victor shakes his head; no.

> LEO
> Hey, Victor. Look what I did.

Leo hangs the clock back up on the wall. It reads 7:35. Same as the Genesee clock.

CUT TO:

INT. PETE AND DOLLY'S TAVERN – NIGHT – LATER

In his booth, VICTOR plays a game of solitaire. He sips at his diet soda.

*The phone rings.* DELORES picks it up.

> DELORES
> Pete & Dolly's. No – we don't deliver – so call
> Dominoes then. Bye.

Delores hangs up. Victor stands. He picks up some trash from a table, looking out through the glass hopefully.

> Maybe this is her way of quitting. She didn't get her
> money. Not that it's any of my business.

Victor nods. He trudges to the back of the restaurant.

CUT TO:

INT. PETE AND DOLLY'S TAVERN – KITCHEN – NIGHT
(CONTINUOUS)

VICTOR pulls a rubber bin filled with grated cheese and a tub of sauce from the refrigerator.

DELORES sticks her head through the order window.

> DELORES
> What's going on?

> VICTOR
> I'm hungry.

Smoking a cigarette, LEO saunters into the kitchen, grabs a handful of cheese from the bin and flops down into DOLLY'S EASY CHAIR. He eats the cheese.

> LEO
> How's life in the old Listerine Factory?

Victor looks over at Leo. Leo is slumped in the easy chair his feet up, his mouth full of cheese.

> What is this look I'm getting? I'm sorry, I'm sorry.
> Here's a dollar.

He slaps a dollar bill down on the cutting board.

*rinnnng. rinnnng.* Out in the restaurant, the phone rings. Delores enters the kitchen.

> DELORES
> Leo, get out of the kitchen. Go answer the phone if
> you feel so goddamned at home.

Leo does not move. He sits there. The phone stops ringing. Delores turns back to Victor.

> So?

> VICTOR
> What?

> DELORES
> What's happening at the hospital? What happening
> with all the tests?

Victor says nothing as he continues making a pizza

The phone starts to ring again. Victor glances at Leo.

> **LEO**
> Ahh, Christ.

Leo stands up, sighs, and walks out of the kitchen.

Delores walks toward Victor. Victor stiffens.

> **DELORES**
> Let him finish his drink, Victor. I need him to drive
> me home. Unless you're gonna. Now, they say it's
> the transmission.

*Looking through the food slot* – Leo answers the phone.

> **LEO**
> (off-screen)
> Pete & Dolly's. Yeah. Can I? . . . Uh huh . . .

Victor turns to Delores.

> **VICTOR**
> It's okay. Go home. Feed your bird. Go to the
> airport with Leo and watch the planes.

Delores grabs Victor's cheek. Hard.

> **DELORES**
> Honey, I don't ever want to do that with him.

*Through the food slot* – Leo hunches over, looking very serious. Still
on the phone, he speaks very softly, almost inaudibly.

> **LEO**
> Two weeks ago? No. It's just that – we – I didn't – I
> mean, I knew but –

Leo glances at Victor. Victor tenses. He turns away, throwing his
pizza into the oven. Unsuspecting, Delores crosses to the far end
of the kitchen, putting the bin of cheese back in the refrigerator.

CUT TO:

INT. PETE AND DOLLY'S TAVERN – NIGHT

The Genesee Cream Ale clock reads 12:05.
The Molson's clock reads 12.05.

At the bar, VICTOR cuts his fresh steaming pie into a grid. He watches the news on the TV. LEO sits down beside him.

> LEO
> (quietly)
> That was Freddie Hubbard. He said he heard that –
> uh – that Dolly . . .

Victor looks up.

> – from his sister-in-law. She's a nurse over at Mid-
> Hudson.

Victor says nothing. Leo smiles a devious crease of a smile. Maybe it's compassion. He gets up, pulling on his hunting jacket.

> Someone's gotta tell Delores.

DELORES emerges from the ladies' room. She pulls on her coat. She snaps off all the lights except the one over the bar.

> What is this – some insurance thing?

Victor says nothing.

> DELORES
> What are you two talking about?

> LEO
> Nothing, Del. Man-talk.

Victor sips at his soda.

> DELORES
> See you tomorrow.

Victor nods. He watches Leo and Delores trudge to Leo's car.

On TV, a Nutri-system weight-loss commercial. He snaps it off. *Suddenly, there are raised voices.* Victor turns.

Through the glass – out in the parking lot, Delores stands, her arms dully at her sides as Leo gesticulates. He struggles to explain something, his voice blurred by the glass and the distance. Suddenly, Delores bolts toward the tavern –

Victor – !

– but Leo grabs onto her coat. She squirms, turning, but Leo takes her tightly by the arm. They tussle, Delores' eyes returning to Victor in the tavern.

The remaining bar light *browns out.* Victor is suddenly shrouded in darkness, lit only vaguely by the pink beer neons. He watches as –

Delores falls still. She turns to Leo, slumped. He gently leads her to his car. He picks up her hat. They drive off.

Victor turns. Sitting there in the pinkish darkness, he begins to eat his pizza. He starts slow – but soon the pace snowballs until he is eating voraciously. He sees himself in the bar mirror, his cheeks filled with pizza He begins to weep. He cries and cries, like a dam has broken.

Suddenly he stands. Running his thick arm across the length of the bar, he pushes everything; bottles, glass, dispensers, to the floor. He kneels behind the bar, beneath the food slot, weeping.

CUT TO:

INT. PETE AND DOLLY'S TAVERN – NIGHT – LATER

*knock, knock, knock.*

There is someone at the front door of the restaurant. It is JEFF. He is standing in the open doorway, lit from behind by the street lamp outside. CALLIE stands behind him.

Jeff steps inside. Callie timidly calls from the doorway.

> CALLIE
> Victor?

> JEFF
> Hello?

Callie steps inside tentatively. Jeff moves past her.

> CALLIE

Victor!

It is dead quiet in the dark restaurant. Jeff walks farther into the restaurant. He notices THE BROKEN GLASS ON THE FLOOR.

> Jeff . . . maybe we should call the police or something.

Stepping over the glass, Callie walks past him – around the bar – toward the place where Victor had collapsed behind the bar.

Jeff turns. He notices –

IN THE SHADOWS, SOMEONE SITS IN THE BOOTH IN THE CORNER.

> JEFF

Callie. (beat) Callie!

Callie's turns. Her face falls, ashen.

> CALLIE

Oh, my God.

Jeff snaps on the television.

VICTOR – AT HIS BOOTH – IS FROZEN IN THE THROBBING LIGHT OF THE TV SCREEN. His eyes are red and wet. He wipes them with his sleeve.

> Victor.

An uncomfortable pause. Callie covers her mouth. She steps toward Victor.

> Victor. Um. I don't –

> JEFF

She's quitting and she wants her pay.

> CALLIE

Jeff.

> JEFF

She's been putting up with all this bullshit and she's had enough.

CALLIE

Jeff! Why don't you just go outside?

Jeff nods. He obediently crosses to the door.

CUT TO:

INT. PETE AND DOLLY'S – AT THE REGISTER – NIGHT (CONTINUOUS)

VICTOR turns from the register, counting cash.
CALLIE stands at the bar.

Outside, Jeff is visible, smoking, through the door.

CALLIE

I'm sorry about your mother. I'm sorry I – got so angry.

Victor holds out several twenty-dollar bills to Callie. Callie struggles to say something.

– It was nice and all for you guys to hire me, but I don't think you really need the help.

Victor nods.

Victor. You're a very special person but – I never meant to –

*bang, bang, bang.* JEFF knocks at the door, impatiently.

I have to go, now.

Victor nods, his eyes filling again with tears.

Callie crosses to the door. She stops at the sound of Victor's voice.

VICTOR

Uh. Maybe you could come by – once in a while.

CALLIE

Yeah. Sure. I'm thinking about going back to school for a while.

Victor nods.

Bye.

Victor looks up at her.

VICTOR

Goodbye.

The door closes slow behind her. Victor looks about the dark restaurant.

*Through the glass* – Callie and Jeff climb into his MUSTANG. The car rumbles away into the darkness.

CUT TO:

INT. MODINO HOUSE – DAWN

*Talk radio plays.*

The dull dark haze of dawn spreads across the sky outside Victor's bedroom window. His bed sheets thrown back. In his robe, VICTOR dumps some meal into NANNY'S BOWL. Suddenly, Victor scrunches his brow, looking about. He snaps off the transistor radio.

VICTOR

Nanny?

AN EMPTY WICKER DOG BED. The dog is not in his mother's bedroom.

CUT TO:

EXT. MODINO HOUSE – DAWN

Holding his bathrobe closed, VICTOR shuffles out of the house. Nanny's chain hangs, the collar empty. Victor looks about, panicked.

CUT TO:

EXT. ALONG THE WATER – DAWN

Dim yellow lights through the purplish trees. VICTOR's slippers scuff scuff along the shoulder of the road. His breath condenses with the icy air. He stops at the place he found the tattered baseball. He looks out toward –

291

THE FROZEN RIVER. There are patches of broken ice leading out into the center where a large spot has broken through.

Victor stares. *A distant whimper.*

NANNY PADDLES FURIOUSLY IN A HOLE SHATTERED IN THE ICE, TRYING TO STAY ABOVE WATER. The ball floats beside her.

VICTOR STEPS ONTO THE EDGE OF THE ICE. Water seeps. He presses down his slippered foot, expecting the thin ice to break through. *But it does not.* He takes another step, his full weight on the ice. It snaps and pops but continues to hold.

VICTOR SLOWLY SHUFFLES ACROSS THE SNAPPING ICE. It is miraculous that this big man does not break through – and Victor knows it. Approaching the hole, he kneels down, and lies out on his belly. HE REACHES OUT TO NANNY, PULLING HER INTO HIS BIG ARMS.

CHILDREN GATHER AT THE SIDE OF THE ROAD, MEETING A SCHOOL BUS. One of the children, THE PUDGY BOY, stares out at Victor.

Victor stands, holding Nanny, pulling at his robe, making his way back. He feels the pudgy boy's gaze.

Suddenly – VICTOR FALLS THROUGH THE ICE. Up to his waist in the icy water, he gasps. HE STRIDES TO THE EDGE OF THE ICE, THE DOG CLINGING TO HIM.

CUT TO:

INT. MODINO HOUSE – MORNING

NANNY lies on her belly, beside her bowl, watching as –

CUT TO:

INT. MODINO HOUSE – MORNING

NANNY (WET) is wrapped in a swaddle of towels. She lies on her belly, beside her bowl, chewing on the tattered baseball. She watches as –

A water puddle spreads from beneath a chair. *drip drop.* Shivering, VICTOR SITS AT THE TABLE IN HIS DRIPPING ROBE.

On the table – THE REMAINS OF DOLLY'S BREAKFAST: FRIED UP EGGS. THE JUICE HAS SEPARATED INTO WATER AND PULP. Victor picks up a piece of toast. There is a single bite taken out of the side. Victor examines it closely. IT IS A CLEAN BITE, EACH TOOTH HAVING CUT AWAY A SMALL ARC, AND EACH TOOTH WITH THE NEXT AND THE NEXT HAVING TOGETHER TAKEN THAT SAME SHAPE, A PERFECT CRESCENT, FROM THE BREAD.

Nanny sits in the water puddle at Victor's feet. She licks his hand. Victor pulls his hand away. The dog looks up at Victor, its head cocked. Victor strokes the creature's wet fur. The dog licks his fingers. Victor smiles gently.

For the first time, this house is quiet; unhaunted by the squawking of the radio or television. *Birds are singing.*

Victor stands. He picks up his mother's OLD BREAKFAST PLATE AND SCRAPES IT OFF INTO THE GARBAGE. He carries the plate and glass to the sink. He turns on the faucet.

CUT TO:

INT. DELORES' APARTMENT – MORNING

We are looking through a doorway into the bedroom. Morning light seeps through the drawn blinds. In a tank top and boxers, LEO is slumped in the bed, asleep.

PAN TO – the living room. Max the PARAKEET sits in his cage. DELORES sits on her lazy boy recliner, in front of the TV. The home shopping network plays. Delores wears her velour wraparound. Her eyes red, she looks like she's been crying. She takes a drag on her cigarette and looks upward as –

*vvvvvrrrrmmmmmm!* – a plane roars overhead.

CUT TO:

INT. WELLES HOUSE – CALLIE'S BEDROOM – MORNING

A worn-out Raggedy Ann sits atop a bedroom dresser. Pictures of Jeff are taped to the adjacent mirror. A Snoopy clock ticks off the seconds.

PAN TO – CALLIE lies face up, asleep in her bed.

*vvvvvvrrrrrmmmmmm!* – the plane roars overhead.

CALLIE OPENS HER EYES, she opens them suddenly, and she looks frightened, as if startled out of a nightmare.

                                                        CUT TO:


INT. MODINO HOUSE – MORNING

CLOSE ON – VICTOR MODINO, his head bent down. A PILE OF CLEAN DISHES sits to the side. He washes the last dish in the sink.

*vvvvvvrrrrrmmmmmm!* – the plane roars overhead.

Victor looks up. Steam rises up around his face, turning yellow with the morning light.

                                                        CUT TO:


EXT. CONVENIENCE STORE/DELI – MORNING

Yellow light sprays through the trees. THE NIKE-CLAD JOGGER runs along the river, his GOLDEN RETRIEVER keeping perfect stride on its tether.

NANNY sits on the steps of the CONVENIENCE STORE – tied firmly.

                                                        CUT TO:


INT. CONVENIENCE STORE/DELI – MORNING

THE CASHIER'S COUNTER: *Darlene is not there.*

VICTOR opens one of the refrigerator doors that line the rear of the store. He kneels, picking out a carton of eggs. He pauses.

THROUGH THE SHELVES, IN THE DARKNESS BEHIND – A WOMAN'S STOCKINGED FEET ATOP A STEP LADDER. One of her toenails has ripped through her stocking. It is painted with sparkling nail polish.

Victor stands abruptly. He removes a bottle of juice, CLEARING A VIEW THROUGH THE SHELF AT EYE LEVEL. He pretends to examine the bottle's label, instead glancing –

THROUGH THE SHELF – THE WOMAN'S TORSO. She is reaching above, obliviously stacking Gatorade. She steps down, out of view, then her chest appears again. Her name tap reads: *Darlene.*

A BOTTLE OF GATORADE teeters at the edge of the shelf above, as Darlene continues stacking. It moves closer and closer to the edge. Suddenly, *it falls.*

Victor catches it in mid air. He looks up. *Another bottle is about to fall,* sliding out over the edge of the wire shelf.

Victor quickly puts the first bottle into his basket just in time to – catch the *next plummeting bottle.*

Then, another falls, *and another* – Victor catching them in his basket, his arms. Then – *smash!* one hits the floor, shattering.

> DARLENE
> (off-screen)

God dammit!

Victor stands, looking about, his arms filled with Gatorade.

Darlene emerges with a broom and dust pan. She blows the hair out of her eyes. She notices –

Victor – replacing the bottles in his arms onto another shelf.

Oh, my God. Did I knock all those off?

> VICTOR

No – just one.

Darlene smirks.

> CUT TO:

EXT. CONVENIENCE STORE/DELI – MORNING (CONTINUOUS)

INSIDE THE STORE – THROUGH THE GLASS – VICTOR kneels, holding the dust pan as DARLENE sweeps up the broken glass.

CLOSE ON – NANNY sits, tied outside on the stoop. The dog turns, watching through the glass as –

*Darlene swishes a mop about on the floor, seemingly wherever Victor is standing. He shuffles about, moving out of her way, awkwardly clinging to his basket. It is almost a dance. She smiles. Victor smiles. She touches his shoulder.*

BACK TO – NANNY, watching impassively as –

Victor and Darlene continue to talk, he leaning on the refrigerator door, she leaning on her mop. *They laugh.*

The sky is gray, with a patch of deep blue in the center. A speck of a plane rumbles overhead.

                                                                    BLACKNESS

# Storyboards

## COP LAND
(see pages 10–12)

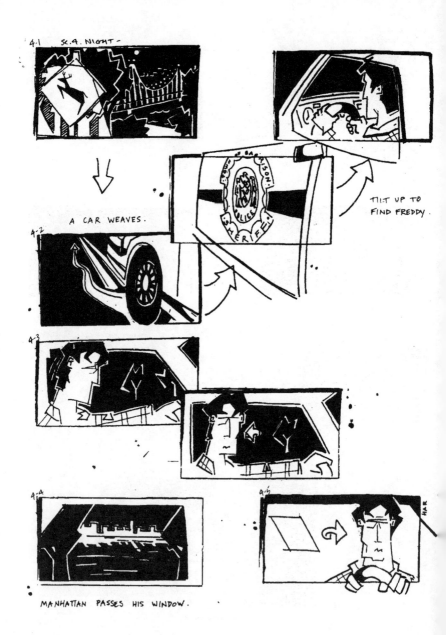

4.1  SC.4. NIGHT —

A CAR WEAVES.

TILT UP TO
FIND FREDDY.

4.2

4.3

4.4

4.5

MANHATTAN PASSES HIS WINDOW.

298

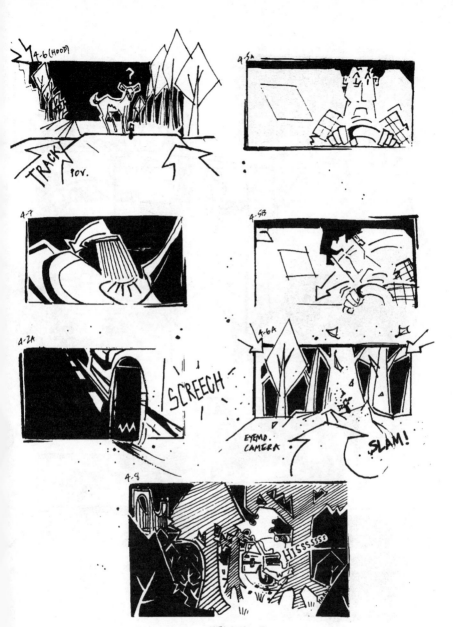

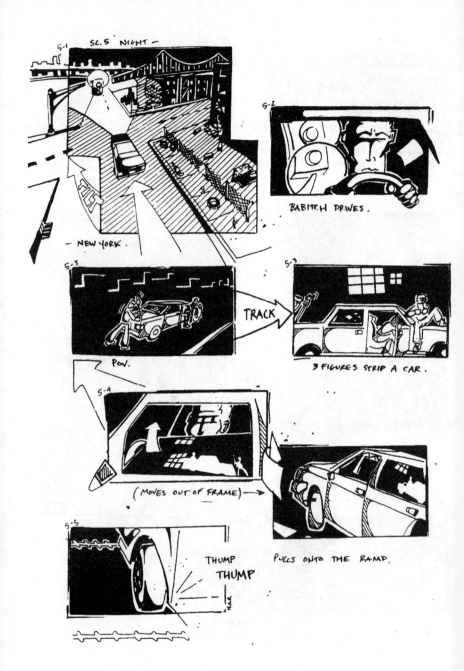

SC.5 NIGHT —
5-1

5-2
BABITCH DRIVES.

— NEW YORK.

5-3
POV.

TRACK

5-3
3 FIGURES STRIP A CAR.

5-4
(MOVES OUT OF FRAME) →

PULLS ONTO THE RAMP.

5-5
THUMP
THUMP

300

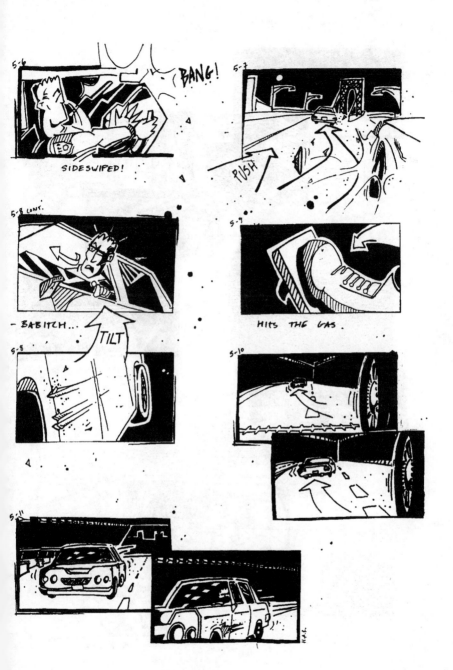

301

5-12

5-11A

NYPD

5-12A

A GUN ?!

302

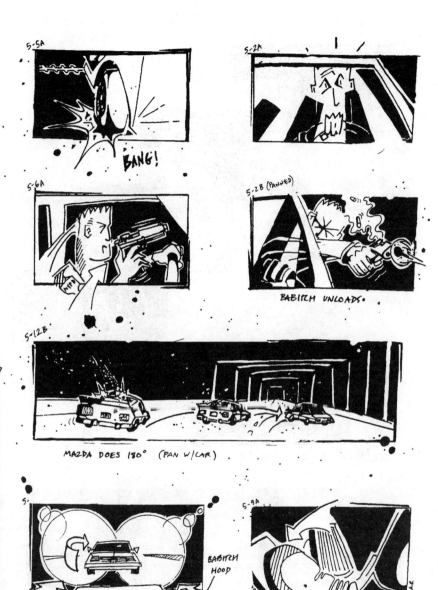

303

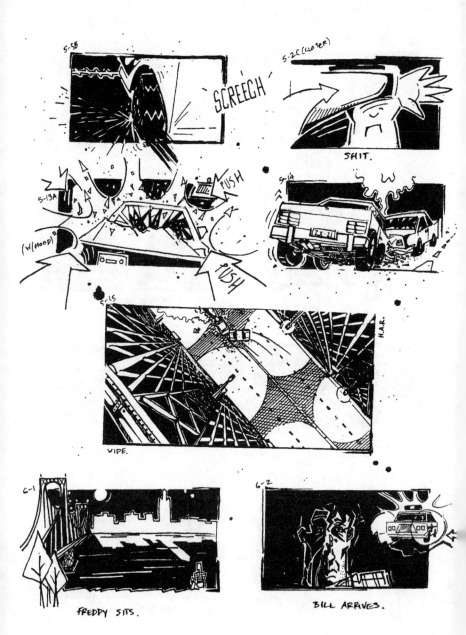

SCREECH

SHIT.

WIDE.

FREDDY SITS.

BILL ARRIVES.

# Storyboards

**HEAVY**
(see pages 223–6)

52.

53.

306

54.

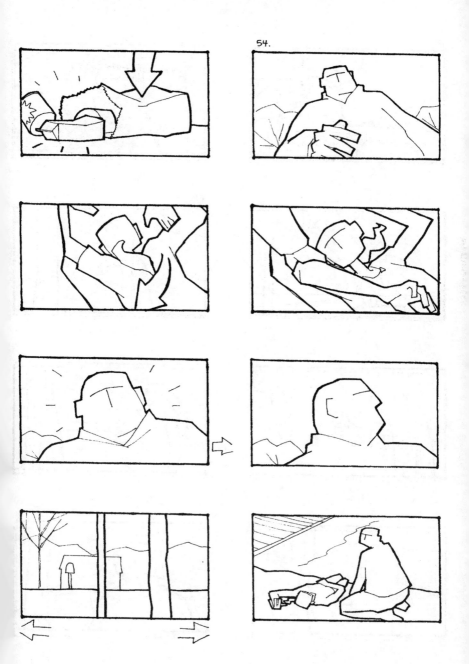

307

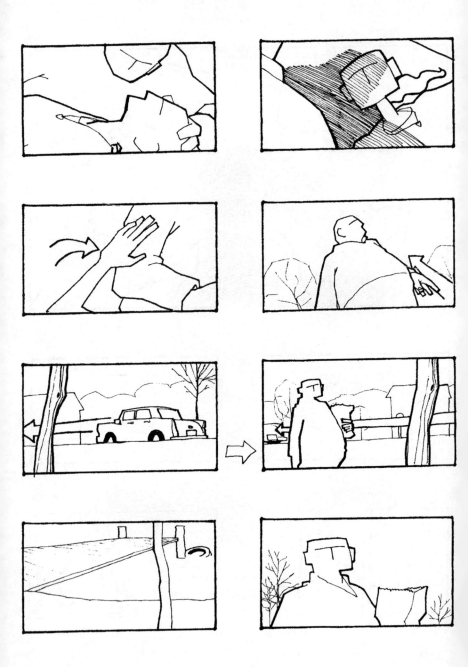

*Heavy* is available on video
from Artificial Eye.